ACT LIKE YOU KNOW

ACT LIKE YOU KNOW

African-American
Autobiography
&
White Identity

CRISPIN SARTWELL

The University of Chicago Press
Chicago & London

CRISPIN SARTWELL has taught at Vanderbilt University and
the University of Alabama. In 1997–98 he is visiting associate professor
of humanities and philosophy at Pennsylvania State University, Capitol College.
His previous books include *Obscenity, Anarchy, Reality* (1996).

The University of Chicago Press, Chicago 60637
The University of Chicago Press, Ltd., London
© 1998 by The University of Chicago
All rights reserved. Published 1998
Printed in the the United States of America
07 06 05 04 03 02 01 00 99 98   1 2 3 4 5

ISBN: 0-226-73526-5 (cloth)
ISBN: 0-226-73527-3 (paper)

Library of Congress Cataloging-in-Publication Data

Sartwell, Crispin, 1958–
    Act like you know : African-American autobiography and white
identity / Crispin Sartwell.
        p.   cm.
    Includes index.
    ISBN 0-226-73526-5 (cloth : alk. paper). — ISBN 0-226-73527-3
(pbk. : alk. paper)
    1. American prose literature—Afro-American authors—History and
criticism.   2. Afro-American authors—Biography—History and
criticism.   3. Slaves—United States—Biography—History and criticism.
4. Afro-Americans—Biography—History and criticism.   5. Whites—
United States—Race identity.   6. Race relations—United States.
7. Autobiography.   I. Title.
PS366.A35S27   1998
810.9′896073
[b]—DC21   97-49139
                                                                    CIP

♾ The paper used in this publication meets the minimum requirements
of the American National Standard for Information Sciences—Permanence
of Paper for Printed Library Materials, ANSI Z39.48-1992.

*This book is for my parents,
Joyce and Richard Abell,
in deep gratitude.*

CONTENTS

ACKNOWLEDGMENTS

My greatest debt is to Judith Bradford, who helped nurture this book from its infant stages. She was particularly helpful on anything to do with gender. She actually revised portions of this manuscript, and I am not clear in every case which sentences are hers and which are mine.

This book arose originally out of a class I taught at the University of Alabama. This intensely engaged group of students provided me with the best experience I have had as a teacher, so I am going to thank them all by name: Reshawna Banks, Anjanette Burkett, Greg Carden, Hayden Childs, Mia Cowan, Niambi Dennis, Amelia Dillard, Takeshia Dozier, Lida Anne Elliott, Ulysses Haynes, Timothy Meadows, Jasmine Montgomery, Mavis Reed, Bryant Sanders, Johnny Skelton, Vincent Strickland, and David Whitney. The philosophy department at Alabama, especially Norv Richards, supported this project and the teaching from which it emerged.

Leonard Harris gave shape to this book by pointing out precisely how the initial proposal was fundamentally misguided.

Nick Murray and two anonymous reviewers for the University of Chicago Press provided many detailed suggestions for improvements, as did my editor, David Brent, who shocked me by believing in this project from the beginning. Naomi Zack also provided detailed comments, and reading her work changed my thinking about race.

David Levering Lewis and Robert Bernasconi, as well as audiences at

Rensselaer Polytechnic and at the University of Maryland, helped me re-think and elaborate my reading of Du Bois. Peter Hare and folks at the Society for the Advancement of American Philosophy did the same for my reading of Hurston.

Elihu Katz, Barbara Grabias, and the rest of the Annenberg Scholars Program at the Annenberg School for Communication provided financial and intellectual support for this project, though I was supposed to be working on something else at the time.

Nicole Keating provided many useful insights and emotional support for my disintegrating, postmodern subjectivity. Leslie Cooksy went to Alice Deal Junior High School with me and affirmed my memories of the place.

Finally, I'd like to thank Willie Singleton, who taught me African-American history when I was in eighth grade at Alice Deal, introduced me to Malcolm X, and taught me something as well about responsibility, passion, and how to think.

INTRODUCTION

Since this book is about autobiography and race, I will begin with an account of some of the experiences that made me a white man.

I grew up in a lily-white enclave of Chocolate City: Washington, D.C. My parents were leftists, and as a child I attended a number of civil-rights demonstrations, including the Moratorium held in the wake of the assassination of Martin Luther King Jr. King's death was a pivotal event in my developing sense of racial situatedness; I was ten years old, and I remember my mother crying when the news of the assassination was announced on television. But I remember also her fear: She speculated that King's assassination would lead to a race war. Nor was she far wrong. That night there was a citywide curfew, and a pall of smoke rose over D.C.; the Fourteenth Street corridor was burning. Thirteen years later, when I went down to that area to try to collect unemployment, it was still burned out, and I wended my way through the ghetto in fear. It was on Fourteenth Street, too, that my brother Adam scored the heroin with which he committed suicide in 1992. At that time, Fourteenth Street was still a black ghetto, though undergoing restoration, and I returned, still in fear, to try to get some of Adam's stuff out of hock.

There was one black kid at Lafayette Elementary School in Chevy Chase; his name was Benjy. When the time came to put on a performance for parents, the elderly white music teacher had a special solo number in mind for Benjy: a pseudo-Caribbean song that was about some bone-headed Jamaican building a house on the sandy ground and watching it wash away. In rehearsals, the music teacher kept telling Benjy how to move in a kind of rhythmic sway, while making exaggerated gestures. And she continually yelled at him to grin, until his face was fixed in a leer. This puzzled me; I did not understand the various signifiers involved. When I told my mother about it, she got angry. But when Benjy performed in front of the parents and kids—all of whom, except Benjy's parents, were white—he brought down the house.

Around the same time, my immediate neighborhood was integrated for the first time by a family of light-skinned black folks who moved in around the corner. I played basketball in the alley with the kids, while their dad watched us from the back porch. They had moved from downtown, and one thing was pretty obvious—they thought that the white kids in the neighborhood were wimps. They told stories of their old neighborhood that sounded to me like something out of a horror film, but they took great pride in the toughness they had developed. This toughness impressed and intimidated me, and these kids kicked my ass continually on the basketball court. No other black families had moved to the blocks near my house by the time I moved out in 1976.

The year I started junior high, 1970, D.C. started a program of forced busing. Alice Deal Junior High School had been over 90 percent white; the year I started, it was about half black. The kids were bused up from Mount Pleasant—by no means the roughest area of the District, but much poorer than Chevy Chase. The racial situation was extremely tense. There were individual confrontations and collective pitched battles. I had to fight or run every day to preserve my lunch money from black guys, whose refrain was "Anything I find, I can have?" I let myself be robbed a couple of times, then started making sure I had other white kids around me as much as possible. Even so, I got into some fights. I also made some black friends (though they never came to my house, nor did I go to theirs; they disappeared on the buses when school let out). But these guys told the other guys to leave me alone. Before very long, I felt pretty comfortable.

Lord knows that Alice Deal was a hard place to feel comfortable. Kids of both races got beaten up regularly. The next year, many of the white families, most of whom lived within walking distance of the school, had pulled their kids out; I'd estimate the ratio at 70 percent black and 30 percent white, with a smattering of Hispanic kids. There were a lot of weapons: small-caliber handguns and knives, mostly. Teachers, many of them white ladies who had been at Deal before busing, had no control of their classes. Students walked in and out at will. A male French teacher took out his frustrations on a Hispanic kid I knew—threw him against a wall and broke a chair over his head. The student disappeared to the hospital for a couple of weeks (after which he reappeared in casts); the teacher disappeared entirely. A black friend of mine, Vertisse, was stabbed in the library with a pair of scissors. Periodically, the paramedics would arrive and drag an OD out of the bathroom; it was the heyday of the (first) D.C. heroin epidemic.

The administration started locking the doors. They hired a bunch of three-hundred-pounders and called them "Community Aides." These bouncers prowled the halls with two-by-fours. One day when I was in eighth grade, the whole school gathered at windows to watch one of the aides chase a black kid who had tried to escape the school. He landed on top of the kid and proceeded to beat the piss out of him with a board. Lockers were subject to random searches, or at least the lockers of black students were subject to random searches. The aides and administrators would gather the weapons and drugs they found into big piles. No one, as far as I could see, was learning much of anything except how to survive.

One rare zone of exception to this was the classroom of a teacher named Willie Singleton. Singleton, a young black man, ruled his history classes with iron discipline, and he taught Marx, Che Guevara, and Malcolm X. He had the respect of his students, black and white, and his course in Afro-American history was both scary and absorbing for me: scary because there were a lot of ticked-off black kids in there learning about me as an oppressor, and absorbing because reading Malcolm X and others made me change my thinking about race in a way that gave me some perspective on what was happening in my life and contributed to a growing political radicalism. I started a "free" paper at Deal (for which I was twice suspended), ran for class president on the "No More Bullshit" platform (I finished second), and led a student walkout when, the following year, the teachers went on strike (demanding, as I recall, a supply of basic materials). Finally, I instituted a terrorist campaign demanding an end to compulsory attendance and grading. My little cell spread a stink solution made of eggs and Drano all over the administrative offices. When I returned to the school three or four years later, the place *still* stank.

I looked at the black kids around me with a mixture of fear and desire that I will explore at length as this book goes on. They were sometimes armed, and sometimes fucked up, and I learned to watch my back. But these kids seemed much older and hipper and smarter than me or my white friends. They seemed to know a whole bunch of stuff we didn't know. In seventh and eighth grade, for example, most of the white kids were sexual *naïfs,* and most of the black kids, including the girls, radiated sexual confidence and experience. I was intensely attracted to some of the black girls, in particular a girl named Jaqui. When I approached her to ask for a date (it had taken me weeks to screw up the courage), she laughed in my face and said something like, "You wouldn't know what to do with me if you had me, white boy." That was true. Meanwhile, several girls from my neighborhood were impregnated by their black boyfriends, which led to real panic on the part of white parents. In the following chapters, I will have some things to say about interracial sexual desire, including my own. Let me just make explicit my awareness that my history and attitudes regarding this matter are, putting it mildly, a problem.

By the time I got into ninth grade, the school was perhaps 90 percent black. That year, too, my brother started at Deal. After he was battered a couple of times, my parents—despite their deep commitment to integration and to public education—moved him to a private school.

The most popular music of the time was black music, and the black kids at Deal seemed to know everything that was happening; they had the best music before I even knew the artist. The Jackson Five were hot, as were such nuggets as "Theme from Shaft," by Isaac Hayes, and a song called "Money Runner." James Brown was probably the most popular artist, and the halls reverberated with "Say It Loud (I'm Black and I'm Proud)"—though that was a few years old—and "Papa's Got a Brand New Bag." I immersed myself in the history of African-American music: I was listening to Muddy Waters, Aretha Franklin, the O'Jays, and anyone else I could get my hands on. The black kids thought that was pretty funny.

I could continue this narrative, but it would consist fundamentally of more of the same; my basic racial attitudes had been set by the time I finished at Deal. (Nevertheless, there are going to be autobiographical bits scattered throughout this book.) Any book about African-American writing by a white man is, obviously, problematic. I cannot hope to escape the possibility that some of what follows—or even all of it—is racist. It should be even more obvious that a white man who has had the experiences just described cannot hope to erase the traces of racism from his own writings. Indeed, if what follows is anything like right, the claim of a white American man not to be a racist is always extremely suspicious and also false. And what follows is written in the *anxiety* that it could be interpreted to express racist attitudes. Indeed, and what is even more problematic, I have ended up spending much of my life in the South (in Virginia, Tennessee, and Alabama) and have developed a kind of redneck persona. A couple of years ago you might have seen me working on my car (ineffectually, it's true) in front of my house in Cottondale, Alabama, tattooed, spitting Skoal juice, and listening to Hank Williams Jr. I feel perfectly comfortable in redneck culture and in fact romanticize it in a way similar to the way I romanticize black culture. But here I belong, or at least pass, and one of the central ways in which people belong to redneck culture is simply by *not being black,* so that even in the midst of poverty, say, there is a sense of membership and of privilege; even in poverty (which admittedly I didn't share) there is the pleasure of power.

I have tried in what follows both to inscribe my own racism and to elide it or even destroy it—a conflict that surely renders this entire text problematic. But I hope that this conflict also serves to clarify the racing of white men; it is a conflict characteristic not only of me, but of us. Both my racial position in the dominant culture and my anxiety about that position are, I hope, legible on every page. This is not a tension I intend to resolve in what follows; indeed, I hope both to intensify and elucidate it. That tension is, finally, what the book is about.

One way in which this tension is manifest is in the selection of materials that I have chosen to discuss. For reasons that will become obvious as the book goes on, white folks have paid a fair amount of attention to African-American autobiography, and relatively little to the theory and philosophy produced by African-Americans. (This fact has been emphasized and diagnosed by Michele Wallace and Patricia Hill Collins, among others.) I think it is a fair generalization that a disproportionate number of the books in the African-American tradition that have been canonized as central texts have been autobiographies. This book continues the white habit of attending to autobiographies of black people, though I will also discuss various theoretical writings by African-Americans on black autobiography.

However, I want to throw the distinction between autobiography and theory quite generally into question. First of all, works of theory are, it seems to me, autobiographical. Certainly this book is autobiographical theory as well as theory of autobiography. For the most part the autobiographical elements in the European and European-American traditions are systematically concealed, and for reasons that track precisely the nature of that tradition and in particular its racial content. Yet, as I have elsewhere urged, each work of theory, though it may purport to be produced from no standpoint, out of no personal history, proceeds necessarily from *some* standpoint, out of *some* personal history. This means, among other things, that it emerges in a particular historical and social location. It is characteristic of European and European-American male theoretical production that it fails to acknowledge its sources in personal experience and in social situations. In particular it fails to acknowledge its location in the social situation of privilege and oppression. The neutral theoretical subject, whose tone is transparent to the argument, is itself a particular raced (and gendered) construction. I take as the models for the form and voice of this book such African-American thinkers as Michael Eric Dyson, Houston Baker, and Patricia J. Williams, all of whom do theoretical autobiography or autobiographical theory and speak with an especial power because they own the sources of their ideas in their experience. These figures show the connection of thought and life in an exemplary way.[1]

We white male philosophers tend to read our own tradition as non-autobiographical, as proceeding from no particular location, and our voices as we write are often designed to disguise the sources of our preoccupations in our own lives. This is true of my own authorial voice, though I have spent years trying to pit myself against that voice, to work against it or away from it. I am constantly slipping into transparency and "objectivity," constantly dragging myself back in fear to passion and particularity, slipping again, and so forth. Left to my own devices, I *disappear* as an author. That is the "whiteness" of my authorship. This whiteness of authorship is, for us, a form of authority; to speak (apparently) from nowhere, for everyone, is empowering, though one wields power here only by becoming lost to oneself. But such an authorship and authority is also pleasurable: it yields the pleasure of self-forgetting or apparent transcendence of the mundane and the particular, and the pleasure of power expressed in the "comprehension" of a vast range of materials.

On the other hand, the white reception of the authorial voices of black cultural production takes place within a set of expectations that removes those voices from the space of authoritative theory. Even those works which display elaborate and compelling theoretical structures get read as the traces of particular lives and social locations. One effect or cause of this way of reading is a segregation of black discourse; we try to make sure we hear you speaking *as* a black person, that we hear you speaking *to* "the black experience." Thus, we attempt to insulate our own discourse from the critique or even destruction which threatens that discourse from its "other." We try to maintain our theory in its "purity," its whiteness, its abstraction. What counts as theory or as autobiography thus proceeds through the racial codes that imaginatively locate white authors as amorphous objective observers and black authors as precisely located recorders of their own lives.

So I want to work toward breaking down the distinction between theory and autobiography or, more precisely, to show that it has already broken down in fact. This occurs in the literature itself that I will be surveying. W. E. B. Du Bois's book *Dusk of Dawn,* which I will discuss at some length, is subtitled *An Essay Toward an Autobiography of a Race Concept.* This explicitly collapses the autobiographical and theoretical dimensions of his authorship. Autobiography has theoretical purposes, theoretical underpinnings, and theoretical effects, and I will certainly, in what follows, take these features seriously in the autobiographies I discuss. Anyone who asserted that *The Autobiography of Malcolm X* or Zora Neale Hurston's *Dust Tracks on a Road* did not emerge from an elaborately developed theoretical framework would have some serious explaining to do. I find a useful alternative to the Western tradition in these works, for they develop theory precisely out of a concrete human context; they acknowledge the source of theory in lived experience and social construction. In the very insulation of our theoretical discourse, we articulate by negation the limits of that discourse and the conditions for its collapse. So I want to use these works, among other things, precisely to throw the distinction between theory and autobiography into question. And the reasons I need to do so are themselves autobiographical.

Houston Baker has worked explicitly on breaking down the distinction between autobiography and theory, particularly in his book *Workings of the Spirit.* He offers this caution to white folks who want to deal with African-American texts and traditions: "'Autobiographical,' in my proposal, means a personal negotiation of metalevels—one that foregrounds nuances and resonances of *an-other's* story. The white autobiographer who honestly engages his or her own autobiographical implication in a brutal past is as likely as an Afro-American to provide such nuances."[2] What Baker suggests is that for a white person to write about African-American literature without acknowledging his own situatedness in a racist culture would be colonializing and disingenuous, and would simply reinforce the "objective" stance and the "neutral" authorial voice which themselves participate in the construction of whiteness.

Hazel Carby has been even clearer on this matter. "In practice, in the classroom," she writes, "black texts have been used to focus on the complexity of response in the (white) reader/student's construction of self to a (black) perceived 'other.'" She continues,

> We need to recognize that we live in a society in which systems of domination and subordination are structured through processes of racialization that continuously interact with all other forms of socialization. Theoretically, we should be arguing that everyone in this social order has been constructed in our political imagination as a racialized subject. In this sense, it is important to think about the invention of the category of whiteness as well as that of blackness, to make visible what is rendered invisible when viewed as the normative state of existence: the (white) point in space from which we tend to identify difference.[3]

Carby deftly identifies the difficulty which this book diagnoses and within which it exists, for I intend in what follows precisely to "use" texts produced by African-Americans in order to construct or reconstruct myself in distinction to the black "other." But I intend also to make whiteness visible as a particular social construction, and by the very same means. If I am right, the most promising strategy for bringing whiteness to visibility is to arrange an encounter with what it has, in imagination, extruded or ejected from itself. And I hope that whiteness can also be *compromised* in this encounter; for one thing, I hope that it can be shown to be a sort of hallucination, though a hallucination with concrete effects.

Therefore I will explore the construction of whiteness elaborately in what follows. I am, I hope, answerable to black folks' descriptions of their own self-understandings. But I am answerable only to myself about my own self-understandings. I cannot be an authority on African-American experiences, but I am an authority on the phenomenology, the inside view, of white racism. And what I say about it might even disconcert black critics—perhaps especially when I speak about its pleasures. I have a fairly extreme self-loathing about the self-constructions that go into making a racist social structure, but by the same token I can neither shed those self-constructions by an act of will nor cease to experience the pleasures of power—even the pleasures of the "objectivity" or "neutrality" (the hallucinated detachment of the voice from the body, of autobiography from theory) that mark the white authorial fiction. Of course, theory and autobiography can be loosely distinguished as literary forms; I only insist that every work of theory is also the trace of some particular life, and I seek for ways to acknowledge that in my own work, which would also be ways of compromising "whiteness" in one of its aspects.

I have never stopped fearing black folks, and I have never stopped romanticizing them. This book is an attempt to explicate and deal with my own immensely complicated racial attitudes. It is an attempt, among other things, to find the racism both in my fear and my romanticization. This book is "about" African-American autobiography in the sense that it is those texts that are quoted and discussed. But it is, above all, a safari to the mysterious heart of whiteness: It is my attempt to locate myself, to make myself visible, as a white man. In this sense, this book takes a place within the growing field of "white identity studies."[4] For strategic reasons, however, I do not deal with that literature in what follows (though I hope to write about it in the future): This book is about the encounter of a white man with texts produced by African-Americans. My identity is raced, through and through, in innumerable ways. But one theme of this book is that while white racism seeks obsessively to render blackness visible in the prescribed stereotypical way, white racism also seeks to render whiteness invisible. One of the major strategies for preserving white invisibility to ourselves is the silencing, segregation, or delegitimation of voices that speak about whiteness from a nonwhite location; above all, we can't stand to be looked at, described, or made specific. I attend to black autobiographies in this way in order to reveal whiteness by hearing what whiteness excludes. I try also—and necessarily with limited success, since I remain white, and thus to some extent unmarked to myself—to *take seriously* what black writers say about white people, about how we look from there. For such reasons, along with sheer constraints of time and energy and creativity, this book is anything but comprehensive. Though the works I write about are, I think, excellent and important, they represent only a tiny fraction of black autobiographical production. I write about these works in particular—some of the slave narratives, some writings of Du Bois, Malcolm X's and Zora Neale Hurston's autobiographies, and some rap music—because I think they are particularly potent in showing how whiteness is made. I also make use of other texts in each chapter as foils or confirmations: works by James Baldwin, Richard Wright, Langston Hughes, and Patricia J. Williams, among others. These works, too, are employed as ways of revealing the interlocking structures of racial identity.

To be a privileged white man in American culture is to be a neutral, all-seeing eye; to be black is to be the object of the gaze. What is "normal" in our culture is always, invisibly, raced white. This fact is crystal clear with regard to recent debates on multicultural curricula, for example. The opponents of multiculturalism often appeal to the hackneyed image of the melting-pot: They ask why we can't all form a single people, and they offer to welcome African-Americans and other minorities into European-American culture with apparently open arms. (As one white student in my

African-American philosophy class put it, "Can't we just forget about race? Let's just all be the same.") But this argument rests on two crucial and intertwined errors. First, it equates American culture with European-American culture, and offers this culture to everyone in the form of the canon of Western literature, science, and philosophy. However, American culture is also deeply African; the identification of the American canon with the Western tradition and American culture with European culture expresses white America's anxious provincialism.[5] We're located at the margins of the Western tradition, and also dead center (well, maybe a bit north of dead center) of the African diaspora.

Thus, second, the "neutral" culture which these folks offer "minorities" is in fact raced white. What is regarded as the neutral content of American culture, into which we are waiting to welcome you, is the very same neutral content that justified your enslavement, your exclusion, your systematic impoverishment. The problem is this: We white folks can't see ourselves as having a race, as taking up by virtue of our skin-tone a perfectly precise place in the ongoing systemic racism of America. Thus, our welcome becomes an assault that seeks to expunge African-American culture; our offering to you of our culture becomes, in terms to which I will return, a premonition of cultural annihilation.

I am not an African-American. But I am an American, and thus I am embedded in a situation in which cultural division and interchange between black and white are fundamental. My race is as central to this situation as is theirs because, as many figures (notably Martin Luther King Jr. and James Baldwin) have shown, our identities are interwoven, are inconceivable without one another. A fundamental contention of this book is that this situation creates and embodies a particular epistemological transaction. Both the oppressor and the oppressed are articulated within this transaction in a way that allows and constrains the production of knowledges. In one dimension, this regime consists of the confrontation of general truth by particular truth: the truth of the stereotype confronted by the particular lives of Frederick Douglass, Zora Neale Hurston, Sister Souljah. In another, it consists of mirrored hypocrisies: the hypocrisy, for example, of the "Uncle Tom," who conforms his behavior to a stereotype while thinking who-knows-what, and the hypocrisy of the professed Christian or democrat who buys and sells people, or lives in and helps maintain a segregated community. I will, thus, contend that the truths of American culture are permeated thoroughly by race relations. The division of inner life and outer enactment, of authentic and inauthentic living, of mind and body as they play out in our culture are incomprehensible outside the structure of black/white relations. In my view, racism is a form of what I will term *ejected asceticism;* white Americans practice the purification or the mortification of the body by ejecting the body imaginatively into black persons, who become associated with the physical *per se:* sport, sex, violence, and dance, for instance. Or as Ralph Ellison puts it, "Being 'highly pigmented,' as the sociologists say, it was our Negro 'misfortune' to be caught up associatively in the negative side of this basic dualism of the white folk mind, and to be shackled to almost everything it would repress from conscience and consciousness."[6] The American self is made in a racial transaction.

One of the fundamental features of the epistemological situation I have just described is that, in it, the oppressed are rendered invisible; their inner lives cannot be expressed in the wider culture's public space (this is obviously thematized, for example, in Ellison's *Invisible Man*). Nevertheless, they are continually "comprehended" under the general truth of the stereotype, or of the social sciences, or of the vast information-gathering machinery of the welfare system. Thus, the oppressor forces the oppressed into concealment, or tries to. More accurately, the oppressor seeks to constrain the oppressed to certain approved modes of visibility (those set out in the template of stereotype) and then gazes obsessively on the spectacle he has created, as the white music teacher and the white audience gazed on Benjy.

On the other hand, the oppressor becomes in this process totally visible to the oppressed, so that (as has often been observed) the oppressed person knows the oppressor better than the oppressor knows himself. This is shown with perfect directness in, for example, Douglass's devastating indictment of southern Christianity, or in King's attack on the hypocrisy of racists who profess to endorse the ideals of the Declaration of Independence. White hypocrites do not, for the most part, know themselves to be hypocrites; American racial oppression supposes a breakdown in self-awareness. In this transaction, then, the European-American becomes invisible to himself, and simultaneously visible to those he oppresses and therefore silences. The silencing of the voices of the oppressed—or, again, the restriction of them to approved modes of audibility—is a strategy that seeks to maintain the epistemological transaction of racism. White oppressors do not know what they are because they do not allow anyone to tell them. One devastating effect of the texts considered here is that, by bringing what is invisible into the space of publicity, they make the oppressor visible to himself as an oppressor. They remove the shroud of generality in which white culture wraps black bodies. Thus, reading these texts as a white man is a particularly dangerous and needful activity. Hearing black voices, if I am right, is the only way for white people to make visible to themselves their own racial self-construction.

That was brought home to me when I taught African-American philosophy at the University of Alabama in the summer of 1994. The class consisted of seventeen students, twelve of whom were black. The first question I asked them was whether they thought racism was a problem at Alabama. This, recall, is the same school where George Wallace tried to exclude black students by force of arms, but it's now about 10 percent black. The white students held unanimously that racism was not a problem anymore, that they themselves were not racists (supposedly shown by the very fact that they were taking the course), and that no one they knew was a racist. They did notice, however, that black students tended to "separate themselves off" and that (due to "paranoia") they resented white students and suspected them unfairly of racism. Then the black students started in. They recounted literally dozens of incidents of discrimination, prejudice, and massive insensitivity, ranging from systemic practices (such as the complete segregation of the fraternity system, absence of black materials from the curriculum, and lack of black professors and administrators) to a hundred specific slights, subtle exclusions, and unintentional insults, including the diagnosis of paranoia made by the white students.

For example, there was often a presumption that black students had unfair advantages because of affirmative action programs, whether or not the students in question had benefited from such programs (which were in any case tentative and ineffective). Black students, especially males, were assumed to be athletes, and athletes in turn assumed to be dolts who took gut classes and passed because of athletic department pressure on professors. The white students did not detect any racism at the university; the black students held it to be obvious that racism was *the* major problem there. The course became a catharsis, as we often forgot about the texts completely or used them as occasions to discuss the issues that the students faced.

What was instructive about this situation was how much the white students learned about themselves. The class became very close; the students partied together, and I'd see the black and white students eating at the same table at the student union (a rare sight at UA). And as the stories multiplied, and the white students began to take the experiences of black students seriously, the white kids slowly became aware of some of their own racist attitudes and, what was much more significant, of their complicity in racist practices (for example, within the Greek system), whatever their attitudes. Again, the only way to learn of such complicity is to hear black voices, but the incredibly elaborate segregational practices in place at Alabama and throughout our culture relieve us white folks precisely of the burden of hearing such voices and provide us with machinery for their dismissal or minimization when they do speak to us.

There was also, as I will discuss below, a reversal of authority in the classroom; I could hardly stand up there and claim to be an authority on the black experience (though I could claim to know something about the forms of white racism). So I had to appeal to my students precisely as the authorities, and this was for me the most refreshing aspect of the course, because I have always had an anxious or perhaps violent response to authority, even my own. I hate being an authority. Now that structure is also going to be enacted in this text; it is the function of my quotations from and references to African-American theorists. I have to appeal to authority in this book in a way that I have always before resisted appealing to authority in my scholarly work (which is conspicuous for having no references at all to "secondary sources"). I *still* resist this kind of authority, whether the authority is black or white, and I may not have addressed the African-American critical tradition adequately in what follows. But I am going to try to appeal to it to whatever extent I can, because to do otherwise would be to fall into the sort of "colonialism" that this book is dedicated both to attacking and to elucidating.

As the works of Malcolm X especially demonstrate, there is, in the cases both of the oppressor and the oppressed, an implosion of the self in which the distinctions of public and private, authentic and inauthentic, break down. The oppressed person may "internalize" oppression, as Malcolm X points out in his passages about African-Americans, including himself, making themselves over to look like white people: They have internalized white standards, and paid a hideous price in self-loathing. But likewise, the oppressor "externalizes" his oppression, shunts it away from himself, seeks to release himself from responsibility for it. Finally, the oppressor no longer knows what he is or what he is doing: he hides himself from himself, as my white students effectively concealed their own racism from themselves. This crisis is personal, public, and epistemological. The notions of truth and of self become obscure, chaotic.

It is in and out of this last crisis that I want to try to locate some contemporary speech, especially rap music—much of which (Ice T, Public Enemy, Kool Moe Dee, Sister Souljah, Biggie Smalls) is, I think, serious philosophy and excellent autobiography—as the construction of a discourse that resists this implosion of self, as an often beautiful reassertion of cultural and personal identity precisely out of the materials of stereotype. Rap is an invasion of silence by the spoken word of the silenced, using the modes of expression to which they have been consigned in order to attack white culture at its most vulnerable points.

Let me make a few general remarks on how I am thinking about race in what follows. Race in the United States has been conceived to be a rigid dichotomy. This dichotomy has had to be *enforced,* by law and by a thousand microdisciplinary procedures and representational practices. For example, in order to *sort* people by race, what counted as black had to be codified, and this codification amounted finally to a conception of whiteness as purity, and a shunting of every "impure" case into the category of blackness by the one-drop rule. Similar principles, most of them no longer codified by law, underpin *de facto* segregation practices in housing and employment, and underpin even affirmative action programs. *You* must turn out to be black or white, and if you seem to slip through the fissure in the dichotomy, everyone involved is likely to be very uncomfortable. Judith Butler has argued that sex is not a fact antecedent to its enforcement; instead, the rigid dichotomy of male and female is applied over a range of biological sexing that forms a continuum, rather than a binary pair. This structure seems even (or much) more obvious in the case of race. The consignment of each person to a racial location, white or black, is a social operation carried out on a continuous range of genetic heritages and skin shades.

As I will go on to argue, this dualistic conception of race is absolutely required, and not only to produce certain desired economic and political results for white people (though certainly and centrally for that, too). It is required by the dualisms that dominate the Western tradition; that is, the specific forms of economic and political hegemony which we practice are articulated through what is essentially a metaphysical construction. The primordial dualisms of the Western tradition are between mind and body, culture and nature, general and particular (and when you cut to the chase, these are *the same* dualism). The dualisms are inscribed in European languages or, it has been suggested (by Derrida among others), are constitutive of European languages. So if black is coded as physical, natural, and particular (all of which, again, amount to the same thing), and white is coded as intellectual, cultural, and general, this calls into service the vast machinery of Western conceptuality that has been developing since the Greeks.

To encode blackness as physical, natural, and particular is to deploy black people into a metaphysically grounded axiomatics. This axiomatics is simultaneously ethical and economic, abstract and brutalizing, and it calls into play the grounding assumptions of Western thought about *what it means to be human,* which at the deepest strata include ideas such as this: that the body entraps the soul (the person), and hence that the body is the other that must be *dominated.* Thus, among other things, in this racial schema black people are bestialized, which has the economic consequences we white folks want (we constrain them to perform cheaply the labor we find degrading).

But our construction of black folks as bestial, as particular bodies, is also our construction of ourselves as pure white souls, as embodiments or disembodiments of "the highest human functions." That is, our selves are made by the exclusions that give them shape. We white folks appropriate to ourselves intellectual pursuits and the exercises of managerial power that are conceived as the functions of "mind" in a *social* body. In our strange metaphysics, the mind *commands* the body to move; the mind must *master* the body's functions and desires. What is physically dependent—cognition—becomes metaphysically independent, and hides its actual dependence on bodily support. In parallel, white dependence on the labor of black people is hidden, while we assume the "necessary burden" of guidance and administration. Thus, what is coded black becomes the sign of the slave and also of desire, the sign of white power and the sign of the origin of that power as emerging from mind to control the human body and the physical world technologically.

In this book, I emphasize the interlocking constructions of race as the product of a metaphysical system for articulating selves. I am not going to try to solve the chicken-and-egg problem about whether this system drives forms of economic exploitation, or whether on the contrary it is driven by them. It is obvious, I suppose, that the dualisms of Western thought start with the Greeks, and perhaps it is fair to say that they were not articulated out of Greek exclusion of Africans (though that is controversial). The Greeks, however, held slaves, and bestialized them in various ways. But the various dualisms are channeled and concretized in very specific configurations starting with the Renaissance and proceeding apace in the Enlightenment. These developments of the tradition, which give it the specific forms it assumes in modernity, coincide precisely with the economic expansion of Europe by colonialism, the slave trade, and the massive exploitation of third-world labor that continues today. The economic arrangements suit our raw self-interest, but they also aid in our self-constructions, and our constructions of the universe, including the notion that the world consists of raw, inert materials that must be made available for technological exploitation. For most of what follows, I describe white self-image as a sort of collective psychodrama, as the building of a metaphysical system, and also as a reflection of that system. But it should be borne in mind at all times both that this metaphysics is designed to have the most direct economic effects, and that it disguises its own economic applications.

Let me make one thing explicit about this construction: It is imaginary, which is a nice way to say that it is luridly false to the situation at hand, though not *simply* false, insofar as it succeeds in manufacturing its own confirmation. First of all, there is no defensible biological definition of race, as we will see Du Bois and Hurston argue. This is illustrated by the example of what it means, in America, to be Jewish (and I am Jewish by birth). Prior to World War II Judaism was considered fundamentally to be a matter of race, and it is still traditional to regard any child of a Jewish mother as Jewish (this I regarded as a great boon when I married a woman from an orthodox Jewish family: I didn't have to deal with the explosive reaction of that family to "intermarriage"). This is analogous to practices of racing in American slavery: Any child of a black woman was to be accounted a slave, so that the master, by acts of rape and threats of punishment could add to his own "stock." And in fact, it is a common claim within the Jewish community that the practice of counting the child of a Jewish mother as Jewish emerged in similar conditions of oppression and attendant rape, though here as a self-defense and means of survival for the people. The point is that Jewish identity in many (though not all) communities began to be regarded, first, as an "ethnicity"—a cultural identification that is not held to supervene on biology—and finally as more or less a religious preference. These shifts are regarded as a loss in some segments of Judaism, are regarded as a threat to Jewish identity, but they also display the fact that racial distinctions can shift or be eliminated. It is my opinion that the distinction of black and white in our culture will endure for a long time; indeed, I will argue that it is roughly as intense as it ever has been at the present moment. But with regard to my Jewishness, I'm either "passing" as a white man, or I simply have a certain ethnic background within the white world, depending on who you're talking to, when, and where. (In fact, I often enough felt, with my wife's family or at a synagogue, that I was "passing" there too; I am neither a goy nor Jewish *enough*, being myself the product of a "mixed marriage.") If nothing else, this displays the fact that races are a cultural construction and one that is fairly liquid.

The conceptual dichotomy of black and white does not, then, supervene on a defensible distinction, on any properties whatever that could be conceived to be intrinsic to the people whom the dichotomy sorts. Second, even within the traditional "scientific" account of race, there are not only two races, but at least three, and perhaps many. Yet when race is deployed in American discourse, there is a continual effort to reassert it as a dichotomy: white and nonwhite. Third, and related to both of the first two points, the racial situation, even if we started out with an opposition of black and white, is incredibly complex. Every possible combination of the races is instantiated over and over again. If race were a dichotomy, there would be many, many more people in the gap between the sortals than could possibly fall into either. As we are going to see, this is an immense problem for any theory or practice that takes race as a dichotomy or a trichotomy—indeed, for any system that deploys any racial taxonomy whatever.

Lastly, race itself is an interactive variable; race does not come neat.[7] The racing of women is not the same as the racing of men. The racing of southerners is not the same as the racing of northerners (for that matter, the racing of Alabamans is not the same as the racing of Tennesseeans, the racing of Birminghamians is not the same as the racing of Mobilians, etc.). The racing of old people is not the same as the racing of young people. The racing of poor people is not the same as the racing of middle-class people. People *fight* to retain the dichotomy in the face of this endless complication, but in fact the situation on the ground is infinitely vexed. I enter into the complications on the ground many times in what follows, but the basic project is to elucidate the content of the imaginary dichotomy itself and the modes of resistance to it mounted by African-Americans. This imaginary dichotomy is the way *we* try to *race ourselves as white*. So if I return again and again to race as a dualism, it is in an attempt to reveal, through the content of white imaginations, us to ourselves.

Even if it were not continually compromised in its application to the situation, the dichotomy could not possibly accomplish what it wants to accomplish. For what it seeks is precisely an *insulation* of the white from the black. This insulation is perfectly literalized in segregation practices, but it has conceptual underpinnings. Descartes imaginatively ejected his body from himself; he argued for an identification of himself with his mind or soul. We white folks seek to define ourselves in insulation from, and to dominate, what we exclude from ourselves in the construction of race as a dichotomy. Yet the terms are perfectly interdependent. White self-image is made out of its exclusions; it is incomprehensible without precisely *these* exclusions. It exists in a continual dependence on that which it segregates from itself, that from which it insulates itself. There *are* no minds without bodies; there is no managerial expertise without labor, no freedom from desire without the mark of desire and its erasure from the semiotic order. If our language is constituted by its dualisms, it is continually implicated in the terms of the dualisms that it seeks to devalue: in body, nature, and particularity.

This, as we are going to see, has the most practical and immediate consequences. We desire what we exclude, for one thing, and this desire is hyperintensified when what we exclude is, precisely, desire. This is elaborated in practices of slumming and spectacle. Forms of dominance are also, covertly, forms of dependence, and if the Confederacy fought for slavery, it was because its economy was dependent on slave labor. In other words, we need what we exclude, both because its exclusion is a fragmentation of the self that leaves a laceration that must be healed, and because we cannot live the life we have made for ourselves without making ourselves economically, socially, and aesthetically dependent on what we have attempted to dominate. For this if for no other reason, the dualism of race has already broken down at the moment of its articulation; it seeks to erase the dependence of the privileged term on the dispossessed term, but it inscribes exactly that dependence in its very possibility.

There is a final complication I want to mention. We white folks articulate what is black by a series of ejections from white selves and white culture. If we now assert (as I have asserted) that racial identities are interwoven, that makes it appear that black selves and black culture are made by white ejections, that the black "other" always merely subserves the white "same." But a notion like that could itself emerge only out of racism. Rather, the conceptual schema inscribes the "logic of the Same," while actual persons inhabit it at various points and with complex tensions.

White culture (despite its own views) did not find a raw, cultureless, languageless human material in Africa, and then make it over technologically into the limit condition of white civilization. On the contrary, what it tried to appropriate to this purpose was already encultured as elaborately as itself, but often in ways that seemed unrecognizable to Europeans and European-Americans. The attempt to make Africans into the other of European culture was quite literally the attempt to achieve a total erasure of African languages, African religions, and African arts. And yet African cultures survived and became means of survival for Africans in the diaspora.[8] What speaks to white people out of "the black experience" is not, or not only, the voice of our own exclusions, but voices that speak out of great cultural resources that we have repressed in order precisely to make an other for ourselves. And so *the very form of our exclusion* is also given form by the antecedent character of what we found; since we require ourselves to be whatever you are not, every event that shows us who you are changes *us*. Further, since the constructed limit is permeable and forms the zone of a transaction of desire and knowledge, we practice incorporations as well as exclusions. For example, one way that young white people can rebel against their parents and their culture is precisely by finding out about black culture, by searching for the intrinsic content of what has been abstractly excluded. Thus, the ways in which black and white identities are interwoven are endlessly complicated and, despite and because of the hegemonic relation, mutual.

The voices in the texts discussed in what follows speak *from* very different locations: different genders, different eras, different regions, different economic circumstances, different individualities. But in some sense they speak *to* the same situation—a situation in which we are all located.

1

TRUTH AND CONCEALMENT
IN SLAVE NARRATIVES

The function of the slave narrative is apparently straightforward: resistance to oppression by speaking the truth.[1] Unlike the later autobiographies we will examine, the early slave narratives were sponsored for a perfectly specific political purpose. Northern abolitionists intended to bring the depredations of slavery before the public by publishing the particular experiences in slavery of escaped or freed slaves. So the slave narrative intends to present the particular truth of individual human beings as a reply to general bromides about the institution of slavery and the childishness and savagery of the slaves themselves; for the myth of the benevolent plantation, in which happy darkies gratefully accepted the protection of fatherly masters, was the basic mode of propaganda in defense of slavery.[2] Such an image could remain comfortably ensconced in the North because Northerners were distant from the actual conditions of slaves. The slave narrative seeks to attack that hazy, generalized picture with the specific truths known by (and perhaps only by) the slaves themselves.

Furthermore, however, the slave narrative constitutes a direct assault on stereotypes of African-Americans. The picture of the Southern slave is of a person illiterate, primitive (as African civilizations were held to be primitive, or rather, not to be civilizations at all), with rudimentary capacities for intellection. The slave is conceived as a raw, cultureless material mined from the dark continent, as a natural resource.[3] Books such as

Narrative of the Life of Frederick Douglass and *Narrative of William W. Brown, a Fugitive Slave* presented, on the contrary, persons of deep intellectual and expressive power. For just such reasons, the authenticity of the narratives was widely impugned, and it was often held that they were the inventions of abolitionists. In the cases of Douglass and Brown, at any rate, the falsity of such claims was manifest as soon as one heard them speak, and in their later writings. Harriet Jacobs's great narrative, *Incidents in the Life of a Slave Girl,* was widely held to be a forgery until 1981, when it was proven to be authentic.

Most slave narratives were published with documents attesting to the trustworthiness of the narrators. To be heard, the narratives had to be authorized as true by white people. Furthermore, the composers of the narratives had to be affirmed, by white people, to be authors, and to be truth-tellers. The authorship function, the use of signs, was conceived to be a white function; it was a mark of mind, and minds in the European tradition, as we shall see, are held to inhabit white bodies. Africans were excluded imaginatively from the symbolic order, because the symbolic order itself was constituted by the dualisms by which Africans were abjected. Thus the notion of black authorship, particularly early on, was vexed: It appeared to many people to be *a priori* impossible; it was as if we had discovered a book by a baboon, or by an inanimate object.[4]

Henry Bibb's *Narrative of the Life of Henry Bibb, an American Slave* was published with a sheaf of documents. In a typical "letter" appended to the front of Brown's narrative, his editor, Edmund Quincy, addressed Brown thus:

> Your opportunities of observing the workings of this accursed system have been singularly great. Your experience in the Field, in the House, and especially on the River in the service of the slave-trader, Walker, have been such as few individuals have had;—no one, certainly, who has been competent to describe them. What I have admired, and marvelled at, in your Narrative, is the simplicity and calmness with which you describe scenes and actions which might well "move the very stones to rise and mutiny" against the National Institution which makes them possible.
>
> You will perceive that I have made very sparing use of your flattering permission to alter what you have written. To correct a few errors, which appeared to be merely clerical ones, committed in the hurry of composition under unfavorable circumstances, and to suggest a few curtailments, is all I have ventured to do.[5]

Such testimony has a double function. It attests to the truth of the narrative and the literacy and intelligence of its writer (in this case, it emphasizes that Brown was exceptional in this regard); it authorizes the authority of the writer, his status as an eyewitness to the events he describes. But it also admits the narrative under white sponsorship. It at once frees the slave to speak for himself and reasserts white power over that expression. This is an instance of a dilemma to which we will revert repeatedly: To enslave and silence you is to disempower you, but to allow you to speak is to empower ourselves. That you speak at all integrates you into the symbolic realm that is conceived as our exclusive domain, and the fact that you speak at all is thus subversive; that we dominate your speech reconfigures the symbolic as again our domain.

That, to repeat, is an imaginary self-construction of whiteness. Taking the thing from the other side, Joanne Braxton argues that, particularly with regard to black women, language has been an instrument of resistance throughout the history of African America: a medium of artistic creation, and a mode of cultural preservation.

> Like the narratives of questing male fugitives, narratives of female fugitives and former slaves echo the values and the language of the founding fathers [we will explore that theme later] as they traverse the path from slavery to freedom, literacy, and self-empowerment. Yet, within this "pregeneric quest" for freedom and literacy lies another myth—that of the female slave (or former slave) trying to protect her family and create a hearth and home for them. Her tools of liberation include sass and invective as well as biblical invocation; language is her first line of defense.[6]

We will see this theme of language and liberation developed very elaborately by Zora Neale Hurston, and it continues today, for example, in the work of various rappers. But initially the relation of black to white language was highly problematic, or rather, ambiguous. The experience of slaves had to emerge into the public linguistic space of the book or pamphlet in order to be represented at all to people who might have the power to ameliorate the conditions of slaves or to abolish the institution of slavery. But the very means of production of these texts could not fail to reinscribe the power relationship inherent in American racism. The texts were printed by white people for white people, even as they were composed by black people as liberatory instruments. And they could not fail also to repress some of the more colorful elements of black vernacular English, particularly its Africanisms, because they had to make a case for the equality of black people with white people in part by a suppression of cultural differences.

The white sponsorship that appears within and before the black text is a very early instance of the construction of authorial voices that I discussed in the introduction. The white voice "neutrally" authorizes the black text; the black voice appears as the narrator of the life of a subordinated person. In fact, the very reading of the slave narrative as a story of subordination is given by the white authority under which it is presented; surely the narratives are at least as plausibly read as tales of victorious resistance that culminate in an ability to tell one's own story and at a location where one can do so. But the appearance of the texts under white supervision seeks to constrain their readings within a theory/practice distinction, a distinction between mind and body, white and black. When Frederick Douglass first started speaking on the abolitionist circuit, he was told by his white sponsors, "'Give us the facts. . . . We will take care of the philosophy."[7] This presents not only the structure of the authorial function of the slave narrative but the structure of American race relations in a nutshell: black and white here are separated as facticity and philosophy, particular and general, speech and writing, raw material and technological mastery. It should be noted that Douglass immediately manifested his discomfort with this situation and was not, ultimately, controllable in this fashion.

Nor can I avoid the sting of my own critique here, for my own authorial voice speaks from on high, and seeks relief from its absence from my own body in the particularity of the black text. I am trying to treat this in myself by this writing, but I am also unavoidably redoubling its intensity, so that to seek a rapprochement with myself by doing theory of African-American autobiography becomes a form of slumming that makes me whiter and whiter until I threaten to disappear completely.

I want to allow the texts I discuss to speak for themselves. But in this book, it is precisely *I* who seek to allow this. I thus arrogate to myself the authority to present these texts; that arrogation is the structure of racial oppression in germ. This text, like the slave narratives, presents black lives under white auspices. The black lives that are presented do not lose, in this process, their subversive possibilities, yet those possibilities are attenuated by the context of presentation. *Could* I be an authority about African-American autobiography, and, if I could be, what would be the structure of that authority in circumstances of systemic racism? Above all, why do I *want* to be an "authority" on this topic? Do I want to help black folks to free themselves? And is wanting that a way of helping them to free themselves, or a way of seizing back white power over black discourse, a seizing that sweeps even liberation into racist oppression?

This problem was brought home to me in the most vivid way when I tried to teach the texts I discuss in this book to a largely black class. I expected to walk into that class as I had into dozens of philosophy classes, presenting myself as an expert on this material with something to hand over to my students, test them on, and so forth. After all, I had read the books carefully and repeatedly and had fit them all into a fairly neat conceptual structure (destroyed in the process of that class). But I quickly learned that to claim expertise on this material was to claim authority over what I really knew very little about: black experience in America. One thing I heard immediately was that this experience was multiple and vexed, that no one speaks for all African-Americans; my students resisted my use of such phrases as "the black experience." I had fundamentalist Christians from rural Alabama, kids from the projects in Birmingham, middle-class suburban kids, a Moslem woman who was a world-class triple jumper. They argued with each other daily about the scope and accuracy of the representations we found in the texts. And as the class went on, the balance of power in the classroom shifted dramatically; my students were the experts, and I learned something from them. Where I finally tried to emerge was as an "expert" on *white* experience. Such expertise itself came only through the leverage yielded by hearing how *we* constructed blackness. And yet one fact was inescapable: I was a white man teaching black voices to black people. I couldn't cease entirely being the professor who designed and was teaching the course; I had to grade the papers of black students writing about black texts.

I will continue to ask questions about my right to speak here and about my angle of vision as I go on, but I am afraid that I will arrive at no answers, and I am afraid that my own answers to these questions about myself would always be tainted, that I am precisely the person who cannot answer such questions when they are posed with regard to myself. I want to *display* these tensions here, rather than resolve them; any resolution that removed the tensions inherent in the racial politics of this project would simply redisguise the problem. To write theory of African-American autobiography that erased the power at work in the positions of author and "material" would be to use that authorial power in its most colonial mode: It would be a strategy for the comfortable reappropriation of the revelations of the texts. There are, of course, major differences between the situation of, say, a white abolitionist authorizing slave narratives and my use of black autobiography; then, the voices that an abolitionist could expect to hear confronting or answering her were all white. Now, however, there is a black critical community, ranging from my own students to the probable reviewers of this manuscript, to whom my writing is accountable and whose voices I cannot avoid. Another obvious difference is that I am hardly bringing to light unknown texts or "authorizing" previously unheard voices. Yet I do not wish to exculpate myself from the dangers inherent in this project, as though the canonic status of these texts or the existence of a black critical community counteracted the racial power structure within which this work is composed and deployed.

The fundamental epistemic strategy of the slave narrative, at any rate, is revelation: a bringing to light of the hidden. The strategy of pro-slavery propaganda was typical of elaborate systems of political or economic oppression: to force the truth into concealment, to throw up around the particular facts the facade of a vague, pleasing picture, and thus to allow the brutality to continue behind the "veil" (the term is Du Bois's). One reason why fugitive slaves were hunted down in the North, aside from their value as property, was that they were bearers of their own experience: They knew, and could be expected to speak, the truth. And Northern or foreign visitors to the South were treated to a parade of appearances, a guided tour of stereotypes, while the slaves were, in various obvious ways, constrained from showing forth the reality. Bringing the truth to light thus becomes associated with liberation, while being concealed behind the veil is associated with enslavement.

But the relation of concealment and revelation to slavery and liberation is, in fact, much more complex than the above sketch would suggest. For *within* slavery, the slave is pulled in just the opposite direction. To reveal one's thoughts to the master was always dangerous. To reveal one's movements to the master put the slave directly under the master's control. In fact, slavery could proceed only by means of an incredibly elaborate system of surveillance in which the white community as a whole cooperated, and into which they also conscripted black people. Henry Bibb, an inveterate escape artist, writes the following from bitter experience:

> I would remark that the domestic slaves [as opposed to field workers] are often found to be traitors to their own people, for the purpose of gaining favor with their masters; and they are encouraged and trained up by them to report every plot they know of being formed about stealing any thing, or running away, or any thing of the kind; and for which they are paid. This is one of the principal causes of the slaves being divided among themselves, and without which they could not be held in bondage one year, and perhaps not half that time.[8]

The strategy is to divide slaves into the watchers and the watched, and hence prevent a community of information through which resistance could be mobilized.

As late as the 1960s, Malcolm X was using the distinction Bibb draws as a powerful trope; he asserted that he was a "field Negro":

> There were two kinds of Negroes. There was that old house Negro and the field Negro. And the house Negro always looked out for his master. When the field Negroes got too much out of line, he held them back in check. . . . And today you still have house Negroes and field Negroes. I'm a field Negro. If I can't live in the house like a human being, I'm praying [for a fire and] for a wind to come along.[9]

Malcolm was referring here to "moderate" African-American leaders of his time—such as Roy Wilkins of the NAACP and even Martin Luther King Jr.—as "house Negroes." He held that such leaders were apologists who sought to defuse resistance in the black community, precisely the function Bibb ascribes to (relatively) privileged slaves. They were approved and rewarded as "black leaders" precisely by the white community, according to Malcolm. He asserted that their privilege was bought, in a structure that will soon be familiar, at the cost of cultural identification; to gain privilege is to identify oneself with white people, that is, with one's oppressors.

Booker T. Washington, himself born in bondage (his autobiography, ghost-written, was entitled *Up from Slavery*) notoriously said this:

> We went into slavery pagans; we came out Christians. We went into slavery pieces of property; we came out American citizens. We went into slavery without a language; we came out speaking the proud Anglo-Saxon tongue.[10]

This certainly repeats various vicious caricatures of African cultures. The notion that Africans had no language, a bizarre assertion that could not have withstood the most superficial contact with Africans, will prove a key to what follows. It is evidently an *a priori* claim, following not from any examination of Africans, but proceeding from European notions of what language was and what it meant to be able to speak. For one thing, to speak is to claim some authority, however slight. For another, and relatedly, mind in the Western tradition is bound up with text, so that to think is to have (our) words. This piece of *a priori* "reasoning" can be traced all the way back to Plato's division between Greeks and barbarians: those who can speak, and those who emit noises. The construction of the African as subhuman, as natural, as body, thus *required*, conceptually, that the African have no language. This construction of the African was the white construction of itself as a text, as the mind that commands the body by issuing instructions. It is not surprising, then, that Washington's approach was extremely successful as a fund-raising strategy directed at white philanthropists, and it is not surprising that most of these philanthropists were industrialists. Ten years after Washington delivered these words at Fisk, Tuskegee was one of the best-endowed institutions of higher education in the United States. (It is worth adding that Washington certainly did criticize the slave system, albeit somewhat ambiguously. He wrote, for example, that "from some of the things I have said one may get the idea that some of the slaves did not want freedom. This is not true. I have never seen one who did not want to be free, or one who would return to slavery."[11])

Slaves could not be allowed to move or speak freely, and this meant not only that they must at some times be shackled, or beaten, or sold to the deep south or away from their families for violations, but above all that they must be watched. To anticipate the extension of this theme into the body of this book, let me point out that this strategy persists today. Sister Souljah, in her autobiography, *No Disrespect,* says this:

> We . . . had to adjust to the welfare system and its bureaucrats. They wanted to know everything, and I mean *everything*. Not just your address and Social Security number and birthdate. They would ask my mother if she had a boyfriend. And if she did, did he give her money so they could deduct it from the extremely small amount of money they were giving her each month. . . . The welfare agency would authorize a social worker to roam freely through your apartment and report "findings." Findings could include men, extra toys, new furniture, et cetera. . . . Some days we had to stand in line starting at eight o'clock in the morning (or until they got ready to open) until four or five in the afternoon, merely to receive two blocks of cheese, butter, and two big steel cans of peanut butter. When you finally got to the front desk you would be asked a whole new round of personal questions in front of what seemed like scores of other people. (There were no private offices.) The welfare worker would talk loudly, to embarrass you. If you responded softly, as though you wanted some privacy or confidentiality, she would broadcast your responses by repeating them loudly.[12]

It is notable here that though slavery is designed for subordination and exploitation, and welfare (supposedly) for charitable uplift, they are both administered by surveillance. We will explore this development in what follows. For now, let us note that white uplift of black folks, like white degradation of black folks, can take the form of slavery. And let us note that the basic forms of race relations and race comprehension that circulate in American culture today persist from slavery.

In this situation it is precisely concealment that liberates, that creates a zone of the private that makes a rudimentary humanity possible in a situation of massive degradation. One of the strategies for concealment is to impersonate subservience, an impersonation which Washington sometimes approximated. Lunsford Lane, who was an inventor and an entrepreneur even in slavery, and who had been able to gather some money (he eventually succeeded in buying his wife, his mother, and his seven children), writes this:

> Ever after I entertained the first idea of being free, I had endeavored so to conduct myself as not to become obnoxious to the white inhabitants, knowing as I did their power, and their hostility to the colored people. The two points necessary in such a case I had kept constantly in mind. First, I had made no display of the little property or money I possessed, but in every way I wore as much as possible the aspect of poverty. Second, I had never appeared to be even so intelligent as I was. This all colored people at the south, free and slaves, find it peculiarly necessary to their own comfort and safety to observe.[13]

What Lane must conceal are precisely those things that construct the self-image of the Southern planter: his property and intelligence. Every expression of such things by Southern blacks is a threat to the self-image of the white man, which is constructed by the extrusion of the black. The first and simplest function of this forcing-into-concealment is the preservation of the appearance of inferiority, and in particular, stupidity, which justifies the slave system. Thus we get a very small epistemic loop: the system is bent on producing the facts that justify it. For example, it was a crime, bemoaned in many narratives, to teach a slave to read; there was a concerted attempt to manufacture stupidity. But true stupidity cannot be manufactured without, say, psychosurgery; forbidding slaves to read could only make intellectual activity more difficult to achieve. Thus the slavemaster attempted to force an *appearance* of stupidity out of the slave, an appearance that the slavemaster tried to produce for his own sake, so that he could describe the slave as animalistic, and hence justify the slavemaster's power. This forces the intelligence of the slave into concealment. When the master "discovered" that the slave was a childish dolt who needed "protection," he discovered an appearance forced out of the slave by the master's own technologies of oppression.[14]

What the slavemaster could not tolerate, then, was the expression of the slave's humanity, as humanity was construed by the master and associated by him with himself. White self-construction is perfectly encapsulated in the function of the *master as a watcher*. The slave becomes a pure datum, a material. The master becomes the pure eye that sees but that cannot see itself, and a will without desire. Patricia Williams says that slavery required "a deep socially embedded schema of self-partialization that was body-centered (as to blacks) and will-driven (as to whites)." And she adds that this "bizarre, even hallucinatory self-partialization" persists today.[15] Knowledge in the Western epistemological tradition is "justified true belief," an operation performed by minds over propositions, an operation that represents the world in the abstracted realm of text. Knowledge in the West is procured precisely in an apparent elision of desire, an elimination of subjectivity that pulls one into the objective realm where knowers are interchangeable, where they have no idiosyncratic content. What knows is a mind, conceived as a series of textual manipulations over propositions, construed in turn as textual or metatextual items. In an empiricist orientation, the materials out of which these propositions are derived, and by which they are justified, are "sense data." The body in this structure is an eye, and the mind a page or screen on which texts are inscribed. Mind in that sense is departicularized, while the data are conceived as particular but are finally themselves arranged taxonomically; they are subsumed under general concepts as they are captured or accounted for in propositions. Then knowledge consists of the *imposition* of comprehensible form on a welter of particulars, though it perhaps describes itself as a mirror of these particulars. The propositional reconstruction of the "data" is an active discipline or administration, but it disguises itself as a sheer receptivity. This procedure itself mirrors or mimics the oppressive social structure, in which the facts that we discover are manufactured by the *way* we discover them, and in which power is associated with a generalization of the particular, a comprehension, a stereotype.

The deepest resistance to slavery from within, then, was accomplished by bringing the truth and intelligence of the slave before the master, that is, by the insertion of the slave by the slave into the realm of mind, knowledge, and language. James W. C. Pennington, who later became the pastor of a major congregation in New York, describes an epochal event in his own liberation. Pennington's father was a particularly "devoted" slave in the sense that he worked hard and did what was expected. His master became enraged one day because several slaves had failed to appear for work on time. The master said this:

> "I shall have to sell some of you; and then the rest will have enough to do; I have not work enough to keep you all tightly employed; I have too many of you."
>
> All this was said in an angry, threatening, and exceedingly insulting tone. My father was a high-spirited man, and feeling deeply the insult,

replied to the last expression—"If I am one too many, sir, give me a chance to get a purchaser, and I am willing to be sold when it may suit you."

"Bazil, I told you to hush!" and suiting the action to the word, he drew forth the "cowhide" from under his arm, fell upon him with the most savage cruelty, and inflicted fifteen or twenty severe stripes with all his strength, over his shoulders and the small of his back. As he raised himself upon his toes, and gave the last stripe, he said, "By the *** I will make you know that I am the master of your tongue as well as your time."[16]

To be the master of someone's time is to control his body; to be the master of someone's tongue is to control his self-presentation. And to seek to master someone's tongue is to seek to expunge him from the order of language, to control his voice as a ventriloquist manufactures the voice of an inanimate puppet. Pennington writes that, after witnessing this event, "in my mind and spirit, I never was a slave" (7). It is not, therefore, enough to enact the fact that one's body has been subordinated; one must produce the appearance that one is satisfied with this fact; one must produce the appearance of subservience and silence as the cowhide produces the fact of subservience and silence. To be subordinated is a pure form of pain; to have to pretend to like it is shattering; and Pennington was reconfigured by his witnessing of that experience into a posture of resistance.

It is obvious, as well, that escape requires concealment, and Sojourner Truth said that she could not escape by day, because she would be visible, nor by night, because she could not see. *The Narrative of Henry Watson, A Fugitive Slave* elaborately describes the various lies Watson had to tell white folks in order to effect his escape.[17] Pennington was captured in Maryland as he tried to escape, and though he claimed to his captors that he was free, he was unable to produce his "free papers." His captors then demanded to know where he was from and to whom he belonged. Pennington says,

> The facts here demanded were in my breast. I knew according to the law of slavery, who I belonged to and where I came from, and I must now do one of three things—I must refuse to speak at all, or I must communicate the fact, or I must tell an untruth. How would an untutored slave, who had never heard of such a writer as Archdeacon Paley, be likely to act in such a dilemma? The first point decided, was, the facts in this case are my private property. These men have no more right to them than a highway robber has to my purse. (22)

Pennington, who was obviously a man of great moral scruples, finally came up with an ingenious series of lies: that he was in a gang of slaves being marched cross-country by a slave-trader, and that there was among the slaves an outbreak of smallpox which killed the slave driver. As people try to keep their distance from the presumably infected Pennington, he effects another escape. But the point of this passage is the relation Pennington asserts between himself and his truth. It is his own private property, his possession, indeed almost his only possession. Other people want possession of his truth as the means and the sign of his enslavement, and to give them his truth is to become again a slave. Knowledge is the sign of authority, and the authority of the sign. Indeed, the only power that Pennington has in this situation derives from his preservation of the privacy of his truth. Escaped slaves in the North of this era faced a similar situation; if their status, hence their history, were known, they would be subject to blackmail and manipulation. Concealment becomes the only possible strategy for nurturing the truth, the only place where a non-enslaved self can be made.

We will see, throughout this book, that concealment is a strategy—though far from the only strategy—by which African-Americans have sought to preserve their culture, their freedom, and their lives against a "system" which constantly seeks to empower itself over them by revealing them, by "understanding" them. Hence, the "truth" of the black American plays a double and dangerous role: It is an instrument of liberation and an instrument of enslavement. There is the general "truth" of the stereotype, or of the pastoral, patriarchal plantation, which is an instrument of oppression. There is the general "truth" of the actual condition of "the slave," which is an instrument of liberation. Both of these are, to a large extent, the productions of white people: both the defenders of slavery and the abolitionists spoke the "general truth" about slavery. But there is also the specific and culturally located truth of the individual or the family in slavery, which is both an instrument of oppression and of liberation, both in its concealment and in its revelation. From the earliest slave narratives, such particular truths were the productions of black people, and the arena in which their lives were conducted.

Thus, from the earliest discourses on the matter, there is in the public imagination a "white" mode of truth-production and a "black" mode. The white mode is associated with generality, hence with comprehension, science, intellect, and so forth. The black mode, on the other hand, seems insistently particular, and hence is associated with primitivism and with the body. This is a fictional distinction, as is more obvious today than ever, given the massive production of philosophy and theory by black people (though this production is not so massive as it should be even now). But again, it is relevant that the narratives were published under white auspices; their intractable particularity both disturbed and confirmed white stereotypes of black people, the content of which, as I will suggest, when finally stripped of detailed elaborations, amounts merely to particularity. That the slave speaks at all subverts the metaphysics and epistemology of slavery. That the slave speaks *only* of particular experiences (which is false, but which even abolitionists tried to enforce) reinstitutes this metaphysics and epistemology. Particularity is at once reviled and desired, and constitutes both a confirmation of white hegemony and the deepest possible threat to it. I will return to these themes at much greater length. For now it suffices to note that these two modes of truth, the concealment and revelation of which always take up a location in a systematics of power, is manufactured by a social system of oppression. The black autobiographical tradition is at once an insertion of the African-American into the order of the sign and the sign of his or her particularity; it contains deep expressions of resistance, but it also in some ways confirms the construction of whiteness.

This social system and its epistemic expressions are by no means limited to American slavery; they informed the entire colonial system, for example, and they pervaded the sciences of the nineteenth century. Indeed the empirical sciences as modes of generalization and comprehension (think here especially of the human sciences, such as anthropology and sociology) are informed by and employ modes of exclusion, oppression, exploitation, and surveillance. Empirical science in this sense extrudes the particular—above all, the body—and makes of it an object of study, but it elides particularity in its practitioners; it is pure minds "grasping" pure bodies. This gets read through the theory of evolution, for example, so that *Homo sapiens* is on a trajectory to pure mind, and any little reminder of embodiment drags one back into the body of a monkey. Thus we construct our spiritual lives out of our construction of the physical lives of black people; we construct ourselves as scientists out of our construction of black people as objects of study; we construct ourselves as civilized out of our construction of the primitive, the unevolved, the apelike.

Of course, the people we are busily accounting for as apes bring with them into our lives rich and complicated arts, religions, and languages. What we found in Africa was anything but a raw human material. Slavery thus depended for its legitimation on the manufacture of appearances. Even the intraregional slave trade depended on the separation of appearances and reality. William Wells Brown worked for several years for a slave trader, and he writes as follows:

> Before the slaves were exhibited for sale, they were dressed and driven out into the yard. Some were set to dancing, some to jumping, some to playing cards. This was done to make them appear cheerful and happy. My business was to see that they were placed in those situations before the arrival of the purchasers, and I have often set them to dancing when their cheeks were wet with tears. (45)

This describes the division among slaves that Bibb credits with being necessary to their continued enslavement, and it is relevant in this context that Brown was very light-skinned, and thus more likely to be a "house Negro" in Malcolm's terms. The actual conditions and interior lives of slaves were hidden from outsiders, and hidden also to a large extent from their masters, who often employed poor whites for the work of physical cruelty. What we want is grinning, dancing idiots, so we simply manufacture them. We then notice that these folks seem to be grinning, dancing idiots, and justify our racism out of our own invention.

Slavemasters, in fact, often set about manufacturing appearances for their own entertainment and edification. Bibb, a highly religious man, describes a plantation sabbath as follows:

> Those who make no profession of religion, resort to the woods in large numbers on that day to gamble, fight, get drunk, and break the Sabbath. This is often encouraged by the slaveholders. When they wish to have a little sport of that kind, they go among the slaves and give them whiskey, to see them dance, "pat juber," sing and play on the banjo. They get them wrestling, fighting, jumping, running foot races, and butting each other like sheep. This is urged on by giving them whiskey; making bets on them; laying chips on one slave's head, and daring another to tip it off with his hand. (68)

This early version of "slumming" provides a diverting spectacle. But it does so simply by a systematic conjuring of a preconceived set of appearances; the master goes to see a particular thing, then pays and constrains the slave to produce it. It must be remarked that we white folks still like to watch black people dance, play music, and fight. It is obvious, I suppose, that this technology of appearance, this systematic production of the desired surface, creates or can create an immense tension between the inner and the outer. It would be no surprise if the outer expression came to be regarded by the slaves themselves as utterly false, and the reality, the authentic life, were pushed inward. Inwardly, it can be concealed and retained. So the epistemic situation of slavery comes to associate the outer with the lie, and the inner with authenticity. Of course, the inner and the outer are connected in many ways, and the attempt to manufacture the desired appearances is always also an attempt to endanger or destroy the inner life of the slave. Just as one proceeds to control black people by turning them against one another, one tries to debase each individual by turning her against herself, by making the appearance she presents a continual self-betrayal. One who is thus debased becomes incapable, finally, of resistance. That this *is* a fundamental mode of domination must remain unknown to ourselves, because the appearances we manufacture must be naturalized; we must take them as showing *what the black person is*. That is, the mechanisms by which we exert power *must* be invisible in order to have the desired effects, and thus we make ourselves invisible *as empowered*. But the slave searches for a zone of concealment in which a self, and hence a possibility of resistance, can be nurtured.

The slavemasters, then, sought the production of appearances not only for the sake of power over the slave; such activities allowed the enormity of their acts to remain to some extent veiled to themselves and to a world that might judge them morally. The Virginia slaveholder George Fitzhugh wrote in 1853 that the slaves

> love their master and his family, and the attachment is reciprocated. . . .
> Southern slavery has become a benign and protective institution, and our
> negroes are confessedly better off than any free laboring population in the
> world.[18]

About half a century later, Booker T. Washington could make a similar claim:

> When we rid ourselves of prejudice, of racial feeling, and look facts in the
> face, we must acknowledge that, notwithstanding the cruelty and moral
> wrong of slavery, the ten million Negroes inhabiting this country, who
> themselves or whose ancestors went through the school of American slav-
> ery, are in a stronger and more hopeful condition, materially, intellectually,
> morally, and religiously, than is true of an equal number of black people
> in any other portion of the globe. (*Up from Slavery*, 37)

Now that is obviously and obscenely false. But what is not obvious is that Fitzhugh and Washington did not themselves believe it. In order to continue to oppress on such a grandiose scale and in such a brutal manner, the slavemaster had to conceal himself from himself as an oppressor, to provide and to some extent believe a series of claims that any detached observer would immediately dismiss as rationalizations. If the slavemaster believed himself to be the brutal oppressor he was, he could not have held on to the image of himself as a civilized, Christian man, and that image was at the heart of the self-construction of the Southern planter. The slavemaster and, later, the "liberal" white philanthropist rewarded the production of appearances that confirmed their image of black folks, and hence confirmed their image of themselves.

Many masters attempted furiously to hold on to a picture of themselves as Christians, and as paternal protectors of childlike slaves.[19] Thus, in order to retain their own view of themselves—in order not to come to the sudden, horrible realization that they were moral and religious monsters of a certain kind—they required that the slave put forward a childlike appearance, an appearance of primitiveness expressed as total embodiment, and an appearance of dumb, simple happiness. So the fundamental motivation for the technology of appearance is not an attack on the slave, but a therapy for the master, a therapy by which the slaveholder's profits can be maximized without the slaveholder having to confront his own endorsement of the inhuman means by which his coffers are filled. This technology requires the erasure of the slave as a speaker, a knower, and a moral agent. But it also requires the erasure of the slaveholder as a physical object implicated in a set of material conditions by which bodies break bodies. The material is "transcended" by the manufacturing of appearances by the master and for the master that erase precisely the material conditions by which the body of the master is maintained and fattened. The selfhood of the slave is constantly endangered by this technology, but the delusory selfhood of the master cannot be maintained without it. (I will argue that we white folks retain this delusory selfhood to this day.) While the technology of appearance renders the slave invisible to the master as an oppressed person, it renders the master invisible to himself as an oppressor. Both of these things are required if the oppression is to continue.

The master thus constructs the interlocking identities by ejection. The black becomes the white's "other." (Even identifying people as white or black is the initial inscription of the dualism: we're dealing with a broad spectrum of colors of differing saturations, ranging from light pink to deep mahogany, but not including either white or black.) But to say that this construction is inadequate to the facts is an understatement: It is a single-minded assault on the facts made possible by and necessitating the assault of the white self on its own materiality. The slave is supposed to have no language, no culture, and no virtue except that which is lent by white culture; the slave is conceived as raw human, or rather not-yet-human, stuff. Then we can make of him what we will, and we make of him a perfect inverse image of ourselves. But meanwhile the raw stuff itself has to be manufactured as raw by incredibly intense disciplines of cultural annihilation, and the production of appearances assures us that these disciplines have been perfectly successful in eradicating African languages, religions, arts, and values. Thus the self/other dualisms are purely imaginary, because they are supposed to be "natural," biological, and so forth, but they have to be *made,* or rather, simulated, by breaking bodies.

The slave narratives confront us with litanies of cruelty, a barrage so intense that one is supposed never to allow oneself to be seduced by appearances again. But the most dramatic epistemic strategy of the slave narrative is to compromise not the appearance that the master imposes on the slave, but the appearance that the master imposes on himself. One of William Wells Brown's most effective strategies is simply to reproduce, at the end of his narrative, without comment, selections from Southern slave codes and newspapers. These simply allow the practices of white people to be seen. That is why Douglass's narratives have tremendous moral power; they expose the hypocrisy, the false self-image of the slavemaster. The master accuses the slave of being a savage and a heathen. But the savagery of the master, beyond anything the slaves could think of mustering, was revealed to the slave every day. And though many slaves were devout Christians, Douglass asserted the Christianity of the slavemaster to be the merest appearance and the most disgusting hypocrisy.[20]

In the famous appendix to his first autobiography, *Narrative of the Life of Frederick Douglass, an American Slave,* Douglass writes as follows:

Between the Christianity of this land, and the Christianity of Christ, I recognize the widest possible difference—so wide, that to receive the one as good, pure, and holy, is of necessity to reject the other as bad, corrupt, and wicked. To be the friend of one is of necessity to be the enemy of the other. I love the pure, peaceable, and impartial Christianity of Christ: I therefore hate the corrupt, slaveholding, women-whipping, cradle-plundering, partial, and hypocritical Christianity of this land. Indeed, I can see no reason, except the most deceitful one, for calling the religion of this land Christianity. I look upon it as the climax of all misnomers, the boldest of all frauds, and the grossest of all libels. Never was there a clearer case of "stealing the livery of the court of heaven to serve the devil in." . . . We have men-stealers for ministers, women-whippers for missionaries, and cradle-plunderers for church members. The man who wields the blood-clotted cowskin during the week fills the pulpit on Sunday, and claims to be the minister of the weak and lowly Jesus. . . . He who sells my sister, for purposes of prostitution, stands forth as the pious advocate of purity. . . .

> We see the thief preaching against theft, the adulterer against adultery. We have men sold to build churches, women sold to support the gospel, and babes sold to purchase Bibles for the *poor heathen*![21]

Throughout his career as a writer and speaker, Douglass reserved his greatest passion for the revelation of hypocrisy. And one of the most passionate things he says about himself is that "I prefer to be true to myself, even at the hazard of incurring the ridicule of others, rather than to be false, and incur my own abhorrence" (36). William Andrews rightly points out about that sentence that it is "a crucial declaration in the history of black autobiography."[22]

Nevertheless, the epistemic structure of the situation is more complicated than mere hypocrisy. For the master not only claims to be what he is not; he claims the slave to be what he (the master) actually is. The relation of nineteenth-century America—particularly in such regions as Alabama, Mississippi, and Arkansas—to high European ("white") civilization (which, to white Americans as to white Europeans, was civilization *simpliciter*) was highly problematic. Slaveowners liked or perhaps needed to think of themselves as highly "civilized," "cultured," "educated," and so forth. But the actual plantations had to be carved out of a hostile wilderness. They were distant from artistic and literary centers. Such institutions of higher education as existed were rudimentary by the standards of Europe or even of New England. Thus one may well suppose that the status of being "civilized"—a status achieved, to whatever extent it was achieved, on the back of slave labor—was one that slaveowners regarded with a great deal of anxiety. Their relation to that status was tenuous. In addition, many of the slaves derived from high African civilizations.

The strategy that was developed to deal with this anxiety was one that we will see repeated throughout the history of American race relations: ejection. The master was civilized, Christian, and so forth, precisely in relation to the slave. The master attributed to and enforced upon the body of the slave those aspects of his own personality that he wished to elide. Thus, the savagery and false Christianity of the master became utterly invisible to himself, while the civilization and religion of the slave were likewise hidden. Among other things, this made the master invisible to himself as an oppressor: Slavery was justified by the intrinsic character of the slaves, who were supposed to be idiotic savages. The slavemaster created himself as an oppressor by the same act by which he made himself invisible to himself as an oppressor; he created himself as the inheritor of high European civilization while becoming invisible to himself as a savage living on a frontier.

By the same token, the savagery and blasphemy of the master were perfectly and continually visible to the slave, who was their constant victim. So the slave knew the master in a way that the master could not possibly know himself while retaining his self-image. The reality of slavery could not be seen by the master, and his own participation in that reality had continually to be repressed, denied, redescribed. But there is no redescribing savagery to its victims; there is no way for them to evade the reality that these people are destroying families, inflicting torture, or using women as sexual possessions against their will. So the slaves were the bearers, in some sense the only bearers, of the truths of slavery and of those who perpetuated it. One strategy that the narratives pursued was a reverse bestialization, in which the masters and mistresses of the South were shown to be the animals that they took their slaves to be. The dictated *Narrative of the Sufferings of Lewis Clarke,* for example, says this about slavemistresses: "I have heard every place I could get into any way ring with their screech-owl voices. Of all the animals on the face of this earth, I am most afraid of a real mad, passionate, raving, slaveholding woman."[23] This epistemic leverage, this visibility of the truth to the slave, is what lends the slave narratives their urgency and their power. They have the power to make white people visible to themselves as oppressors, visible to themselves as heathens, visible to themselves as savages, visible to themselves as hypocrites. That is a fearsome power indeed.

This is the first appearance to white America of the power of black autobiography, a power that we shall see made manifest again and again and channeled in different directions. In displaying the imaginary white construction of the black both *as imaginary,* and as having the most concrete material effects in segregation, exploitation, and cultural destruction, black voices reveal not only the white construction of the black, but the white construction of the white. They reveal this construction, first of all, to be itself imaginary and thus hypocritical. But they display for us most emphatically the *optionality* of this construction; they denaturalize our image of ourselves. Every attack on white constructions of blackness becomes a revelation of white constructions of whiteness. *I didn't know,* except in the most abstract general sense, that I was a white person, until I heard myself called a honky (and I was called a honky many, many times, over a period of years) and then started to find out in a variety of ways what people meant when they called me that. The word *honky* is a reversal of the machinery of cultural attack; it is an example of a counter-invective made as a response to white "racial epithets." But one effect of this is that when one is called a honky, one has the sudden realization that one *has* a race, that one is not simply the abstract general human being.

And the content of *honky* is interesting: it means, first, "oppressor," but second, it encapsulates a critique of white culture for its soullessness, its coldness, its physical clumsiness and repression. A great moment in this reversal of discourse was Richard Pryor's *imitation* of a white man, with a doofy white walk and white talk. The actual content of a hundred years of blackface was instantly revealed.

And make no mistake: Within the slave narratives, this rendering-visible of oppression extended not only to the slavemasters, but to the whole of white American culture. The slave narratives were aimed, above all, at bringing the situation home to white Northerners, and they continually emphasized, to this end, the complicity of the whole white nation in slavery. Brown writes as follows, with regard to Nat Turner's revolt:

> But for the fear of northern bayonets pledged for the master's protection, the slaves would long since have wrung a peaceful emancipation from the fears of their oppressors, or sealed their own redemption in blood. . . . The countenance of the people of the north has quieted the fears of the slaveholders, especially the countenance they receive from the northern churches. . . . Slaveholders hide themselves behind the church. A more praying, preaching, psalm-singing people cannot be found than the slaveholders of the south. . . . Their child-robbing, man-stealing, woman-whipping, chain-forging, marriage-destroying, slave-manufacturing, man-slaying religion, will not be received as genuine; and the people of the free states cannot expect to live in union with slaveholders, without becoming contaminated with slavery. They are looked upon as one people; they *are* one people; the people in the free and slave states form the "american Union." Slavery is a national institution. The nation licenses men to traffic in the bodies and souls of men; it supplies them with public buildings to keep their victims in. . . . The American slave-trader, with the Constitution in his hat and his license in his pocket, marches his gang of chained men and women under the very eaves of the nation's capitol. And this, too, in a country professing to be the freest nation in the world. They profess to be democrats, republicans, and to believe in the natural equality of all men; that they are "all created with certain inalienable rights, among which are life, liberty, and the pursuit of happiness." . . . The people of the United States, with all their high professions, are forging chains for unborn millions, in their wars for slavery. With all their democracy, there is not a foot of land over which the "stars and stripes" fly, upon which the American slave can stand and claim protection. (87–88)

The tropes that Brown employs here would be used again a century and a quarter later by Martin Luther King Jr., and they have the effect of puncturing the words and appearances of freedom with the pervasive reality of oppression. They show the Northerner to himself as a hypocrite, as a conspirator in enslavement. Indeed, the concealment practiced by the slave did not end with her escape to the North; quite the contrary. The escaped slave always needed to remain concealed from agents of her master or from bounty hunters. Thus, though Northern whites attempted to insulate themselves from slavery by concealing their own participation from themselves, the slave narratives attempted to display this complicity to them.

Perhaps the greatest of the slave narratives, considered from the point of view of this convoluted epistemic situation, is the shocking and spellbinding book *Incidents in the Life of a Slave Girl,* by "Linda Brent" (Harriet Jacobs). In his introduction to an edition of this book, Walter Teller briefly discusses the relation of Jacobs to her editor, the abolitionist Lydia Maria Child. Child herself had written that "such changes as I have made have been mainly for purposes of condensation and orderly arrangement." Teller writes:

> If here and there the editorial pencil has also added a literary, moralizing, or didactic touch, these embellishments are easily distinguishable from the stark realities of Linda Brent's life and straightforward narration. Her first-hand knowledge of slavery speaks for itself.[24]

This represents the *a priori* judgment, directly contradicted by Child herself, that everything of general import in Jacobs's text is written by Child, whereas the straightforward particular narrative was composed by Jacobs. Teller, that is, meticulously and "easily" separates the authentic narrative from its theoretical grounding by meticulously and "easily" separating the bits of the text that are raced white (the general, theoretical observations) from the bits that are raced black (the unadulterated narrative of a life). In fact, Jacobs emerges in this text as a moralist who was perfectly capable of issuing general indictments of slavery, and who would have been very likely indeed to have done so.

Jacobs, who describes her parents as mulatto, grew up as a "house" slave. Like most of the other slave narratives, Jacobs's work describes various tortures inflicted by white people on black people, including many by her master, whom she calls "Dr. Flint." These are harrowing, but—despite her privileged position in comparison with many other slaves—Jacobs's own story is more harrowing yet. It displays, first of all, the basic conditions under which power operated in slavery; more specifically, it displays the particular form of sexual power that white masters exercised over their female slaves. This power, though always backed up by the specter of physical beatings and blackmail (if the woman had children, for example, she was constantly reminded that they could be sold elsewhere), was fundamentally epistemic. Dr. Flint sought to make Jacobs available for sexual use by surveillance; she sought to resist being used by concealment. In Jacobs's narrative, hiddenness is the only sort of resistance available; every fact about her that becomes known is an instrument whereby she can be controlled sexually.

Flint begins his assault on Jacobs when she is fourteen. She describes herself at this point as very naive and very religious, and writes as follows of the first such incident:

> It was on a lovely spring morning, and when I marked the sunlight dancing here and there, its beauty seemed to mock my sadness. For my master, whose restless, craving, vicious nature roved about day and night, seeking whom to devour, had just left me, with stinging, scorching words; words that scathed the ear and brain like fire. . . .
>
> When he told me that I was made for his use, made to obey his command in *every* thing; that I was nothing but a slave, whose will must and should surrender to his, never before had my puny arm felt so strong. (16)

Jacobs indeed mustered superhuman strength in resistance to Flint, as we shall see. Nevertheless, her basic situation seemed without recourse:

> He peopled my young mind with unclean images, such as only a vile monster could think of. I turned from him with disgust and hatred. But he was my master. I was compelled to live under the same roof with him—where I saw a man forty years my senior daily violating the most sacred commandments of nature. . . . My soul revolted against the mean tyranny. But where could I turn for protection? No matter whether the slave girl be as black as ebony or as fair as her mistress. In either case there is no shadow of law to protect her from insult, from violence, or even from death; all these are inflicted by fiends who bear the shape of men. The mistress, who ought to protect the helpless victim, has no other feelings towards her than jealousy and rage. (26–27)

One thing that this passage displays, and to which I will return at length in the chapter on Du Bois, is that race is a social construction rather than a biological fact. Being raced as black was not a matter of skin color, but of illegitimacy or impurity of a certain sort. Jacobs was quite light, and her brother is described as easily passing for a white man in his escape from slavery. But marriages among slaves, first of all, had no legal sanction, and could be broken at the whim of the master. The children were his property, and the light-skinned children who continually appeared on plantations and farms of the South were, by law, to "follow the condition of the mother" as slaves. Thus, the blackness of black people was not a matter of skin color but of social location, and though the slave trade had a stake in the biological characterization of race, the actual circumstances in which it was conducted made a mockery of this pseudoscience. William Wells Brown describes several slaves who for all the world appeared white.

The mistress of slaves often found herself in the position of seeing slave children grow up around her who resembled her husband, and the cruelties that were practiced by such mistresses on their husbands' victims and their children are described by Jacobs with horror. For Jacobs, the mistress was the first station of the system of surveillance that came to envelop her life completely. It is worth mentioning that Jacobs's mistress was the foster-sister of Jacobs's mother: Jacobs's grandmother, a central character in the book, had nursed them both together, and had weaned her own daughter early to provide milk for the other child. Jacobs writes,

> Mrs. Flint possessed the key to her husband's character before I was born. She might have used this knowledge to counsel and screen the young and innocent among her slaves; but for them she had no sympathy. They were the objects of her constant suspicion and malevolence. She watched her husband with unceasing vigilance; but he was well practiced in means to evade it. (29–30)

Mrs. Flint thus constructs a system of surveillance around her young female slaves and also around her husband; Dr. Flint finds various means of slipping away, or slipping Jacobs into his room. At one point, Mrs. Flint makes Jacobs swear on a Bible that she has not had sex with Dr. Flint.

> She now took me to sleep in a room adjoining her own. There I was an object of her especial care, though not of her especial comfort, for she spent many a sleepless night to watch over me. Sometimes I woke up, and found her bending over me. . . . At last, I began to be fearful of my life. It had often been threatened; and you can imagine, better than I can describe, what an unpleasant sensation it must produce to wake up in the dead of night and find a jealous woman bending over you. . . . How often did I rejoice that I lived in a town where all the inhabitants knew each other! If I had been in a remote plantation, or lost among the multitude of a crowded city, I should not be a living woman at this day. (33–34)

At this point, Jacobs is being continually watched, even in her sleep. Her life depends tenuously on the epistemic community in which both she and her mistress are, tenuously, located; if she were to die, it would be only too obvious why and by whose hand. Here is also the structure of the slave narrative in germ: the disease is falsehood achieved by concealment; the cure, publicity. Indeed, Jacobs writes that she knew of two mistresses who urged their husbands to free their children by slaves, and says of the marriages involved, "Concealment was at an end, and confidence took the place of mistrust" (p. 35).

Nevertheless, though Jacobs did not lack an epistemic community, this community was largely a community of black people, and hence lacked power to shield her from those with epistemic and physical hegemony; even had her situation been known, there was no one with the power to transform it. In fact, fully to share her situation with other slaves or with free black people would have been to endanger *them.* Obviously, had her mistress killed her, the mistress would not have stood trial for murder. Jacobs depends on this community for whatever resistance she mounts, however, and as Andrews points out, it is a community of women, including Jacobs's grandmother and the sympathetic mistress of a nearby plantation. Andrews also points out that the autobiographical act itself is an attempt to establish a community that can valorize and perpetuate forms of resistance.[25] Henry Bibb, who was sold again and again in various states and to various masters (finishing off with the best of the bunch, a Native American in Oklahoma), felt the limitations of epistemic community acutely:

> I was in a far worse state than Egyptian bondage; for they had houses and land; I had none; they had oxen and sheep; I had none; they had wise counsel, to tell them what to do, and where to go, and even to go with them; I had none. I was surrounded by opposition on every hand. My friends were few and far between. I have often felt when running away as if I had scarcely a friend on earth. (72)

And though Bibb ran away repeatedly and ingeniously, this sort of isolation was a tool of control on several levels. First, isolation debilitates one for individual, and obviously prohibits one from collective, resistance. Second, the master retained his slaves, particularly his male slaves, who were most likely to run, by the threat of isolation: one's family was held hostage.

It is obvious, I suppose, that slaves were isolated from the larger epistemic communities which (with mixed success) guarded and enforced the rights of American citizens. In *My Bondage and My Freedom,* Douglass writes:

> Public opinion in such a quarter, the reader will see, is not likely to be efficient in protecting the slave from cruelty. On the contrary, it must increase

and intensify his wrongs. . . . [The] plantation is a little nation of its own, having its own language, its own rules, regulations and customs. The laws and institutions of the state, apparently touch it nowhere. The troubles arising here are not settled by the civil power of the state. The overseer is generally accuser, judge, jury, advocate, and executioner. The criminal is always dumb. (*My Bondage*, 150–60)

The isolation of the plantation from the institutions of justice, of course, bespeaks the collusion of those very institutions in the slave system. And what this isolation constitutes is an epistemic regime in which the slave is systematically severed from those who could use a knowledge of his situation to protect him, and in which the slave is silenced. Thus slavery relied, as we have already seen, on a destruction of African-American community and on an isolation of it from wider communities. Slavery relied on the creation of tiny dictatorships with their own languages, and then on the silencing of the slaves even from those languages. And if this regime could not annihilate the actual community and communication of slaves, it could force it into concealment, surround it with dangers of betrayal and discovery that freighted trust and openness between slaves with fear.

And though, for Jacobs, concealment within the elaborate family system of the Flints' household is a threat—it would leave her at the mercy of her mistress, for example—the problem as Jacobs sees it is precisely a lack of concealment. She is watched, even as she sleeps. She lacks an epistemic community that is empowered to help her, though she depends for her survival on the community she has. But she utterly lacks private space, a zone of the personal. This, first, is a constant reminder that she is property; or rather, property itself is an epistemic concept here to some extent: being chattel means that one is always, if the need arises, available to be seen, that one cannot, ultimately, conceal oneself. The ejection of the other that constitutes the imaginary dualism of race and hence constitutes whiteness is achieved in large measure by the white gaze, a gaze that objectifies black bodies as the specular negative images of itself and that, hence, abstracts the white person into an abstract knower. The term *overseer*, which remains in black vernacular (where it is often punned or identified with "officer"), is perfectly appropriate: Authority over the slaves is exercised by seeing, with the constant backup of the lash. Indeed, a "field nigger" has no motivation at all to work, and thus must be watched at all times.

The notion that black folks are "lazy," for example, derives from this source: They will slack off as soon as they cease to be observed. This fact is stated with extreme clarity in the *Narrative of Sojourner Truth*. In 1810, Isabella, the woman who came to be known as Sojourner Truth, was sold in New York for seventy pounds to a woman who had not previously owned slaves:

> Mrs. Dumont, who had been born and educated in a non-slaveholding family, and, like many others, used only to work-people, who, under the most stimulating of human motives, were willing to put forth their every energy, could not have patience with the creeping gait, the dull under-standing, or see any cause for the listless manners and slovenly habits of the poor down-trodden outcast—entirely forgetting that every high and ef-ficient motive had been removed far from him; and that, had not his very intellect been crushed from him, the slave would find little ground for aught but hopeless despondency.[26]

Now it may well have been true that slaves were by and large despondent, and certainly they had little opportunity for intellectual development. But what is missing here is an acknowledgment (an acknowledgment made by Lane, for example) that such manners are modes of resistance. First, one resists work by listlessness; one does everything just as slowly and ineffi-ciently as one can, in order to keep one's labor from being efficiently ex-ploited. And the dullness and listlessness of the slave is a mode of epistemic resistance. One conceals oneself behind a screen of apparent stu-pidity so that the master and his minions do not have access to one's in-ner life. This is both a confirmation of and a resistance to the specular regime that makes white people white, and it institutes a particular divi-sion of the inner and the outer that we will explore as we proceed. But for now it must be noted that this division originates as a strategy for self-preservation. The zone of privacy that is constantly being violated finally retreats into the self, and while the surface appears blank, the inner per-son seethes, as all these narratives attest.

The Narrative of Sojourner Truth explores these themes with utmost intensity. For even the internal life of the slave could, finally, be contami-nated by seeing, so that one became the watcher of oneself. This is an-other theme that will be explored as we go on, especially in relation to Malcolm X: the notion of "internalized oppression." In slavery, the in-ternalization of the master's eye finally becomes a motivation to labor, so that the epistemic attack can, occasionally, actually achieve its economic aim: an extremely productive laborer. Here is Sojourner's version:

> She became more ambitious than ever to please [her master]; and he stim-ulated her ambition by his commendation, and by boasting of her to his

friends, telling them that "*that* wench" (pointing to Isabel) "is better to me than a *man*—for she will do a good family's washing in the night, and be ready in the morning to go into the field, where she will do as much at raking and binding as my best hands." Her ambition and desire to please were so great that she often worked several nights in succession, sleeping only in short snatches, as she sat in her chair; and some nights she would not allow herself to take any sleep, save what she could get resting herself against the wall, fearing that if she sat down, she would rest too long. These extra exertions to please, and the praises consequent on them, brought upon her head the envy [?] of her fellow slaves, and they taunted her with being the "*white folks' nigger.*" . . . At the time, she looked upon her master as a *God;* and believed that he knew and could see her at all times, even as God himself. And she used sometimes to confess her delinquencies, from the conviction that he already knew them. (32–33)

Now this exemplifies Truth's superhuman will and industry, displayed throughout her life. But it also demonstrates the possibility of an internalized eye of the other, a wielding of power over oneself that is the reflection or intensification of the specular power that is wielded over one. She later came to "look back in astonishment" at her commitment to being a good slave.

It is interesting that, in a charge that continues to be leveled at people to this day, Truth was called a "white folks' nigger." She was subject to this charge precisely because she did not engage in the well-understood forms of resistance: the manufacture of an appearance of laziness and stupidity. She was subject to the charge, finally, because she allowed the white folks, as it were, inside her head, because she had "internalized her oppression." This compromised her identity as an African-American in the eyes of African-Americans precisely because she failed to maintain a zone of the personal inside herself. Later, this took different forms; for Malcolm X, a "white folks' nigger" is a black person who tries to "act white." And these days, African-Americans who are upwardly mobile in white-dominated society are told to "stay black." But here what is in question is not the production of a white person in a black body, but the too-perfect fulfillment of white expectations for a slave. Sojourner drives herself to be as ruthlessly exploited as possible, out of certain forms of self-division.

She signaled her victory over this internalized specular power when she *named herself* "Truth," when she claimed a place, and a privileged place (truth) in the system of signs. Recall that one of the first moves in enslavement was to take away the name of the slave and to claim the power to name the slave. William Wells Brown, for example, makes of his names a symbol of his journey from slavery to freedom. The removal of the name, or arrogation by the master to himself of the right to name, is a removal of the slave from the language, or rather, an assertion of the right of the master to control the manner in which the slave appears in the language. To claim the right to name oneself, to place oneself into the language, is thus both to resist white power and to attack its underpinnings in the semiosis of domination that marks the West's science, philosophy, and technology. And it is, furthermore, to *change the language itself,* to mark or make a zone in the language that exceeds or resists the West's semiosis of domination.

We return now to *Incidents in the Life of a Slave Girl:* Jacobs falls in love with a free black man, which enrages her master. He strikes her, and she tells him that she despises him.

> For a fortnight the doctor did not speak to me. He thought to mortify me; to make me feel that I had disgraced myself by receiving the addresses of a respectable colored man, in preference to the base proposals of a white man. But though his lips disdained to address me, his eyes were very loquacious. No animal ever watched its prey more narrowly than he watched me. (40)

Jacobs eventually urged the man she loved to leave the area, for a marriage would have had no sanction, and no effect on Flint, who would continue to have her under his control.

Flint seeks to isolate Jacobs under his gaze by building her a house where he can "make a lady" of her, where she can be kept for his use out of the sight of his wife and of Jacobs's family.

> In the blandest tones, he told me that he was going to build a small house for me, in a secluded place, four miles away from the town. . . . Hitherto, I had escaped my dreaded fate, by being in the midst of my people. When my master said he was going to build a house for me, and that he could do it with little trouble and expense, I was in hopes something would happen to frustrate his scheme; but I soon heard that the house was actually begun. I vowed before my Maker that I would never enter it. I had rather toil on the plantation from dawn till dark: I had rather live and die in jail, than drag on from day to day, through such a living death. . . . And now, reader, I come to a period in my unhappy life, which I would gladly forget if I could. The remembrance fills me with sorrow and shame. It pains me to tell you of it; but I have promised to tell you the truth, and I will do it honestly, let it cost me what it may. (53–54)

The desperate (by her own account) expedient that Jacobs hit upon was yielding sexually to an unmarried white man of the area, a man who later became a U.S. Congressman. She places herself under his protection, and when Flint tells her that the house is ready, she says that she is pregnant. Eventually, she has two children, a boy and a girl, by the future legislator. "There is something akin to freedom," she writes, "in having a lover who has no control over you, except that which he gains by kindness and attachment" (55). (This passage makes me wonder why and whether Jacobs *was* ashamed of this relationship, which she describes using terms reflecting love and commitment. What she expresses when she expresses shame, however, is that she is a *good woman;* she claims the right to be treated with the respect due to a virtuous lady. I will return to this point.)

Jacobs describes the general redoubling of epistemic control over the lives of slaves that followed the revolt of Nat Turner: houses are searched, and the only public meetings of black folks—modest Sunday church services—are banned. Furthermore, the facts about the revolt itself are assiduously repressed; knowledge of the actual events by the slaves would be dangerous. This public activity perfectly mirrors the continuing effects of Flint's control over Jacobs: He seeks to control her by controlling the knowledge she possesses, and by possessing knowledge of her. Indeed, as is a constant theme of slave narratives, Jacobs repeatedly emphasizes that the slaves are controlled by lies.

> Slaveholders pride themselves upon being honorable men; but if you were to hear the enormous lies they tell their slaves, you would have small respect for their veracity. I have spoken plain English. Pardon me. I cannot use a milder term. When they visit the north, and return home, they tell their slaves of the runaways they have seen, and describe them to be in the most deplorable condition. A slaveholder once told me that he had seen a runaway friend of mine in New York, and that she besought him to take her back to her master, for she was literally dying of starvation. . . . I afterward staid with that friend in New York, and found her in comfortable circumstances. She never thought of such a thing as wishing to go back to slavery. . . . I admit the black man *is* inferior. But what makes him so? It is the ignorance in which the white men compel him to live. (42–43)

Superiority and inferiority hence correspond to knowledge and ignorance. Power accrues to comprehension, sight, literacy. After Jacobs leaves Flint's house, and even after she has escaped to the North, he tries to manipulate her to return with lies, that is, he tries to render her ignorant, and to use her ignorance to *possess* her.

Thus the truth of the public world, information, and education become very direct instruments of resistance, or rather, conditions for the possibility of resistance. One supposes that the abolitionists who urged the freed or escaped slaves to record their experiences often found them eager to do so, and that the former slaves themselves experienced their narratives as a liberation. Much, however, remained concealed. For example, and typically, Jacobs changed her own name and those of everyone else involved, suppressed geographical details, and certainly avoided giving any specific information about the route of her escape. Such information would immediately have placed her family and friends—both those still in bondage and those who were fugitives—in peril. Indeed, such information would probably have placed herself and her children in peril.

Despite her efforts, Jacobs finally ends up under constant watch. "I rarely ventured out in the daylight," she writes, "for I always went in fear, expecting at every turn to encounter Dr. Flint, who was sure to turn me back, or order me to his office to inquire where I got my bonnet" (70). And, in an attempt to break her from the father of her children, "He came morning, noon, and night. No jealous lover ever watched a rival more closely than he watched me and the unknown slaveholder. . . . When my grandmother was out of the way he searched every room to find him" (83).

Finally—because, in my reading, being the object of the gaze had become intolerable—Jacobs resolves on flight. She spends a horrible series of nights in hiding, and is sheltered for awhile on a nearby farm, the mistress of which is sympathetic. Finally, she comes to believe that the situation puts her protectors in too much danger. She finds a place of concealment in her grandmother's house: a garret over a shed. In a dark room, seven feet by nine, and *three feet tall* at its highest point, without even the space to turn over in bed because of the slope of the roof, she sequesters herself. Jacobs was to spend the next *seven years* hiding in this dark "loophole." Her children lived in the same house.

> I was not comfortless. I heard the voices of my children. There was joy and there was sadness in the sound. It made my tears flow. How I longed to speak to them! I was eager to look on their faces; but there was no hole, no crack through which I could peep. (117)

Eventually, Jacobs made some chinks in the wall and was able to watch her children at play. One supposes that was one reason why she did not try to get to the North much more quickly; she wanted to remain near her children. Imagine the torture, however, of seeing and hearing them without being able to communicate with them or touch them.

My immediate reaction to this horror (Jacobs's limbs atrophy to the point where she is crippled, for example; the roof leaks, and she is by turns soaked, frozen, and fried), is that she was much worse off after than before her escape, that virtually any course of action, and certainly sexual pliability, would have been preferable to such a fate. But for Jacobs at this era of her life, freedom is worth any price whatever, and freedom here means simply and solely concealment. Valerie Smith remarks that "given the constraints that framed her life, even the act of choosing her own mode of confinement constitutes an exercise of will, an indirect assault against her master's domination."[27] Jacobs herself writes,

> This continued darkness was oppressive. It seemed horrible to sit or lie in a cramped position day after day, without one gleam of light. Yet I would have chosen this, rather than my lot as a slave, though white people considered it an easy one; and it was compared to the fate of others. I was never cruelly over-worked; I was never lacerated with the whip from head to foot; I was never so beaten and bruised that I could not turn from one side to the other; I never had my heel-strings cut to prevent my running away; I was never chained to a log and forced to drag it about, while I toiled in the fields from morning till night; I was never branded with hot iron, or torn by bloodhounds. On the contrary, I had always been kindly treated, and tenderly cared for, until I came into the hands of Dr. Flint. I had never wished for freedom till then. But though my life in slavery was comparatively devoid of hardship, God pity the woman who is compelled to lead such a life! (118)

Notice that darkness and light have a double metaphorical and actual function. They track the black/white dichotomy, and they mark the trope by which knowledge and ignorance are articulated in the West. But though darkness connotes ignorance and entrapment, it also suggests concealment and nurturance. Notice, too, that Jacobs subjects herself to analogues of the various abuses she describes; she renders herself unable to move, for example. But it is crucial that she does this by her own choice instead of experiencing it at the hand and under the eye of another.

It is crucial also that Jacobs asks God's pity for "the *woman* who is compelled to lead such a life." For Jacobs's enslavement was not primarily a thing of whips and chains, though these always lurked in the background, but a thing of continual surveillance and continual attempts at manipulation. Flint does not *rape* her, he attempts (with the shadow of force and control of her children) to *seduce* her, to "make a lady of her." He attempts to control her *emotional* life; he compromises her internal independence from him. Jacobs resists him and describes her resistance through the tropes of virtuous purity; she appeals to a European ideal of virtuous womanhood to assert her right not to buckle under to his min-istrations. She seeks to make herself comprehensible, to find a language for herself by which to make herself understood to white people (to her master's family and later to her readers), in the only way possible: by lo-cating herself in the discourse of white femininity. This enrages Flint, but is also comprehensible to him, and perhaps pulls him up short of the ac-tual physical attack that he continually seems to contemplate.

In fact, Flint's desire for Jacobs, and its particular expressions, stand in some need of explanation. Presumably, for example, there were other slaves that he could have used with less difficulty. But Flint never stops, never lets up at all. Even after Jacobs has escaped, Flint pursues her for a decade. This is hardly a case of romantic love. But it reads comprehensi-bly through the structures of love to some extent, precisely because Jacobs constructs herself as a woman with the right to sexual resistance, as "un-available" in precisely the same manner that upper-class white women were supposed to be unavailable to men other than their husbands. Flint's desire, in fact, is fueled by a sort of witches' brew of conflicting impulses that I will explore at much greater length in the chapter on Malcolm X. For now it suffices to say that the desire of the master for the slave is a de-sire born in part of difference; the slave is alluring in her strangeness, her exoticism, her primitiveness, and so forth: the very stereotypical features that suit her to be a slave in the first place, the very blackness we consti-tute by constituting ourselves as white through ejection. But Jacobs is less different than most; she is light-skinned, and beautiful, we may well sup-pose, precisely by European standards. And in addition, to repeat, she as-serts herself in the familiar tropes of respectable womanhood. Thus, she is tantalizing as being different, but she is nevertheless comprehensible: a devastating combination, and one that continues today in white appreci-ation of black female beauty.

The very subordination of the slave, her status as property, makes her a sign of masculine power; male domination of women in slavery could hardly be read except as an intensification of male domination of women in patriarchy; the very fact that *they are dominated* makes female slaves especially explicit signs of the dominating power of male sexuality: male sexuality is, in part, constructed in patriarchy as the pleasure of domi-nance. And yet here too is the alluring doubleness, for what makes Jacobs irresistible to Flint is precisely her heroic resistance to him in circum-stances in which resistance is well-nigh impossible. She is simultaneously his property and recalcitrant to his transformations. This is literally mad-dening; it maddens Flint with desire. He possesses her, but he cannot *know* her, and he both compensates himself for this lack and tries to make it good by trying to know everything about her, to become omniscient with regard to her.

I understand this desire and this pleasure, as I have already said. What we white men find in black women is what we have systematically sought to eliminate in ourselves. To begin with, all traces of subordination must be eliminated (imaginatively) in the construction of ourselves as masculine. And what blackness *means* here—physicality, particularity, and so forth (precisely the aspects Teller uses to sort out Jacobs's text from Child's)—is what we seem to lose in the construction of ourselves as certain sorts of authorities (slavemasters) or certain sorts of authors (introducing slave narratives, or writing books on African-American autobiography). When I wanted Jaqui, the girl I asked out in junior high school, I wanted her in a different way than I wanted the white girls around me; I wanted her exoticism, her heightened presence in her own body: things I constructed about her out of racial signifiers. But Jaqui was also "pretty" by white standards. She was both comprehensible to me as a sexual object and resistant to comprehension as a sexual object, and this is what made the erotics of the situation so intense.[28]

This situation eroticizes the essentializing and naturalizing functions of race dualism. It *uses* the content of this dualism as a technique for intensifying desire. It eroticizes dominance and difference (the dominance *of* what is different). The imaginary white excisions of body, spontaneity, and particularity are experienced as absences, as places where the self is lacerated and hence yearning to be made whole. And yet interracial erotics also displays the fact that this dualism is always in the process of being breached. Certainly it displays the fact that we white guys are as embodied as anyone else, and the matings across the dichotomy are of a character that is only possible between members of the same species. Furthermore, though it is difference that is eroticized, this difference cannot be understood in its erotic function as a dualism. For the forms of white male desire require not only what is perfectly ejected or incomprehensible; they require also proximity, so that the search is on for partners that are different but possible, partners that are interstitial, that fall between the established categories, and hence embody the impossibility of race as dualism. And of course, interracial sex is precisely one way in which interstitial persons are made. So the eroticization of difference both supposes the construction of race by white ejection as a dualism, and shows that construction to be impossible. I will return to this theme at length.

Jacobs's concealment is certainly not a physical freedom from bondage. It is an emotional freedom from manipulation, an assertion of virtue which is the claiming of a place in the semiotic system, and a construction and preservation of her knowledge of herself. It is, among other things, a resistance to being Flint's property, a defiance of his claim to be her master. Hence, it takes the form of an assertion of equality to, for example, Flint's wife; it is a claim to be treated as a lady (Sojourner Truth: "Ain't I a woman?"), to insert herself in white femininity. This self-construction throws the hypocrisy of *white* female self-construction, exemplified in the plantation mistress, into high relief. White women, in the racial discourse of the day, represented purity: race purity, as mothers of white children, and sexual purity, as virtuous women innocent of desire. But the exercise of Mrs. Flint's power over Jacobs shows the brutality of her attempt to preserve "purity" in her family. Jacobs clearly indicts Mrs. Flint for failing to support her, and underscores the way white women's self-constructions depend on their treating black women as diabolical sexual temptresses. Indeed, the way Jacobs defended herself against Flint may have threatened Mrs. Flint's understanding of herself: If white women are "pure," it is because black women hold the place of the body, of sexuality, and are the source of race contagion. The black woman's claim to sexual virtue, expressed in her resistance to Flint's advances, threatens her mistress's self-image in the same way that a male slave's manifestation of intelligence and civilization threatens the self-image of his master.

It is finally Jacobs's claim to feminine virtue, though complicated by powerlessness, in which her interstitiality resides. Her heroism is her extreme endurance of horrible conditions in order to preserve herself, sexually and epistemically, from her master's domination. As her constructions of herself as female take up an interstitial position in the dominant discourse of black and white womanhood, so her body becomes *literally* interstitial, as she hides in the space between the walls. Her experience of her enslavement was the experience of being continually forced into visibility; freedom becomes invisibility, so that she spends seven years, recovering from her epistemic availability by a retreat into the nurturing darkness and aloneness. Jacobs becomes something that cannot be seen, but which can see; she sees her children, and every day sees Flint himself passing to and fro. This is her perfect vengeance upon him, though he is unaware of it: she sees him without being seen by him, knows him without being known by him. She ceases to be chattel, which in this case means the object of the gaze, and becomes a pure eye; her body atrophies, but she *sees*. And she then begins to manipulate Flint, through his desire for her return and for her sex, and even lures him by a series of false letters to look for her in the North. The power she resists is epistemic and linguistic, and so, finally, is the power she constructs for herself out her virtue and her concealment.

2

VEIL AND VISION

KNOWLEDGE IN DU BOIS

The slave narratives established a discourse about truth and knowl-edge. The persons who wrote the slave narratives brought their knowledge of the particular conditions of slavery to bear in an enuncia-tion of the truth about slavery, and sought by this exercise to transform the conditions that had oppressed them. They attempted to shatter the lies in which slavery concealed itself by an assertion of knowledge: knowledge both of the conditions under which African-Americans lived and the con-ditions by which they were oppressed. Most especially, they sought to shatter the lies that enshrouded not black degradation but white domi-nation. Their knowledge was an instrument of resistance. Even to *claim* knowledge was a subversion of the dualism that sought to eliminate the voices of black bodies from discourse.

Now as Foucault has shown us, knowledge is bound up with power. For example, the notion of race, the division of the world's people into races, is a discursive construction which arranges around itself and per-meates a whole field of "knowledge": a physiology of racial types, an an-thropology of race-conditioned or race-symptomatic cultures, a sociology of racial conditions, a psychology of particular faculties or talents, and so forth. In fact, it is fair to say that many of these sciences were invented largely for racial purposes; that, for example, whatever the current range of its application, anthropology originated as a comprehensive taxonomy of the races.[1] And of course such sciences harbor and subserve various normative programs; they are anything but purely descriptive: early scientific anthropology was a site of white self-construction through nonwhite abjection. As soon as the races of the world are scientifically distinguished, there is the possibility of racial "purity," of miscegenation, of physiological or psychological anomaly, all of which become vectors of power.

In the writings of W. E. B. Du Bois, there is an attack on these fields of scientific knowledge, which takes the form, first, of a rejection of various scientific results and methods. But I am going to argue that, more, there is in Du Bois an attack on the very notion of knowledge deployed in these discourses, and the revelation of an alternative site of knowledge, an alternative that seeks, in a more systematic way than do the slave narratives, to transform knowledge from a locus of oppression into an instrument of resistance to domination. The resistance to the forms of knowledge that are instruments for the oppression of African-Americans opens up the possibility of alternative knowledges, and perhaps an alternative account of knowledge. Now, though I attribute this opening to Du Bois, it must immediately be said that his own relation to the move from knowledge to counterknowledge was ambiguous and volatile. In fact, it is precisely for that reason (among others) that he is an exemplary figure.

In my view, knowledge as power in the West is a structure of comprehension, in which particular facts are ranged under general facts, formulated as generalizations. The particular facts are gathered, categorized, and then presented as freed from their particularity, as released into the general. In the case of sociology, which is above all in question here, the particular is abstracted into the statistical. In a reverse reification, things and persons and situations are relieved of their concreteness. The particular facts that are so relieved and inserted into a taxonomy are already articulated in "research" by the concepts under which they are subsumed, so that the taxonomy is always present, even in the initial encounter with the concrete situation. No fact is recalcitrant to comprehension, because there is a place in the taxonomy for all genuine possibilities; anything that stands outside of or is interstitial to the taxonomic grid is ignored or effaced. The application of the taxonomy, in a procedure which we will examine more closely but have already seen in operation, constructs the facts it discovers.

Notice that this shows that modern science is raced. The mode of thought that deals with the particular by subsuming it, that ranges particular bodies and events *under* general concepts, and that identifies that as knowledge, has already performed the sort of ejection that makes races. One problem with the particular is the complexity and recalcitrance with which it resists the transformations of human will (just as *one's own body* resists the transformations of one's own will, and thus opens the possibility of sin and evil). To subsume the particular under the general is to *make it available for use,* to subsume it not only under one's concepts, and not only into one's language, but also thereby to subsume it under one's will. This introduces the particulars so subsumed into the realm of profit, turning them to economic use. We learn this by enslaving other people, and we learn to enslave other people by this.

Power flows in the opposite direction from knowledge here; while knowledge is (apparently) constructed by generalizing the particular, power is exercised in the application of general principles to particular situations. The purpose of the research is a conceptual and, finally, a physical leverage over the situations de-reified (relieved of their "thingliness," or particularity) in the taxonomic structure. Thus the possibility of the human sciences is precisely the possibility of human taxonomies in which we arrange people by income level, age, state of health, race. The human sciences seek to "grasp" the messy situation in order to provide the possibility of specific reconfigurations of it.

Furthermore, the scientist himself is transfigured in this process. As the wielder of the objective and objectifying taxonomic grid, the wielder of the publicly authorized language, the scientist is manufactured as an objective observer, is freed from his own particularity. He wears a white coat and reports the data, erasing his own idiosyncratic voice from the scientific discourse in which everyone is supposed to sound the same. The knowledge he produces is public property, and claims a neutral position; it is the sheer reflection of the antecedent facts. By erasing himself, the scientist races himself, claims a race for himself, bleaches himself.

The social sciences are, in part, a mode of surveillance; they gather information about people: their characters, movements, productive and reproductive activities, their deaths. This information yields very direct forms of leverage; one cannot control what one does not know. For just this reason, slavery was an epistemic disease as well as a physical brutalization. In general, the social science trained on African-Americans throughout this century has aimed, by its own account, at their "uplift." It seeks to accomplish this aim, among other things, by their medicalization: it seeks to diagnose their "pathology" in anticipation of a cure. But time and again, as we will see, what appears to white America to be uplift appears to African America to be cultural destruction. Diagnosis and cure come to be both charitable acts and assertions of power; your need of my charity is my power over you, enforced and articulated in a regime of information. You are safe neither from my prying eyes nor from my good deeds. (It should of course also be emphasized that much early American sociology was anything but charitable, often putting itself in the service of directly racist propaganda.) If you were the sheer object of science, you could not contest my descriptions of you, whatever my intentions were in so describing you. The attempt to convert you into the object of science is the attempt to replace your voice with mine, to authorize myself as the voice of your experience.

Yet such direct exercises of power through surveillance and uncontested description are not the only mechanisms by which power circulates. Surveillance (as Foucault has pointed out, and as was thematized in Sojourner Truth's narrative), when it is thorough enough, or when one is not sure when one is being watched, may become self-surveillance. One produces the desired appearance even when one is not being watched, at first because one does not know when one is being watched and finally because the eye of the watcher has been internalized; one becomes the watcher of oneself. At this point, power can operate not only nakedly and physically, but invisibly. As we are going to see, it is this very thought that drives much of Du Bois's writing. And as we are also going to see, it is this thought that drives much black authorship in this century (paradigmatically, Malcolm X's), and often the particular modes of resistance to white power taken up by African-Americans.

The social sciences come to "know" about people by shoving them into the right pigeonhole, and those who use this information exercise power by the taxonomy. Power—power that operates by scientific comprehension or generalized surveillance—does not have the time or inclination to deal with particular situations, or the people in them, so its method is a constant assault upon particularity in general: finally all particular things are, if they are anything at all, mere examples of general principles—in this case, statistics. In that sense the notion of race is top-to-bottom knowledge as a propaedeutic to power. I remember that in the natural history museum of my youth there were mannequins arranged in tableaux showing the "characteristic" Eskimo, Pygmy, and so forth (missing: the average white European). One aims here for a "general picture" and presumes a certain audience, an audience that itself evades being pictured in this way. The scope of power is increased by taking in as many particulars as possible, and this "taking in" is subsumption, comprehension, or what is called, in the Western tradition, knowledge. This requires, to say the least, radical simplification of the particular situation: its remaking into something that can be comprehended and hence controlled. And it will motivate disciplines that not only simplify the situation, but exercise power by *imposing* this simplification on concrete situations.

This mode of knowledge as comprehension is not an instrument. It is an entire comportment in the universe; it is a way of life. It is a way in which all information can be processed, all relationships conducted (the taxonomy of roles), all activities pursued. It is a way of encountering the world, or rather a way of mitigating the poignancy of the encounter with the world. But it is also a way of gaining power over the world; knowledge as comprehension always makes the comprehended object into a potential instrument. Thus, though not itself an instrument, knowledge as comprehension makes of everything else an instrument. This sort of comprehension enslaves, for example, though there are other ways to enslave.

Of course, such considerations bear directly on the conduct of the "Negro problem" in the late nineteenth century, which was the golden era of truth as comprehension: of the most simplistic scientism, for example, and the most facile hosannahs to the power of human intelligence. In the gathering of statistical knowledge bearing on the "Negro problem," the taxonomy of race itself is taken as an assumption: That *there are* races about which information can be gathered is the initial empowering articulation of a taxonomy. The early sociology of "the Negro problem" has no place for people who are ambiguously raced; it presumes the same taxonomy that was, for example, fossilized into laws concerning slavery in the South: that any detectable black ancestry rendered one black, so that "whiteness" meant simply "purity" of blood—having no known black ancestors. That the child of a black person and a white person is a black person is of course not something we discover, but something we stipulate for reasons that emerge directly from power relations.

There were, nevertheless, two ways in which the science of the races as an instrument of white power could be resisted. One was simply by turning it around and showing it to be a failure on its own terms. This was actually done: Various idiocies about cranial capacity, slope of the forehead, and the physiological or intellectual causes of poverty were simply scientifically refuted, so that the taxonomies had to be rearticulated. (We are not yet finished with this process; see *The Bell Curve*.) Du Bois himself turned truth by comprehension against itself as an instrument of power; in his elegant sociological studies at Philadelphia and Atlanta, he attacked general truths with general truths, science with science. And in

Dusk of Dawn, he drew this conclusion, which he had long labored to establish:

> It is easy to see that scientific definition of race is impossible; it is easy to prove that physical characteristics are not so inherited as to make it possible to divide the world into races; . . . that the possibilities of human development cannot be circumscribed by color, nationality, or any conceivable definition of race.[2]

The passage not only attacks the scientific taxonomy of the races but goes on explicitly to state that the taxonomy is deployed for the sake of power.

> All this [he says] has nothing to do with the plain fact that throughout the world today organized groups of men by monopoly of economic and physical power, legal enactment, and intellectual training are limiting with determination and unflagging zeal the development of other groups. (*Writings,* 654)

That is, the racial grid is, among other things, a pretext under which the real mechanisms of power are operated.

I should quickly emphasize that Du Bois himself had an ambiguous relation to this conclusion. In his now notorious early essay "The Conservation of Races" (1897), for example, he wrote this:

> The history of the world is the history, not of individuals, but of groups, not of nations, but of races, and he who ignores or seeks to override the race idea in human history ignores and overrides the central thought of all history. What, then, is a race? It is a vast family of human beings, generally of common blood and language, always of common history, traditions, and impulses, who are both voluntarily and involuntarily striving together for the accomplishment of certain more or less vividly conceived ideals of life. (*Writings,* 817)

Du Bois did not fully free himself of the concept of historical races with ideal destinies until the middle of his long career, and perhaps not even then. Yet, as the previously quoted passages from *Dusk of Dawn* demonstrate, he resisted this idea as well. (This resistance is already present even in "The Conservation of Races," where Du Bois appears to be poised between the notions of race as culture or ethnicity and as biological destiny, a "blood" on which culture supervenes.[3])

Du Bois's own race was a case in point; he himself traced at some length his white ancestry (this is reflected in each of his autobiographies). In fact, the "talented tenth" which Du Bois celebrated as the hope for the leadership of African America was largely made up of persons of mixed race, many of whom had been educated at traditionally white universities in the United States or, as was Du Bois, in Europe. In Du Bois's struggles with Booker T. Washington and the "Tuskegee Machine," there was a constant underlying theme of racial tension; Washington and his followers were suspicious of the "talented tenth's" light skin, European mannerisms, and European models of education and literary composition.

Du Bois's mixed racial location is reflected in what is perhaps the deepest mark of his thought: its continual ambivalence, or as he himself puts it, his "twoness" or "double consciousness." Du Bois's ambivalence about race in general as expressed in "The Conservation of Races" is absolutely typical of his literary production in a wide variety of respects, and one way to read the subsequent development of African-American narratives of self and culture is as a series of explorations of the various locations that this ambivalence makes available. The notion, for example, central in particular to Du Bois's early writings, that the black race has a grand destiny is itself a mode of resistance to white supremacy. Malcolm X (see chapter 3) used just such a structure of thought for just such a purpose; he sought to *assert* the history and destiny of the black race as a mode of counterknowledge. Zora Neale Hurston (see chapter 4), however, asserted with the Du Bois of *Dusk of Dawn* that races were the creatures of myth; then she sought to free herself of the constraints of racial construction, even as she explored and celebrated African-American culture. These two fundamental approaches to a rearticulation of race in American culture are both present in germ in Du Bois.

Du Bois's attitude toward the centrality of science as a mode of "uplift" also oscillated, sometimes in the course of a single essay. This aspect of Du Bois's authorship has been discussed in an exemplary way by Robert Stepto. First, Stepto develops an analogy and contrast of Du Bois's use of science with the use of "authenticating" documents in the slave narratives. The scientific material that Du Bois deploys still takes up a certain place in the system of racial signifiers, but now the authenticator of Du Bois's experience is himself, the sociologist. With regard to *The Souls of Black Folk*, Stepto writes,

> Du Bois wants that [authenticating] space for his own voice, his own array of narrative modes, his own arsenal of authenticating evidence, whether it be empirical in scientific terms, or "twice-told" or archetypal in literary terms. He seeks to create an eclectic mode of self-initiated authentication in which exterior documents to be pieced into a tale are largely forsaken in favor of a scheme of documentation that reinforces the tale by becoming an integral part of the narration.[4]

This accounts elegantly for one of the most conspicuous aspects of Du Bois's various autobiographical writings: his oscillation between highly particularized narrative and statistical sociology. If I am right about the racial content of sociology, this oscillation is more problematic and more closely related to the authentication procedures of the slave narratives than Stepto perhaps believes. Nevertheless, the authenticating materials that Du Bois brings to bear on his narratives are his own production, and that is a very significant divergence from the slave narratives, even where the notion of slave narrative is extended as far as Washington's *Up from Slavery,* which, as Stepto argues, participates in the earlier modes of authentication even as it forms the basis of the body of texts to which Du Bois's *The Souls of Black Folk* responds.

Certainly, Du Bois began as a sociologist and toward the end of his life embraced a Marxist vision of total social comprehension by science. In *The Autobiography of W. E. B. Du Bois: A Soliloquy on Viewing My Life from the Last Decade of Its First Century,* he says of his undergraduate days at Fisk University in Nashville, "I was determined to make a scientific conquest of my environment, which would render the emancipation of the Negro race easier and quicker."[5] And of his work in Philadelphia he writes,

> The Negro problem was in my mind a matter of systematic investigation and intelligent understanding. The world was thinking wrong about race, because it did not know. The ultimate evil was stupidity. The cure for it was knowledge based on scientific investigation. (*Autobiography,* 197)

It is worth noting that Du Bois here turns the language of medicine around; he hoped to cure not primarily the pathologies of the Negro ghetto, but the pathology of white ignorance. This is a deft reversal of the uses of science in identifying and treating pathologies; it is the assertion of a form of counterknowledge, because it seeks to render the "white man" visible by the skillful use of the white man's own strategies, one of the functions of which is precisely to conceal the content of whiteness.

Du Bois's use of science and his distinction as a scientist were themselves subversive, for they certainly showed that a black man could engage in the generalizing discourse that was central to white self-construction. To take hold of scientific discourse, to master *it* and to use it as a method of resistance, were unprecedented and radical reversals of the white word. Much was made, in this regard, of the lightness of Du Bois's skin; he must have, somewhere, gotten a white mind, that is, a mind. The attempt was made to *discredit* Du Bois as a black man by accrediting him as a white man, but he resisted this move with obvious success, simply by insisting on his own blackness and by putting his science into the service of black people. To be a black scientist even now (not to speak of 1900) is to take up an ambiguously raced location and hence to throw the dualism of race into doubt.

During the course of his life, Du Bois developed both a suspicion of "scientific conquest" and a very different mode of authorship. A turning point in this development was his experience of lynchings and race riots while he was teaching in Atlanta. He says that "one could not be a calm, detached scientist while Negroes were lynched, murdered, and starved" (*Autobiography*, 222).

So although Du Bois was a masterful sociologist and, for a time at least, a believer in the concept of race, he was acutely aware of the limitations of the approach of pitting science against science, general truth against general truth. One of these limitations was that white sociologists found many ways to ignore or confine his results. (The U.S. Bureau of Labor actually destroyed the only copy of his sociological study of Lowndes County, Alabama, which it found politically problematic.) As a scientist, and despite the obvious quality of his research, he was successfully marginalized. He found another such limitation, however, in the very "scientificity" of sociology, and thematized his discomfort even in describing his Philadelphia research:

> We must study, we must investigate, we must attempt to solve; and the utmost that the world can demand is, not lack of human interest and moral conviction, but rather the heart-quality of fairness, and an earnest desire for truth despite its possible unpleasantness.[6]

Du Bois's technique in conducting his Philadelphia research was unconventional at the time; he lived in the impoverished area he studied while he conducted his survey.

> With my bride of three months, I settled into one room in the city over a cafeteria run by a College Settlement. We lived there a year, in the midst of an atmosphere of dirt, drunkenness, poverty, and crime. Murder sat on our doorstep, police were our government, and philanthropy dropped in with periodic advice. (*Autobiography*, 195)

He implicated himself thereby not only in the statistical information he gathered, but in the lives of the people he gathered it about.

The power that accrues to scientific knowledge as comprehension requires precisely an erasure of "human interest and moral conviction." The scientific study is precisely "objective," "neutral," and so forth; that is why it is taken to constitute knowledge in the Western tradition, where knowledge is traditionally opposed to interested opinion. This appearance of neutrality is essential to conceal the mechanisms of power which scientific comprehension makes possible; it de-reifies the object of study; it de-reifies its own power; it attributes its own power to abstract general conditions, just as it understands itself to be comprehending the particular by articulating just such conditions.

About a later and much larger project concerning African-Americans in the whole nation, Du Bois said in *Dusk of Dawn,* "Social scientists were then still thinking in terms of theory and vast and eternal laws, but I had a concrete group of living beings artificially set off by themselves and capable of almost laboratory experiment" (*Writings,* 600). The point here is not a radical critique of sociology, but a suspicion that scientific truth and the truth of experience—eternal law and concrete living beings—can come apart. Even at his most "scientific," Du Bois returned continually to "living beings."

As we have seen, beginning with the slave narratives, there has been an imaginary construction of a "white" mode of authorship and of a "black" mode. The white mode is, in the Du Boisian sense, scientific. The black mode is a particularized narrative. (Recall once again the way the voices of Harriet Jacobs and her editor were sorted out.) Du Bois engaged in both modes of authorship with the utmost devotion. And right now I am myself engaged in a white authorship and also in the project, at moments at least, of trying to throw off white authorship, of tearing myself, my voice, apart.

When I was a teenager, I saw a black man on Florida Avenue in D.C. with a small boy whom I took to be his son. The man was literally dragging the boy down the street by his leg, and as the boy cried, the man screamed at him, "Get tough! Get tough!" This was a way of making the black boy a black man. My father tried to make me a white man, and by a similar technique. On a camping trip, when I was nine or ten years old, I got into an argument with my father about whether Napoleon was a great man. Now I knew almost nothing about Napoleon, and neither of us had any stake whatever in the outcome. Yet we argued in the most extreme way for what must have been an hour or so. He yelled at me about Napoleon, interrupted me, and finally crushed me with a combination of facts and intellectualized insults. I cried, which meant I lost. I kept trying to argue through my tears, but I had been beaten and humiliated. At that point, he might as well have yelled at me to "get tough." What this and many similar incidents taught me was how to argue like a white intellectual, in the "scientific" mode; eventually, I had so little emotional or personal stake in any given argument that the thought of being brought to tears would have struck me as absurd. I learned to argue from "on high," to mimic the voice of God. The black man in D.C. was toughening his child physically, so that he could withstand physical pain and manifest physical toughness. My father was teaching me to be a philosopher. Of course, the content of this difference is classed as well as raced: it concerns not only the difference between white and black but between intellectual and manual labor. But then again, the class system is itself raced as well.

The hazing I went through in graduate school was a refinement of this technique. We were taught in great detail to make our prose perfectly transparent (at least to those who had undergone similar trainings), as if emerging from nowhere and everywhere simultaneously. We were taught to play at intellectual puzzles in which we apparently had no emotional stake whatever. We were taught that the problems of our discipline arose at a level of the highest generality, and that we need have no allegiance to anything but the construction of logically valid arguments that would help us arrive at the neutral truths of the matter. The voice I learned there is, I think, the voice that still speaks here, though it speaks against itself in those same measured tones. And the atmosphere of the graduate programs I attended was purely white: pure white knowledge taught to the pure white students who had been admitted to the program. We became what we were by a series of systematic exclusions.

Beginning with some of the essays collected in *The Souls of Black Folk,* Du Bois became much more entangled in this problematic. Here, he pops the blimp of comprehension with the pinpoint of particularity; he asserts his own life and the lives of people he knows as responses to general assertions. At the end of "The Forethought," he announces his repudiation, for the time being, of sociology: "And, finally, need I add that I who speak here am bone of the bone and flesh of the flesh of them that live within the Veil?"[7] Here Du Bois, in the most emphatic terms, inscribes his own interest in the matters at hand, as he had done implicitly by a commitment to live with his Philadelphia population. This is an abnegation of the pretension of objectivity, of the scientific stance. It is also, therefore, a negation of comprehension, an abjuration of power. In a way, this is a shocking move, because for Du Bois, achieving the power of the neutral voice was an achievement accomplished by overcoming seemingly insuperable obstacles. But the move is profound: a relocation of the center of knowledge, and hence of truth and power, a receiving of knowledge back into the body, back into the particular. It is the enactment of a different power, the assertion of a "theory," or rather a location of knowledge. In the context of Du Bois's own continuing picture of himself as a scientist, it amounts to a critique of Western sociology and the conception of knowledge that it deploys; or at a minimum it displays Du Bois's realization of their limitations. It says that Du Bois's writing is *for* something, against the self-understandings of the science that serves its interests by purporting to serve no interests. It is an affirmation of the particular in the face of the unending, insufferable onslaught of the general by which Du Bois's people were kept down.

We have seen the parallel move made in the slave narratives: the assertion of the particular against the stereotype (and between the stereotypes and the social sciences there was often then, and is often now, little to choose). But in Du Bois, the same move constitutes quite an explicit resistance to the Western model of knowledge as comprehension. It is no coincidence that Du Bois studied at Harvard with William James and George Santayana, both of whom also had profound misgivings about the Western conception of knowledge because of its elision of particular experience and of the irreducible plurality of the world. So Du Bois takes up an African-American tradition framed in autobiographical narratives (paradigmatically, for Du Bois, those of Douglass). But he places it into relation with an ongoing American intellectual tradition of mistrust of comprehension that includes such figures as Emerson and Whitman. He then seeks to use the voice developed out of these elements, not merely to tell his own tale (though he does that), and not merely to attack Western "scientism" (though he does that also), but to transform contemporary racial conditions. The movement, then, is autobiographical and conceptual, but above all political.

It is, first, a philosophically radical shift, and it is, second, carried out beautifully; Du Bois's writing always becomes compelling to the degree that it becomes personal and particular. (He loses momentum when he becomes "scientific," though his sociology is exemplary, or when he becomes grandly "literary," a lifelong temptation, often yielded to.) For notice that the very conceptual center of racism, the transcendental condition of its possibility, is generality. The stereotype is simply an inductive inference that makes use of visual imagery; it is a "general picture." It is not based on no information at all, nor is it simply ignorance; it is, rather, a comprehensive generalization based on a problematic taxonomy. Like all science as comprehension, it simply ignores, displaces, or expunges the fact for which it has no category, and like science at its most thorough, it detaches itself from *any* particular fact. (What is generalized and detached here is the "knowledge" of the other and, more important, the knower himself.)

Furthermore, in the social sciences it is a constant difficulty to separate the "discoveries" from the constructions. We have seen that the notion of race as a dualism had to be *manufactured* in order to be discovered. The demand to produce a certain appearance, enforced in a thousand direct ways, enables the "discovery" of the character and problems of black people. Here, science and stereotype collapse into one another; the stereotype is enforced as a regime of appearances, backed by force; the science then naturalizes, examines, elucidates, and diagnoses precisely those appearances. Further, the means by which the information is gathered becomes part of the technology by which the appearance is enforced, as in the use of sociological data within the welfare system. The "discovery" *is* the construction. The fact that it is most often *we* who are studying *you* is a reinforcement of the initial articulatory taxonomic dualism: As those who study, we are neutral, objective observers of material conditions; you *are* the material conditions. White sociology trained on black people makes us invisible to ourselves as particular objects and objectifies the other by the scientific gaze. Thus the structure of sociology itself helps to manufacture what it pretends to discover and covertly *imposes* a false dualism on the "data." The appearances that confirm this dualism must then be *elicited* by applications of power, and subsequently codified and enforced.

Persons who are constantly subjected to stereotypes, who are constantly departicularized by means of stereotypes, ought to become suspicious not just of this or that generality, but of generalities; not just this or that concept, but of concepts. One is in the eerie situation of being oppressed not by particular people, but by Platonic forms, such as the Platonic form of the happy darky or, on the other hand, the Platonic form of the abjected, dispossessed, ignorant black body studied to this day by white sociology and "uplifted" by educational and social programs for its remediation or integration. The Platonic form that one is oppressed *by,* finally, is the Platonic form of the white man, for *each* white man conceives himself as a Platonic form insofar as he conceives of himself as white.

This is a movement in the "abstraction" of power that is central to modernity. Taking the stereotype as true allows the white man to divest himself of responsibility for his power; it explains privilege by the character of the oppressed. It yields the pleasures of power and comprehension without the guilt of oppression. It attributes the power relations not to anyone's desires or activities but to "the way the world is" construed in a comprehensive generalization. The abstraction of power embodied in the stereotype both informs and is reflected in scientific practice; we "explain" the condition of the Negro by studying not ourselves, but the Negro. The scientific approach is not merely a stereotype; it bends (we may hope) to actual information; it is corrigible in a way that the stereotype is not (though stereotypes are also corrigible in certain ways). Yet in its comprehension, sociology also attempts to free power from its actual human embodiments, and hence to free people from their implication as oppressors in oppression.

The problem is not simply bigotry; the very same construction of inductive logic or stereotypes is enacted by "liberal" whites. The classic essay "Of Our Spiritual Strivings" begins like this:

> Between me and the other world there is ever an unasked question: unasked by some through feelings of delicacy; by others through the difficulty of rightly framing it. All, nevertheless, flutter around it. They approach me in a half-hesitant sort of way, eye me curiously or compassionately, and then, instead of saying directly, How does it feel to be a problem? they say, I know an excellent colored man in my town; or, I fought at Mechanicsville; or, Do not these Southern outrages make your blood boil? At these I smile, or am interested, or reduce the boiling to a simmer, as the occasion may require. To the real question, How does it feel to be a problem? I answer seldom a word. (*Souls of Black Folk,* 3–4)

To his white acquaintances, Du Bois was a "representative of his race." Hence, he was "a problem" rather than a particular human being: he was "an issue," "an example" (of what black men could accomplish, or of the infiltration of communism into African-American leadership, or of something). He came to embody for his white acquaintances the whole field of truth about the races. He was generalized, an experience from which he found relief only during his studies and travels in Europe; briefly, at midlife, in Jamaica; and, more deeply, late in his life in Africa. In the United States, where the construction of race was thorough and (in theory) absolute, he *could not* be regarded as particular by whites, that is, by power, whether this power sought to celebrate or to expunge him.

In this structure of power, in which we are still caught up, to be white is to be neutral, a mere eye, an observer, while to be black is to be a "problem" under observation. For, as we have seen, the other side of the stereotype is this: It not only constructs the stereotyped persons as general facts—comprehends them—but it constructs the oppressor as an abstract object. The deployment of the stereotype is always a way of refusing to acknowledge one's own empowerment, precisely at the moment that power becomes conceptually animate. The purpose of domination, finally, is not the dehumanization of its object (if to be human is to be a particular mammalian body, which I think it is), but rather its abjection and exploitation. What is dehumanized is the subject of power: the "white man." The stereotype by which oppression is accomplished sets up the oppressor as a neutral subject, as more or less a scientist engaged in the hands-off business of comprehension. It makes the oppressor absent from his oppression, which is now a matter of general truths comprehended by minds, rather than me winding a rope around your neck. The stereotype degrades or brutalizes the oppressed person, but it denatures or superhumanizes the oppressor, making him over into a disembodied, neutral something: bodiless, raceless, a voice without a particular mouth. In this sense, power is a forgetting of the particular, and power in the age of comprehension is also a self-forgetting. That is a *pleasure* of power: the pleasure of an escape from embodiment, limitation, and sin by systematic amnesia.

I know this pleasure extremely well; I sought a career in philosophy, or even to identify my life with philosophy, because the comprehension that philosophy allows is of the widest possible scope. Few people are as "white" as the male academic philosopher of the West; our dominant tropes are precisely the illumination of the darkness and the ocular constructions that arise out of the objectifying gaze. The universe, all of it, is a tool for the use of the philosopher; the tone of the philosopher is a completely abstracted neutrality. And I sought this mode of self-construction precisely because I found encounters with particular people too poignant to be easily borne (the only people I dislike, other than myself, are *other* people) and perhaps even as a way to assure myself and everyone else of my whiteness (certainly as my way to make it in the white world). A friend of mine in graduate school told me that I was the only white person she had ever known with a completely black body language and vernacular repertoire. I'd had that since junior high school. But already by the time she told me that, acting black was a little transgressive game I played within the bleached academic institution. It is difficult to state how odd it sounds in a graduate seminar to describe Plato as a "sucka." But I emerged a whiter person than I went in, and if you meet me at an academic conference these days, you won't find me pretending to be a rapper. The pleasure I take in writing this book is, in part, a nostalgic revisiting of the pleasures I knew before my bleaching, but it is also the firmest possible way to construct myself as white: by assuming authority over black discourse, by providing a general structure in which it can be understood from a white perspective.

Finding his pleasures just here enables the white man to retain his picture of himself as an ethical person, or as an advocate of American ideals of equality and freedom, or (as we have seen with regard to the slave narratives) as a Christian, while continuing the day-to-day business of oppression and exploitation. Racism can hum along quite nicely even in a case where no one takes himself to be a racist. "Black rage" then comes as a puzzlement, and something in turn to be sociologically or physiologically diagnosed, as in the search for the elusive "violence gene." You know where the scientists are looking for *that:* in black bodies; our own violence, practiced continually on a worldwide scale, is absolutely invisible to ourselves, a theme to which I will return in the last chapter. If you're looking for a violence gene, start with *Congress,* or the boards of directors of multinational corporations. Since we have loosed our power from its mooring in our bodies, we are continually surprised to find ourselves the objects of resentment. Thus we are enabled to preserve both our image of ourselves and the benefits of our oppression, while we make every act of resistance, in proportion to its violence, seem to ourselves arbitrary and incomprehensible, an occasion for diagnosis of *black* problems. The history of racism in this country is, in part, the history of this abstractive performance, which grows ever more subtle, and both justifies and engenders more violence.

Du Bois's fundamental approach to this situation—which in some sense is the only possible approach—is the same as that of the slave narrative: telling the truth. In his magazine *The Crisis* he wrote,

> Awful as race prejudice, lawlessness, and ignorance are, we can fight them if we frankly face them and dare name them and tell the truth; but if we continually dodge and cloud the issue, and say the half truth because the whole truth stings and shames; if we do this, we invite catastrophe.[8]

As David Levering Lewis remarks, these sentences were written directly as an attack on Booker Washington. A central aspect of Washington's "accomodationism," for Du Bois, was its epistemic cowardice and duplicity. What made Washington *dangerous* was precisely that he failed to tell the whole truth, that he knuckled under to the epistemic regime of white supremacy. This consisted, above all, in Washington's confirmation of stereotype, in his allowance of the stereotype to comprehend himself and his people, and to articulate their educational, professional, and political locations. Here Du Bois thematizes racism as a generalized epistemic strategy, a turn in his thought that is central to the modes of resistance he enjoined.

Doing better sociology is a perfectly good attack, for example, on particular stereotypes. It is absolutely useless, however, as an attack on the structure of consciousness which stereotyping requires, because it enacts that very structure. So when Du Bois erupted out of the history of the slave trade and the condition of the Negro in the Philadelphia ghetto and into his own experience, he erupted out of knowledge as comprehension and into knowledge as openness to the particular. He continually returned, and he moved between these two "worlds," even sentence by sentence. *The Souls of Black Folk* is really the node of this doubleness; Du Bois swings chapter by chapter from raw sociological data about "The Negro" in the South to the most vivid personal experiences. "Of the Meaning of Progress," for example, which one would expect to be a polemic on African-American uplift, or perhaps a rehearsal of economic statistics of the sort he mounts in "Of the Quest for the Golden Fleece," is instead a perfectly personal, perfectly particular tale. It describes an epochal experience in Du Bois's life.

Though Du Bois's father had been absent from his childhood, and though he and his mother lived for a time in dire poverty, Du Bois had been raised by and large in marginally comfortable circumstances in a community without great racial tensions by American standards: Great Barrington, Massachusetts. But then he went south to attend Fisk. In order to "penetrate beyond the veil," he taught in African-American communities in rural Tennessee during the summers, a common practice among those attending traditionally black colleges in the South. But his encounter with real live rural Southern black folks was a radical and radicalizing experience. In the essay, Du Bois does not describe this radicalization. He does not state the conclusions he draws except in a brief final paragraph: "How hard a thing is life to the lowly, and yet how human and real! And all this life and strife and failure—is it the twilight of nightfall or the flush of some faint-dawning day?" (*Souls of Black Folk*, 62).

Even these observations are otiose, though simple and compelling. But his description of the life of Josie, who, when he arrives, is "a thin homely girl of twenty," bright and full of love for learning, tells more than any general conclusion could. Josie never is able to follow her dream of going to Fisk; she works herself hard and harder for her family, and finally dies young, as Du Bois found out on a return visit. Throughout the book, the statistics and the literary flourishes are placed into relation to particular human situations. But throughout the book, it is the situations that are memorable; the flourishes and statistics are often interesting, but they are forgotten long before Josie. Du Bois's most compelling moments, it seems to me (and it *would*), constantly pull us back to the particular situation.

Indeed, as I have said, if there is one feature of Du Bois's entire corpus that is conspicuous, it is his own "double consciousness." In "Of Our Spiritual Strivings," the double consciousness of African-Americans described by Du Bois is consciousness of both being American and being attacked and despised by Americans: belonging both to a culture that hates one and to a subculture in which one is nurtured. The world, says Du Bois, yields the African-American no true self-consciousness. It pollutes his relation to himself. In *Dusk of Dawn*, Du Bois would call this "inner spiritual slavery" (*Writings*, 654). But in "Of Our Spiritual Strivings," he puts it this way:

> It is a peculiar situation, this double-consciousness, this sense of always looking at oneself through the eyes of others, of measuring one's soul by the tape of a world that looks on in amused contempt and pity. One ever feels his twoness—an American, a Negro; two souls, two thoughts, two unreconciled strivings; two warring ideals in one dark body, whose dogged strength alone keeps it from being torn asunder.
>
> The history of the American Negro is the history of this strife—this longing to attain self-conscious manhood, to merge his double self into a better and truer self. In this merging he wishes neither of the older selves to be lost. He would not Africanize America, for America has too much to teach the world and Africa. He would not bleach his Negro soul in a flood of white Americanism, for he knows that Negro blood has a message for the world. (*Souls of Black Folk*, 5)

The last sentence of this passage (a passage which is justly one of the most famous in American letters) broaches again the notion of historical races and their destinies that Du Bois had taken up in "The Conservation of Races," and this picture informs at least his early treatments of double consciousness. It is as though this destiny, trapped in the bodies of black folk, seeks to emerge into a context in which it cannot be allowed to be visible, and hence becomes stunted and ingrown.

The passage, of course, need not be read only in this rather grandiose fashion. Double consciousness reflects, among other things, the application of comprehension to African-Americans, the surveillance by which oppression is "internalized." The African-American conforms to the demands of the stereotype by producing, for white folks, the desired and demanded appearance (of humility and subservience, for example; cf. Booker Washington's "manner," his fund-raising trump-card). The production of this appearance is enforced in a thousand ways; one is offered rewards to produce it, and starved or lynched for failing to produce it. But producing the appearance splits consciousness; the appearance leaks into the "private" space of mentality. Emerging from slavery, black people entered more completely the regime of disciplinary power that relies on subjects' freedom in order to make them participants in their own subjugation. If we can teach you to police yourself, then we can *allow* you to be "free," to have political rights, for example. At the turn of the century, this process was still *beginning*, especially in the South, but it has developed very elaborately indeed as integration has become the dominant strategy of "liberation." It was true however, of Du Bois well before it was true of most black folks; he had undergone (and resisted) a full-fledged institutional incorporation. This regime divides people against themselves in a way that is itself an instrument of oppression; it makes them, by comprehensive surveillance (a sort of raw sociology), oppressors of themselves and one another, and short-circuits their resistance. The epistemic regime here operates by compromising selves in such a way that certain knowledges are rendered invisible and silent.

The silenced knowledges are, first, cultural; the effect is to circumscribe a segregated cultural space in which African-American religion, arts, and celebrations can be contained. As I have said, the very notion that Africans *had* cultures that they brought with them to the United States and the fact that these cultures continued their traditions and their creative ferment in the diaspora were the objects of erasure. And the silenced knowledges are personal as well as cultural; what is silenced is the articulation of the *particular* story, and each such story that does leak into white space is treated as an "exception." The "Negro" in American discourse is the *sign* of particularity, which we use in the generalization of ourselves. But to be made over into a sign is precisely to be attacked epistemically *in* one's particularity; to be a sign of particularity is to be generalized. Du Bois was himself such a paradoxical sign. When we use you as a sign of particularity, we cannot just let you do whatever idiosyncratic thing comes into your head; we have a *particular* particularity in mind. We're not going to be too pleased, for example, if your preferences or talents draw you to the academy, as Du Bois's did. At that point, we've either got to get rid of you (and despite everything, the academy is still a very white place and a damned hard place to be black) or extend honorary white status to you. That's got to be a hard, hard pill to swallow, and Du Bois faced this dilemma earlier and more intensely than most. The particular particularity we require out of you in order to make you a sign of particularity and thus both insert you into and eliminate you from our semiotics is the particular particularity that is the specular opposite of our self-construction as white. We require of you that you serve us, not only by cooking and bringing us dinner, but by making us into what we (already, antecedently, naturally) are: white folks.

Du Bois himself enacted double consciousness with a pure intensity. He regarded himself as being in a unique position to "draw back the veil" and show the races to each other, because he moved competently (to say the least), though not always comfortably, through both worlds. I am asserting that one way this played out in his writings was in the struggle between "white" knowledge, that is, knowledge as comprehension, sociology, abstraction, and "black" knowledge, that is, knowledge as situation, as particularity, as embodiment. And there is a doubleness, too, in how these knowledges are spoken; indeed, the voices are inseparable from the forms of knowledge they express and the subject positions from which they can be spoken. For one thing, there is a concerted attempt to erase "black" knowledge altogether from the order of the sign. But this erasure cannot by definition be accomplished, because black knowledge is inscribed in the order of the sign in its very erasure. The erasure leaves a mark.

In speaking sociologically, Du Bois interpellated himself as (white) subject of knowledge; in speaking from behind "the Veil," as object of knowledge. Du Bois's ability to identify double consciousness emerges from his own doubled voice, doubled background, doubled training, mixed race. Forms of knowledge production embed and produce forms of consciousness and forms of words to their own requirements. The knowledge possessed by the oppressor is of the general truth, truth about everything in general and nothing in particular; the maker of such truths cannot speak in a particular voice. The very same conceptuality that constitutes this knowledge opens the possibility or even the necessity of a counterknowledge in the oppressed; the knowledge possessed by the oppressed is a seizing of particularity. This particularity, which in the West amounts above all to embodiment, can be used in resistance as the defiant assertion of the particular into the context of the general, an assertion that confronts the oppressor not only with the particularity of the oppressed, but with his own particularity and embodiment—which, for privileged white folks, is the most feared and desired of confrontations. But Du Bois, all his life, moved in an unreconciled tension between these truths, tried to use both of them as liberatory instruments, and spoke in different voices.

Du Bois's own tension, which embodies the confrontation between body and mind, particular and general, takes on its tremendous force because it *exposes* the essentializing and naturalizing dualism of race as a farce. It does this, first, because it is only possible from a place that the dualism cannot admit to be possible: a place of ambiguity or of mobility between the terms of the dualism; it shows that the exclusions in question have not been and cannot be perfectly performed. And it articulates very directly an attack on racial dualism as fictional, because it seeks to *confront* white people with their own embodiment and particularity, things that are not possible for a living human being truly to eject. In this sense, white culture is a culture of death; disembodiment, finally, is possible in only one way. And all of the things we "find" in black culture are symptoms of life: play, celebration, sex, spontaneity, violence, and so forth. What we imagine ourselves to be in the construction of racial dualism is something that is already dead. Meantime, we remain alive, at least for now, and experience a relation of fascination and fear to the "place" where we have "put" our bodies in our conceptual scheme.

In his magnificent biography of Du Bois, Lewis points to perhaps the most subversive use of double consciousness; it becomes, in Du Bois, itself an instrument of resistance, a particular form of epistemic leverage. Lewis writes,

> The race [Du Bois held] must learn the lesson of the Veil by cultivating the moral and creative energies that lay hidden in the conditions of its very alienation. Scorned and exploited throughout its history in the land of opportunity, his people had gradually undergone a halving of identity, acquired a unique angle of vision, and become habituated to a psychic subordination that handicapped it in the past but could be turned to strengths in its future.[9]

This again takes up a theme of the slave narratives: that the oppressed gain in their oppression an "epistemic privilege" (to use a phrase developed in feminist epistemology). But it motivates this insight with a precise and powerful phenomenology of oppression, and applies it with great specificity and systematicity. In a passage from *Dusk of Dawn* that deserves to be a classic, Du Bois writes,

> Indeed, perhaps the greatest and most immediate danger of white culture, perhaps least sensed, is its fear of the Truth, it childish belief in the efficacy of lies as a method of human uplift. . . . We [!] deliberately and continuously deceive not simply others, but ourselves as to the truth about them, us, and the world. (*Writings,* 664)

One place where this "childish belief in the efficacy of lies as a method of human uplift" is both held and resisted is in the arena of scientific knowledge against scientific knowledge: worse versus better taxonomies. But another is the very concept of knowledge itself, or its location: the general "knowledge" embodied in the stereotype or the sociology versus the particular knowledges located in particular human experiences. Du Bois was here formulating an epistemology of social location. He wrote,

> In this dilemma the sociologists of earlier years took refuge in inventing a new entity, the group, which had action, guilt, praise, and blame quite apart from the persons composing it. It was of course a metaphysical hypothesis which had its uses in reasoning, but could not be regarded as cor-

responding to the exact truth. No such group over-soul has been proven to exist. (*Writings*, 678–79)

(Note that this is opposed to the line pursued in "The Conservation of Races.") It is hard, however, to see how sociology could possibly proceed at all if it settled for "exact" truths in Du Bois's sense. Thus this passage becomes an attack not on this or that conclusion, but on the possibility of finding exact truths by generalization.

Du Bois's cultural location—ambiguous and equivocal at all times—is perfectly captured in the essay "Of the Faith of the Fathers." He begins by contrasting the relatively staid religious services of his youth with his experience of a revival in rural Tennessee:

> The people moaned and fluttered, and then the gaunt-cheeked brown woman beside me suddenly leaped straight into the air and shrieked like a lost soul, while round about came wail and groan and outcry, and a scene of human passion such as I had never conceived before. (*Souls of Black Folk*, 155)

Du Bois was fascinated, repelled, and, finally, absorbed. He was absorbed, especially, by the conversion of oppression and passion into art in gospel music, "the most original and beautiful expression of human life and longing yet born on American soil" (*Souls of Black Folk*, 156). That is not at all a ridiculous characterization, and one of Du Bois's many achievements is that he was one of the first intellectuals to recognize the greatness of African-American art (though similar passages can be found in Douglass's writings). He was enabled to do this, in part, precisely by his notion of racial destiny, which as we have seen, was still present when he wrote *The Souls of Black Folk*. This notion can be used to make visible the *cultural* locations in which art and religion occur.

Making such places visible opens up a profusion of strategies for and weapons of resistance, as we will see in the last two chapters. There is, first, the possibility of the confirmation of stereotype (for example, in the physicality and musicality of African-American Christianity), but also its simultaneous revaluing, so that we say, for example, that black Christianity is alive and white Christianity is part of what I have called our culture of death. Here we appropriate the articulating taxonomy, but use it in attack. In addition, however, since white self-construction entails the association of culture with ourselves and of nature with black folks, bringing forth black culture into public space (especially since we have tried to *annihilate* that culture) throws the dualistic structure into confusion. That dualistic structure can be reconstructed, so that we associate *their* culture (their art and so forth) *with* nature, and *our* culture *with* culture, but even that rough formulation demonstrates that every such reconstruction complicates the niftiness of the simple dualistic exclusions that it reimposes.

At any rate, "Of the Faith of the Fathers" juxtaposes the personal and the sociological in a characteristically Du Boisian manner, giving statistics on church membership and so forth. It leaves no doubt about the centrality of religious institutions in the public life of African-Americans. Perhaps because of Du Bois's intensely equivocal response to Southern black religion, he moves at the end of the essay back into the "doubleness" of African-American consciousness, but this time he explicates it in a slightly different way. Here we see clearly the construction of the oppressed as the oppressor of herself: the internalization of surveillance that splits consciousness. But here we also see consciousness split not into black and white, per se—not even, per se, into particular and general—but into truth and lie.

> It is the same defence which the Jews of the Middle Age used and which left its stamp on their character for centuries. To-day the young Negro of the South who would succeed cannot be frank and outspoken, honest and self-assertive, but rather he is daily tempted to be silent and wary, politic and sly; he must flatter and be pleasant, endure petty insults with a smile, shut his eyes to wrong; in too many cases he sees positive personal advantage in deception and lying. His real thought, his real aspirations, must be guarded in whispers; he must not criticise, he must not complain. Patience, humility, and adroitness must, in these growing black youth, replace impulse, manliness, and courage. With this sacrifice there is an economic opening, and perhaps peace and some prosperity. Without this there is riot, migration, or crime. Nor is this situation peculiar to the Southern United States—is it not rather the only method by which the undeveloped races have gained the right to share modern culture? The price of culture is a Lie. (*Souls of Black Folk,* 166–67)

This passage is aimed squarely at the educational projects pursued at Tuskegee and Hampton, but I quote it at length because it is absolutely central to Du Bois's thought, to African-American thought, and indeed to American thought in general.

First, it is squarely in the line of Emerson: it demands truth, authenticity, self-reliance, "manliness"; it expresses, at any rate, respect for these. But it places these demands, which in Emerson confront each person alone, or confront each person with himself, into the context of the political. It shows how power operates, necessarily, by forcing the person over whom it is exercised to live in a lie. Power as comprehension always falsifies; it demands first and last that the disempowered not show himself, that he conceal himself: that, if possible, he be only what he is allowed to be, so that what he is allowed to be can be claimed to be his nature, his essence. It operates as the demand, enforced by the most explicit economic and sheer physical limitations, to manufacture the appearance that confirms the comprehensive taxonomy. (Recall, for example, Lunsford Lane concealing his property and his intelligence.) It produces the field of knowledge which it then "studies." For this is the dark side of power as knowledge: when knowledge/power is conceived as a subsumption of the individual under the general, only the general in the individual can be allowed to be visible; traces of particularity in the object of knowledge must be expunged. This is true even of the construction of the African-American as a "generalized particular," as the sign of particularity in the Western discourse of comprehension. The African-American is *stereotyped* as particular. That is a paradox, and welling up from it is the possibility of the exposure of the contradictions in the notion of comprehension as a way of life for particular creatures. This places absolute limits on the amount and sort of knowledge that can be gathered; thus, power constituted as knowledge requires concealment; and in what is concealed, in the particular, lurks the possibility of resistance.

The last sentence of the quotation expresses the final, radical development of Du Bois's epistemology. Culture in the Western sense is the subsumption of the particular by the general: politically, scientifically, technologically, and so forth. Thus culture is constituted at its center by its forcing-into-concealment, its making of lies. Here, and directly in connection with the total embodiment exemplified in African-American religion, Du Bois offers a devastating account of oppression, and the devastating conclusion that Western culture simply *is* oppression; that it is made to be what it is—scientifically, politically, technologically, religiously—by oppression, that is, by lies.

Du Bois, in other words, makes use of a distinction which is central to the Western tradition: the distinction between appearance and reality. Indeed, these notions only make sense in opposition to each other; they arise together, in the Greeks. In the American development of this tradition, and particularly in Emerson and Thoreau, the distinction becomes the basis of an ethics, or perhaps it becomes the end of ethics. For Emerson, appearance is evil, reality good. But it is doubtful that Western ethics could survive this move without resorting to its most traditional escape, *identifying* the real with the good, and denying reality to what is not good. But this apparent escape is idiotic; there *exists* too much that we call evil, and the Western tradition is left with the position that to say of something that

it is evil is to say that it *ought* not to be (or, in the most intensely pathological forms of idealism, simply to declare the unreality of the world we
experience in this life). But to identify, provisionally or rhetorically, goodness and the reality of *this* world is to attack the entire notion of ethics.

Du Bois's double consciousness of the oppressed gives this Emersonian
destruction of Western ethics a peculiar urgency; it motivates it with precision. For here, the white world demands a certain appearance; it takes
the reality for granted, or perhaps it is simply not concerned with the reality at all. The white world forces black personality, black authenticity,
black culture, into hiding, demands that it remain invisible. It accom-
plishes this concealment directly out of its construction of values; Western ethics is characterized by generalization (consider, say, Kant, or Mill)
and the abstraction of the white body. Its construction of stereotypes simplifies this process and makes it more emphatic: Simply conform yourself
to this template, and all will be well; what you do in your home, in your
bar, in your church—we are perhaps not so concerned about that.

In fact, segregation is imposed not, or not simply, to insulate whites
from sex and commerce with blacks, and not only for its concrete economic effects, but also to create a context in which appearances can be
maintained, in which appearances can be fully insulated from reality, in
which private need not contaminate public, and in which we need never
hear *what you say about us*, while we are free to speak on and on about
you, even in your presence. This process of circumscribing conceptual
ghettoes has been subtilized as black folks have gained voice, but is just
as virulent in the contemporary discourse. When we are forced to hear
what you say about us, we reduce it to invalidity through various ascrip-
tions of bias. Witness the response on the part of white cultural authorities to the "revisionism" of multicultural history texts. The view that
white people were aggressors on this continent is greeted as a ridiculous
reduction of our real importance, as obviously biased and politically motivated "revisionism." Columbus the hero, on the other hand, is a neutral
fact emerging from no particular point of view. When we hear that we are
oppressors, we dismiss the claim.

Thus white power proceeds by externalizing the oppressed person, by
pushing everything to the surface, or rather by recognizing only the surface, and thus by creating a vast subterranean "authentic" life. Seeking
total knowledge as generality over the oppressed simply constructs the oppressed as a stereotype. The mode of resistance to this is too obvious even
to need explicit enunciation; any act that defies the stereotype, any act that
brings the hidden, "authentic" self to the surface, becomes a subversion
of the oppressor's knowledge.

I place "authentic" in quotes here because, though it is accurate enough phenomenologically, it appears again to naturalize or essentialize the particular. But the experience of certain zones of oneself as "authentic" here presupposes the specular structure of the dualism; since that structure is a manufacture of surfaces, whatever is not brought to the specularized surface lies at the core of the self. Inversely, the "authentic" white self *is* at the surface; it is the specularization itself. But both of these emerge only in the vexed transaction of power, desire, and knowledge by which people are raced. Resistance becomes, simply, the expression of "authenticity," which in turn is simply a defiance of the expectations or the taxonomies that specifically structure the specularization, that govern what *should* be seen by the standards of racial dualism.

When the "authentic" self emerges into public space, it is subject to the specular; it can be "studied" sociologically and so forth. As soon as it reaches the surface, it becomes the occasion for the subtilization of the knowledge/stereotype by which power is exercised. As soon as a voice is heard, it becomes the object of interpretation within the dominant discourse. The history of race relations in America in this century is largely this history: the history of a coming to appearance of the authentic African-American self; then the reconfiguration of templates (by which I mean stereotypes as they are subsumed under racial taxonomies) to regain comprehension, then a further eruption of strangeness, and so forth. Thus, in the struggle, the imaginary dichotomy of race is always breaking down as a dichotomy, denaturalizing and de-essentializing itself, and it is also always in the process of being reimposed in a reassertion of comprehension, in a new sociological study or explanation. As this process continues, power becomes less and less obvious; the stereotype at work is no longer the humble, grinning darky but, say, the jive-talking hoodlum: a stereotype of considerable complexity (is he smart or stupid, for example? threatening or amusing?), but nevertheless a specular template for control of individuals by comprehension.

Martin Luther King Jr. often asserted that the fates of white and black in America were intertwined, and James Baldwin maintained that American culture was constituted by this particular difference, and that the races were utterly interdependent. In *Notes of a Native Son,* Baldwin writes,

> The question of color, especially in this country, operates to hide the graver question of the self. That is precisely why what we like to call "the Negro problem" is so tenacious in American life, and so dangerous. But my own experience proves to me that the connection between American whites and

blacks is far deeper and more passionate than any of us like to think. . . .
The questions which one asks oneself begin, at last, to illuminate the world,
and become one's key to the experience of others. One can only face in others what one can face in oneself.[10]

If, as I have urged, the races are constructed by ejection from the white
self, then really coming face to face with the reality of black lives could
only proceed if we came face to face with ourselves as savages, bodies,
mammals, sexual omnivores, and so forth. Our confrontation with you
would be a confrontation with ourselves. Indeed, our confrontation with
you as we have imagined you *is* a confrontation with ourselves, a fact that
we are always trying to disguise. The only way to reveal to ourselves what
disguises ourselves from ourselves is to hear *you* speak about what we
have tried to make you and, always in excess to what we have made you,
about what you are.

But the division of self which is common to Americans, black and
white, is obviously not precisely the same in each case, though the cases
are mirror images. The structure of double consciousness as developed by
Du Bois can be used to show precisely how this is the case, for the specularization of the oppressed, with its simultaneous demand for visibility
and concealment, also constructs or arises out of a double consciousness
in the oppressor.

Frederick Douglass's deepest attack on white America was for its
hypocrisy: He attacked the slaveowners and those who tolerated them by
confronting them with their own Christian beliefs. This was, in essence,
also King's technique, though King used the texts of democracy. In the "I
Have a Dream" speech, for instance, he quotes the Declaration of Independence, "My Country 'Tis of Thee," and "The Battle Hymn of the Re-
public." (That was a strategy we have also seen employed by William
Wells Brown.) King seeks, that is, to confront the oppressor not with new
values, but precisely with the oppressor's own values. Of the dream he describes, he says that "it is a dream deeply rooted in the American
dream."[11] By an assertion to us of what we take to be *our* values, King
explodes the essentialization of race by appealing across the dividing line
to our similarities.

The oppressor and the oppressed, in these circumstances, both become
hypocrites, and hypocrisy in each case sets in motion a series of internal
tensions, a double consciousness. These tensions run along different lines
in the two cases, though in both cases they play out as a dissonance between "appearance" and "reality," and between the "internal" and the
"external." In the case of the oppressed, the behavior is "false" and the

internal life "true." The grinning, cooperative, bone-headed Negro, conforming his behavior to the specularizing stereotype, is thinking who knows what as he enacts his role. Perhaps he's contemplating violence. Perhaps he's contemplating the promised land. Perhaps he's internalized the stereotype to the point that he's no longer conscious of the tension. In every case, however, the external behavior is in some sense false and produced by the situation in which his survival depends on his appearance.

In the case of the oppressor, however, truth runs the opposite way. Here, one tries to hold on to oneself as a Christian, as an advocate of democracy, and so forth. But one is (say) "forced" by the particular circumstances to buy and sell people, or cooperate in segregation or discrimination. Here the "inner" life is false, while the "outer" life shows the truth (though the external enactment depends on the falsifying racial dichotomy). One *is* a racist and so forth, whatever one may believe about oneself, or even about the races. Again, oppression in the era of comprehension requires self-forgetting. There are various ways to bring these two things into alignment subjectively, various rationalizations, or the whole thing can proceed in perfect unconsciousness of its own structure. Thus, while the external life of the African-American is falsified as it is made the object of knowledge, and the inner life forced into concealment, the internal life of the European-American is falsified as it is made the subject of knowledge. Racism sets up a situation in which the power relation is, obviously, asymmetrical, but in which every person in the culture is dichotomized and turned against herself in one way or another by the imaginary imposition of our acultural essences.

One interesting feature of this is that the inner, "authentic" self of the African-American is forced into concealment, so that the African-American becomes "invisible." But the truth of the European-American, on the contrary, is there on the surface: It is the beliefs that are compromised and falsified. So while the African-American is rendered invisible to the European-American by the specularization of the former by the latter, the European-American is forced into total visibility to the African-American by the same process. Baldwin writes that "it is one of the ironies of black-white relations that, by means of what the white man imagines the black man to be, the black man is enabled to know who the white man is."[12] In Du Bois's essay "The Souls of White Folk," he writes,

> Of them I am singularly clairvoyant. I see in and through them. I view them from unusual points of vantage. . . . I see these souls undressed and from the back and side. I see the working of their entrails. I know their thoughts and they know that I know. This knowledge makes them now embarrassed, now furious! (*Writings,* 923)

Indeed, this preternatural knowledge of the oppressor by the oppressed, this preternatural availability of the oppressor to be known, constantly motivates greater efforts at control and specularization, and hence intensifies itself. The oppressor may appeal to many noble principles, may himself take himself to believe them, but the oppressed know the truth about the oppressor's deepest self, which is constantly expressed in oppression. Putting it mildly, this knowledge is dangerous and is constantly attacked, degraded, and excluded in further acts of oppression. Black folks wouldn't countenance the sort of stuff we white folks believe about ourselves, but we white folks can't allow ourselves to know what black folks know about us. That is why our only hope for ceasing to be oppressors is to listen to what black folks are saying about us.

No figure has seen this with so much clarity as Baldwin, and certainly no figure has written about it as compellingly. The first part of *The Fire Next Time* consists of a letter from Baldwin to his brother's son.

> I know what the world has done to my brother and how narrowly he has survived it. And I know, which is much worse, and this is the crime of which I accuse my country and my countrymen, and for which neither I nor time nor history will forgive them, that they have destroyed and are destroying hundreds of thousands of lives and do not know it and do not want to know it. One can be, indeed one must strive to become, tough and philosophical concerning destruction and death, for this is what most of mankind has been best at since we heard of man. (But remember: *most* of mankind is not *all* of mankind.) But it is not permissible that the authors of devastation should also be innocent. It is the innocence which constitutes the crime.[13]

The oppression that we white folks inflict destroys lives. But what is absolutely intolerable is that we systematically deflect responsibility for this oppression, that we do not view it as our own doing. As we exploit, as we turn people against themselves and against one another, we remain innocent in our own fantastic psychopathology. We have lost track of what is most obvious in ourselves. Indeed, we had to do so, or face the fact that we were destroyers: not Christians, not democrats, but destroyers. "This innocent country," Baldwin writes, "set you down in a ghetto in which, in fact, it intended that you should perish" (*The Fire Next Time*, 7).

Baldwin continues,

> You, don't be afraid. I said that it was intended that you should perish in the ghetto, perish by never being allowed to go behind the white man's definitions, by never being allowed to spell your proper name. You have, and many of us have, defeated this intention; and, by a terrible law, a terrible

paradox, those innocents who believed that your imprisonment made them safe are losing their grasp of reality. But these men are your brothers—your lost, younger brothers. And if the word *integration* means anything, this is what it means: that we, with love, shall force our brothers to see themselves as they are, to cease fleeing from reality and begin to change it. (9–10)

The condescension that Baldwin musters from his position of epistemic privilege is more devastating than any indictment. And his elucidation of the epistemic situation is perfect: We intended that you should perish when we tried to destroy your ability to name yourselves, but in the process we lost *our*selves, and made you name yourselves, finally, with all the more urgency. We tried to erase you from the order of language and culture by arrogating to ourselves the power to describe you; if we were successful, then you would perish as yourselves even if you remained alive. But if we had been successful, we would also have floated free of reality; in a sense, that was precisely what we were trying to accomplish; that is how we were trying to remake ourselves. In the next chapter, we will see exactly what Baldwin means when he says that white people did this in order to be safe, but, finally, as we face riot and crime and resistance, we should begin to learn that in seeking to make ourselves safe by destroying you we have endangered ourselves beyond reckoning. Our violence may be returned upon us by the people who know us as we are in reality.

It is close to right to say that the culture constructs itself wholly around these epistemic dichotomies or paradoxes, fighting for their preservation or for their destruction. Whatever authenticity may be, this gives rise to a situation in which no one can be authentic except by heroic measures (and perhaps not even then) both of self-consciousness and of external enactment.

To the extent that European culture centers around the distinctions between the inner and the outer, the subjective and the objective, the reality and the appearance—to that extent it is a reflection of or a strategy for oppression. In *Dusk of Dawn*, Du Bois writes, concerning World War I,

> As we saw the dead dimly through rifts of battle smoke and heard faintly the cursings and accusations of blood brothers, we darker men said: This is not Europe gone mad; this is not aberration or insanity; this *is* Europe; this seeming Terrible is the real soul of white culture—back of all culture—stripped and visible today. (*Writings*, 929)

What Du Bois sees is that European culture is a deathbound culture, that in seeking a release from embodiment and particularity, we seek death.

Thus the crowning irony: seeking to make a people totally visible forces them into concealment, and simultaneously makes *you* totally visible; the specularization of the oppressed is always the specularization of the oppressor; it is always where the truth of the oppressor is rendered visible. And it must be admitted that European thought, for example, coalesces around these notions; consider Descartes's epistemology, or Hume's, or Kant's. Consider European aesthetics, the science of appearances, wherein the essential distinctions are form and function, art and craft, and so forth. Such developments reflect lives pitted against themselves, lives lived in double consciousness, which in turn reflect conquest, colonialism, slavery, the subjugation of women. Even the overweening anxiety, perhaps expressed as strongly here as anywhere, about the truth in science and philosophy is the trace of oppression, an empty reflection of its structure.

I would like to pause at this point to formulate some provisional conclusions that will be useful as we go on. First, the relation of knowledge to power is certainly not one of simple correlation or identity, as Foucault has sometimes been interpreted as holding. Power in modernity seeks knowledge of the object over which it is exercised, or over which it is defined as power. But this very specularization becomes the occasion of concealment. Thus, this power is at once a gathering of knowledge and a forcing into hiding. Second, knowledge is both an instrument of power and of resistance. For example, there is general knowledge pitted against general knowledge in Du Bois: *The Encyclopedia of the Negro* pitted against the stereotype, better sociology against worse, and so forth. But there is also the knowledge that wells up continuously and ubiquitously from the particular, which power tries to seize by comprehension, but which rends the fabric of comprehension.

Third, one might go so far as to say that truth always escapes comprehension, and hence that knowledge can never be the instrument of power. For now, however, I want to leave this provisional for several reasons. First, we would certainly have to deploy a distinction here between "true truth" or "authentic" knowledge and what people in a given circumstance might *call* truth or knowledge. The knowledge-claim, and the effort to gather knowledge, are certainly instruments of power. But white power is or becomes invisible to itself. Power proceeds by a falsification of its object, and finally by a falsification of itself; the self-knowledge of those who wield power in the age of comprehension is always compromised, always imploding; power is always concealing itself to itself. As it does this, it renders itself perfectly visible, so that to those who stand outside it, and especially to its victims, who conceal themselves in its interstices, it becomes more and more available as an object of knowledge. Fourth, however, this last conclusion depends, in the above discussion, on a failure to problematize the distinction between appearance and reality. The distinction is critical here, but if it ultimately breaks down, or is itself an artifact of a specularization, then all these conclusions must be suspended for the time being. For we must depend on the inner authenticity of the Uncle Tom, and on the outer authenticity of the racist; we must locate the truth of the Tom in his inner life and the truth of the racist in his outer actions. But even the very notion of double consciousness, the very notion that a person can be turned against herself, can lose herself, reveals a variety of ways in which this simple-minded distinction between authentic and inauthentic selves can break down. Whether we now can hold that the true truth and the real knowledge evade power is obviously up for grabs. We need, in other words, at this point to expose or devise a different vocabulary by which to reconstruct the epistemic and psychological situation. I will argue that one such vocabulary of racial and self-construction—and a particularly compelling one—is developed in the writings of Zora Neale Hurston.

3

DIVISION AND DISINTEGRATION

MALCOLM X ON THE SELF

The "truth" of the oppressed person is pushed inward by the necessity of maintaining an outer appearance acceptable to the dominant culture, while the "truth" of the oppressor is pushed outward by the necessity of maintaining a self-image acceptable to the dominant culture. That situation would be relatively simple if we could hold on to the distinctions between authentic and inauthentic consciousness, or between inner truth and the outer enactment of hypocrisy. Even in Du Bois, however, these distinctions are endangered, for he does not develop a distinction between what one thinks and how one behaves (though it often enough seems to amount to that); the distinction is between forms, or portions, or aspects of consciousness. And now we must begin to ask the vertiginous questions: Should we think of this as two persons (members of different cultures, say) inhabiting a single body? Has a single consciousness undergone fission, split into two consciousnesses? Could we trace the originary consciousness into one of its two descendants, or are they simultaneously originated by the same act or within the same conceptuality? Or are they, perhaps, "sides" of a single consciousness? Are they lost to each other? Do they leak into one another? Are they mutually dependent? Could they hate each other? Could they be reconciled? Are the consciousnesses conscious of each other? If two consciousnesses inhabit a single body, from what point of view could we term one of them authentic, or privilege its claim to its body?

Such questions are not addressed very elaborately in Du Bois; it would have been achievement enough for Du Bois to have identified the self-division, and to issue a call to racial pride, a call to the invisible to make themselves seen. Of course, that is both hope and danger: to make yourself visible entangles you in various power relations. Consider, for example, the ambiguous legacy of integration (toward which Du Bois's attitude was . . . ambiguous; in the *Autobiography* he praises "voluntary segregation," by which I assume he means voluntary on the part of African-Americans). When you become visible to us, place yourself into our institutional contexts and so forth, you make yourself vulnerable to our power in certain ways that you were not before, though you empower yourself in other ways: economically, for example. This politics of visibility has its roots in slave society, but mutates in the new political situation, where white power and black resistance must adapt to changed conditions.

In the works of Malcolm X, these themes are explored with single-minded ferocity. It was Malcolm's insight, an insight that is present in germ in Du Bois and had been developed by Marcus Garvey, Frantz Fanon, Ralph Ellison, and others, and that is now so familiar as to be banal, that oppression is "internalized," that oppressed peoples take up precisely the values by which they are oppressed, not only as an external act, but in a pollution or destruction of the self. Du Bois's texts are variously magisterial and impassioned; his voice is partially shaped by his successful route through the white educational institutions of which he was one of the first and greatest black products.[1] Malcolm's texts also show the traces of being shaped by an institution: the prison. Thus they have very different relations to "white" values: Du Bois's trip through Harvard was an accomplishment which he sought as a demonstration of black abilities and of his personal abilities; Malcolm's trip through the courts and the "corrections" system was forced on him in an attempt to break him. (Though both men read the white canon, Du Bois read it as a student at the most prestigious university in the country; Malcolm read it as an inmate at Norfolk Prison Colony.) So it is comprehensible that whereas Du Bois for much of his life sought a reconciliation of consciousnesses (for example, in his debates with Washington over curricula), Malcolm sought to *purify* himself of white values.

Oppression, when it is not the sheer, immediate application of force, operates by deploying values that are, in the age of comprehension, regarded by the oppressor as transparent, or self-evident, or neutral. To the extent that these values are successfully installed as universal, an operation that is uneven and contested, they are installed among both oppressors and oppressed. Notice again that our ethics, like our sciences, proceed by ranging actions into categories, by finding the right ethical pigeonhole for a particular act; the evaluation of that act will then "follow," effortlessly. Ranging these actions into the correct categories is an act that is supposed to transcend individual bodies and cultures; it is the act of Reason (and its attendant, free will) or of some other faculty that subsists generally in human nature. The Western tradition tends to valorize this faculty into the ethical agent per se. Thus to the extent that one acts ethically, one acts in exactly the same way as all other ethical agents, which is no accident, because pure reason, or moral intuition, or happiness, is supposed to be exactly the same in each. Thus the irremediably particular (which we have sought to make you by our comprehension) must be associated with transgression, or sheer obscenity; the assertion of particularity has no place at all in our ethics except as that which must be overcome and excluded. In our articulation of you as the generalized particular, therefore, we make of you the sign of transgression itself, even as we seek to reinstate you into the ethical economy. We construct our pure moral agency by the exclusion of what we construct you to be: particular, appetitive, passionate, incapable of reason, incoherent.

Oppression operates by inculcating values in those whom it uses in the service of oppression: in the white middle class, say—in the "overseer." But it operates, finally, by inculcating those values in the oppressed people themselves, with several effects. First, this operates as a promise: If you live in a certain way or conform yourselves to a certain template, you will ascend into the oppressing classes, and your particularity will, like ours, disappear, since no one will be allowed to point it out. You will gain a share in our power. This serves various obvious economic purposes and creates a momentum toward "equality" or "integration," though always under the aegis of the dominant culture: always, that is, at the price of the existence of the dominated culture, or at least at the price of its manifestation in individuals. But it pulls in precisely the opposite way at the same time: It debilitates people from action by inculcating self-loathing. This is especially true because, though it imposes these values on the people it excludes, it also excludes them systematically from the realm of value altogether; it has made of them the sign for itself of transgression. What is transgressive is thus both incorporated and extruded from the order of ethical signification. It is incorporated *as* what is extruded, as the object of the ejection that manufactures the ethical. And in being absorbed, what makes the transgression most deeply transgressive is lost:

precisely its evasion of signification as generalization. Thus, by the very same act, transgression is signified, condemned, ejected, and attenuated.

The correspondence between these two things is always precise: Self-loathing is inversely proportional, *ceteris paribus,* to the capacity to act. If people can be turned against themselves, they police themselves; they destroy themselves. That is the most efficient technique by which to dominate people; it hobbles people and turns them against each other at minimum expense. In addition, since this operation calls itself by many distracting names (like "education"), it is hard to notice it for what it is: a technique of destruction through cooperation. We will change you from what you are by "offering" you the chance to make yourselves like us. This mirrors the general structure of the ethical ejection: We will sweep you up into significance; we offer you a name: *our* name. But as we inscribe ourselves on you, we erase you.

The inculcation of self-loathing is a perfect form of domination in the case of race. Malcolm learned, he says, to hate himself, to hate the way he looked, the way he talked, and the visible and invisible signs in and on himself of cultural difference and hence cultural membership. One of the most famous passages of *The Autobiography of Malcolm X,* describes "conking" hair with lye in order to straighten it:

> This was my first really big step toward self-degradation: when I endured all that pain, literally burning my flesh to have it look like a white man's hair. I had joined that multitude of Negro men and women in America who are brainwashed into believing that black people are "inferior"—and white people "superior"—that they will even violate and mutilate their God-created bodies to try to look "pretty" by white standards.
>
> Look around today, in every small town and big city, from two-bit catfish and soda-pop joints to the "integrated" lobby of the Waldorf-Astoria, and you'll see conks on black men. And you'll see black women wearing these green and pink and purple and red and platinum-blonde wigs. They're all more ridiculous than a slapstick comedy. It makes you wonder if the Negro has completely lost his sense of identity, lost touch with himself.[2]

This is not to say that there could not be reasons other than racial self-loathing for straightening hair. Indeed, such play with racial signs might have various subversive capacities, as is suggested by Kobena Mercer.[3] It can often be read as an attempt at self-empowerment through play with the symbolic order of whiteness. One of its effects is to denaturalize race, to demonstrate that race is a system of signifiers and not a genetic fact. Within a limited scope, cosmetics, hair products, and clothing offer racial mobility in either direction. If you see me in my hockey jersey, wearing a pair of loops in my ears (and that is possible), you will know, it is to be hoped, that I'm trying to "code black." And I am subject at that moment to my own version of the self-loathing that Malcolm describes; I'm a traitor to my race. There are, however, limits to this treason; I'm awfully blonde and blue to be black (though there are some blond and blue people who count as black in our racial economy—a fact pointed out as early as the mid-eighteenth century by figures such as William Wells Brown and Harriet Jacobs). And black people are going to find it very suspicious that I want to pretend to be black. They ought to find that suspicious. I can wear all the hockey jerseys I like, code myself as black, but I don't *have* to, and I can stop when it gets uncomfortable. I can instantly bring myself perfectly back into white codes, and regain all the privileges of that position (in fact, I never lost them, even for a moment). Or I can come out on the other end and code "redneck." But in my view, self-loathing is not a *black* thing; white people avoid self-loathing as oppressors only through massive strategies of self-deception, and we employ oppression as a strategy for avoiding our own particular embodiment. We try to teach you to hate your blackness, and thus we learn to hate *our own* "blackness": our bodies, our desires, our violence. To say it better, we teach you to hate your blackness *because* we hate our own blackness; our oppression is our self-hatred ejected.

Likewise, both white folks and black folks are going to find it suspicious when a black person "codes white." Such a person will be taken, by white folks, as an *example* of something in need of explanation ("How did you get to talk like us? We should do more of whatever it was!"), but ultimately as something reassuring, especially to white liberals. In either case, one looks to be "trying to be what one is not" (although this can be taken as proof of either corrigibility or betrayal), and to say that is to reinstitute race as a dichotomy. But we are very far indeed from *ceasing* to conceive of race as a dichotomy; I suggest that ceasing to think of race as a dichotomy would be, for Americans, to cease thinking of race at all, and the discourse of race in this country is as intense as it has ever been, as are the practices of exclusion and exploitation bound up with that discourse.

In such a situation, race mobility could be a subversive play of signifiers, but it could also be a system of self-betrayal, of turning away from one's own identity as that is articulated in the social constructions of race. One becomes a "traitor to one's race," which is also to say a traitor to oneself, a traitor to one's family, a traitor to one's community. To be accused of treason in this way is one manner in which the dichotomy is *enforced,* but it is also a means of cultural preservation and pride. This yields a picture of the dilemma that arises out of the dichotomy: to free oneself from the dichotomy is self-liberation, but to free oneself from one's race (the very same act) is self-betrayal. Thus, we attack the dichotomy in a liberatory project (the politics of humanism or integration), but we preserve the dichotomy in a project of authenticity (the politics of identity). This introduces a structure to which we will return: The races require one another in proximity, and require also segregation from one another, as ethics requires transgression, and transgression requires ethics. We are nowhere near emerging from this problem.

At any rate, there is no doubt that racial self-loathing is possible and expresses itself aesthetically. Consider Michael Jackson, who has tried to transform himself surgically into a white person, and who, when a film biography was in the works, suggested that he be played by a young white man. What one has learned is a *principle:* that "African" hair, or whatever it is that marks you as black, is repulsive, or is a "mark" of powerlessness. But that turns you not only against yourself; it turns you against everyone who is similar to you, to precisely the extent that they are similar to you with regard to racial signifiers. Your hatred of yourself constitutes a hatred for your family, your home, your friends. Richard Wright puts the matter very clearly:

> Color hate defined the place of black life as below that of white life; and the black man, responding to the same dreams as the white man, strove to bury within his heart his awareness of this difference because it made him lonely and afraid. Hated by whites and being an organic part of the culture that hated him, the black man grew in turn to hate in himself that which others hated in him. But pride would make him hide his self-hate, for he would not want whites to know that he was so thoroughly conquered by them that his total life was conditioned by their attitude; but in the act of hiding his self-hate, he could not help but hate those who evoked his self-hate in him. . . . Like any other American, I dreamed of going into business and making money; I dreamed of working for a firm that would allow me to advance until I reached an important position; I even dreamed of organizing secret groups of blacks to fight all whites. . . . And if blacks would not agree to organize, then they would have to be fought. I would end up again with self-hate, but it was now self-hate that was projected outward upon other blacks.[4]

Here, Wright's raced relation to himself becomes immensely complicated; he is both implicated in and excluded from "the American dream," and he experiences vividly both the need for resistance and the difficulty of mounting resistance in that situation.

Wright here displays the leakage of consciousnesses that both collapses and reinstitutes the dualism of race: One is hated by the culture of which one is also a part; excluded from that in which one is simultaneously embedded; segregated, but segregated in the geography one shares with the dominant culture. One cannot help but absorb the values of that culture (consider the continuing white dominance of media and educational institutions), but as one coded as the transgressor of those values. These days, when white politicians want to talk about race, they talk about *crime* (words that make race explicit are themselves now transgressive). And no one thinks they're talking about, say, criminal bankers: "criminal" means junk dealer, not junk-bond dealer. Segregation in this sense, whether it is of a city or of a consciousness, is not simple exclusion or ejection; it is exclusion and simultaneous incorporation; it is exclusion as a particular mode of incorporation. We need your labor, for instance, so we must have access to you, on our terms, even as we insulate ourselves from you. The consciousness fragmented in the racial situation is likewise both divided and pulled together by the very mode of division; each bit needs what it excludes. As I will argue, we white folks *yearn toward* what we have, imaginatively, ejected.

To hate yourself as black is to hate anyone who looks like you, talks like you, dresses like you. So if there is black-on-black murder, that should be no surprise. Some black-on-black murder, at any rate, is made in the making of double consciousness, which is in turn made by economic and social exclusion. Many writers, however, have objected to this assessment of the "black experience." Even Du Bois, at times, viewed double consciousness as an opportunity as well as a burden, as something that yielded epistemic leverage. And Zora Neale Hurston, as we will see, simply denied that this whole dynamic was in play in her life, as has, more recently, Molefi Kete Asante.[5] Nevertheless, many African-American autobiographies (among them, obviously, Wright's and Malcolm's) centralize and attack various forms of self-division.

Another feature of these forms of division is a hierarchical arrangement in the black community by skin color:

> This religion [Christianity] taught the "Negro" to think that black was a curse. It taught him to hate everything black, including himself. It taught him that everything white was good, to be admired, respected, and loved. It brainwashed this "Negro" to think that he was superior if his complexion showed more of the white pollution of the slavemaster. (*Autobiography,* 188)

Malcolm had a particularly visceral reaction to the aristocracy of color within the black community. His mother's mother had been raped by a white man, and his mother favored her darker over her lighter-skinned children; Malcolm was the lightest. "If I could drain away *his* blood that pollutes *my* body, and pollutes *my* complexion, I'd do it! Because I hate every drop of the rapist's blood that's in me!" (*Autobiography,* 232). Thus, Malcolm's project in the formation of Malcolm X out of Malcolm Little, his project of taking a name for himself, of making a self in resistance to white hegemony, is conceived by him as a project of purification, of rejecting his "white blood." This project is the perfect mirror image of the basic process of white self-construction, and its very familiarity and the power of its reversal present a direct threat not only to white power, but to the white self that holds power. Of course, it also supposes and enforces race as a dualism made by ejection.

This also shows something of the complications that are endemic to any situation that systematically calls forth self-loathing. It is possible, indeed likely, that one learns to loathe not only the black in oneself, but the white. (That is reflected in the passage from Wright above, for example.) Loathing for the white man is an expression of racial pride. But in a situation in which the races have intermingled for centuries, often in ways that reflect the oppression of African-Americans (rape, for instance)—but also in ways that reflect resistance to that oppression (love, for instance)—loathing for the white man can also be self-loathing, especially for light-skinned blacks. The situation would be much simpler if the racial identifications were clearer; Du Boisian double consciousness, however, breaks down from both ends simultaneously, so that one may be neither black nor white enough for an unqualified identification with race or culture. The fluidity of the races—which racist dogma, some of it codified into law, is dedicated to denying—must reflect fluidity of consciousness in a culture which inculcates hyperawareness of racial identity.

Shirley Taylor Haizlip, in her autobiographical discussion of racial mixing, *The Sweeter the Juice,* writes,

> I do not lust after my whiteness. More often than not, I feel ambivalent about the white part of me and those circumstances, both known and imagined, that resulted in the mix. I am not really sure what the white portion of me means, if anything. Is it a separate self? Does it think differently from my black self? Does it have a subconscious racial memory? How can I love it when it may not love me?[6]

The mixture in Haizlip's background divided her family against itself as those who appeared white sought to insulate themselves from the darker members of their family, and hence from their own blackness.

Three of my grandparents died before I was born. The remaining one, my mother's father, William Morris, whom my mother called "Willmorris" (I heard it as one word), was inaccessible to me. As a "white" man who could not admit colored people into his world, he lived a distant life in a distant place. I knew he was alive, because whenever the subject of her father came up, my mother, with uncharacteristic venom, referred to him as "Willmorris that-bastard-in-Maryland." I never met him, but his absence was a presence in my life. (32)

This situation institutes an apartheid within families and an apartheid within the self, as one seeks racial insulation: the "absence" of oneself from one's family, and the "absence" of oneself to oneself. But this absence, as always in apartheid, itself becomes a presence that arises precisely from the all-too-vivid dependence of the races on one another in a cultural/sexual/economic situation in which, as we shall see, loathing and desire maintain an intense interrelation.

The most beautiful attempt I know by a black writer to come to terms with this is found in Patricia Williams's book *The Alchemy of Race and Rights*. Williams investigates in some detail the circumstances that led to her particular racial mix, circumstances that are in some ways similar to Haizlip's but are also similar in some ways to Jacobs's or Douglass's. At the end of the book, she develops the figure of the polar bear to represent the white in herself and outside herself (actually, that is a simplistic reading, but it gets the gist of the thing). The book ends as follows:

> I pursued my way, manumitted back into silence. I put distance between them and me, gave myself over to polar-bear musings. I allowed myself to be watched over by bear spirits. Clean white wind and strong bear smells. The shadowed amnesia; the absence of being; the presence of polar bears. White wilderness of icy meateaters heavy with remembrance; leaden with undoing; shaggy with the effort of hunting for silence; frozen in a web of intention and intuition. A lunacy of polar bears. A history of polar bears. A pride of polar bears. A consistency of polar bears. In those meandering pastel polar-bear moments, I found cool fragments of white-fur invisibility. Solid, black-gummed, intent, observant. Hungry and patient, impassive and exquisitely timed. The brilliant bursts of exclusive territoriality. A complexity of messages implied in our being.[7]

Any attempt to explain this passage only lessens its power, but I will venture this much: Williams learned to let herself and thus her polar bears be: to see herself and them whole without hating or hunting them. I hope that this observation will echo in the next chapter, when we come to consider Zora Neale Hurston and her insistence that "we's uh mingled people."

As Haizlip's text makes clear, apartheid of the self reaches a high pitch of intensity in the case of African-Americans (as racially identified within the practices of European-American culture) who "pass" as white. (The classic text here is James Weldon Johnson's novel *The Autobiography of an Ex-Colored Man,* where the internal price of "passing" is represented as being enormous or all-consuming.[8]) Here the "promise" of integration is perfectly fulfilled: The individual literally "ascends" from the subordinate to the dominant race, often collecting the perks of dominance (power, money, prestige) along the way, becoming visible as white in white culture. This integration appears to overcome the racial dichotomy. But the visible surface may be produced at the cost of massive self-denial or self-forgetting—self-denial and self-forgetting that entail the existence of the dualism itself (again, that is what Johnson's text thematizes). Often, as again in Haizlip, this includes shunting away members of one's own family. Malcolm writes,

> I'm told that there are in America today between two and five million "white Negroes," who are "passing" in white society. Imagine their torture! Living in constant fear that some black person they've known might meet and expose them. Imagine every day living a lie. *Imagine* hearing their own white husbands, their own white wives, even their own white children, talking about "those Negroes." (*Autobiography,* 318)

Here one both overcomes and tolerates one's own oppression; one becomes the oppressor of oneself; one *is* both white and black in a culture obsessed with keeping these apart and subordinating one to the other. In such people (and who among us is racially "pure"?—we're all passing), the structure of oppression is perfectly crystallized, but it is also overcome or deconstructed. The very concept of "passing" employs assumptions that "passing" bodies deny: that races are distinct, that you "are" one or the other. The very operation of *consigning* bodies to one or the other category shows those categories to be social constructions. That is, the dualism must continually be enforced and reinstituted in the face of racial fluidity. To be both black and white is to embody and to make impossible a racially polarized culture. Racially mixed people are, thus, both central and marginal: They are the *locus* of transaction, and form the traditional "black aristocracy," but they are also regarded with suspicion by both racial communities. They reflect the fact that the races are not distinct: a needed sign, but also a threat to the basic fabric of American culture. Racially mixed people stand as visible markers of white rape of black women, of love and marriage between the races, of the fluidity of identity and the conventionality of racial conceptual structures. They both embody our self-divisions and overcome them. The anxiety with which such persons are regarded (which *are* they?) shows forth our participation in the social operations of the consignment of persons to races.

The various forms and symptoms of self-loathing that Malcolm describes do not result from a "conspiracy" among the oppressors; they do not result from any specific strategy or plan, where we white folks sit down and ask ourselves how to make these people hate themselves. With regal neutrality we deploy a set of ethical and aesthetic values that is in fact incompatible with the values of African and African-American cultures. Thus the barrage of images of Caucasian beauty is not an attempt to turn African-Americans against themselves; it is an attempt to sell blue jeans or whatever. On the other hand, the process does not simply happen, "innocently," to constitute the occasion for self-division. The functions of oppressor and oppressed are here, as everywhere, mirrored. The way images circulate in European-American culture, for example, is not for the most part "aimed" at attacking African notions of beauty. Nevertheless, these images could not circulate in the way they do unless they had their function as oppressive "instruments." Their content, their aesthetic surface, and the ways they are created and presented are permeated by their role in the oppressive machine (though there are zones here of resistance, even within the commercial imagery of "consumer capitalism"). Images of Caucasian beauty are attempts by white people to articulate themselves to themselves; thus, in the American situation, they *must* also perform an ejection of what is constructed as black. *Our* ideals of ourselves are incomprehensible except in relation to our erasure of you from those ideals.

Oppression is, or sometimes is, "internalized" by oppressed persons. But oppression is, or sometimes is, "externalized" by oppressing persons. The point will be familiar from the last two chapters. Oppression is released by the oppressor into an "objective" realm, where it is not anyone's doing in particular, but just a feature of the external facts. While the oppressed person takes it in, the oppressor eliminates it, gets rid of it, makes it a feature of objective conditions, blames the victim, or blames the economic situation, or simply denies its existence. For example, while the "black" person who "passes" pays an internal price for self-denial, the "white" person with black ancestry simply does not acknowledge her blackness to herself. Another example: a couple of years ago I saw a televised debate in which Robert Bork asserted that racism is no longer a significant problem in this country. The camera then panned to Cornel West, whose chin just about hit the table at which he was seated. Bork's claim is ridiculous, insane, but also absolutely typical: Only a few crazy neo-Nazis are racists, because only a few crazy neo-Nazis still use the prohibited locutions that make racism explicit. One of the kindest men I have ever known once expressed to me his puzzlement about black poverty and crime in a culture that has overcome its racism. The externalization of oppression has proceeded to the point of a total loss of contact with reality, a sort of psychosis that could only be manifest in us oppressors. We do not even notice the ease with which we arrogate to ourselves the right to say *what counts as racism,* and to declare that it does not exist, since we do not see it in ourselves. What we *are* able to detect, bizarrely and appropriately enough, is the "reverse racism" in *your* attitude.

The forms of white self-construction by ejection manufacture a subject that is massively lost to itself, unable to see its own relations because it has "floated free" of reality. That is, in fact, what white self-construction is *for,* to float free of the material, to forget the body, and to forget the body's implication in, among other things, the machinery of brutalization. I speak here as one who knows, as a spokesman for the white man. (Though all of us white men who speak publicly are spokesmen for the white man, the only people who are actually described that way are Klansmen or Nazis. That's because the extremists are the only white men who don't speak their race under erasure.) To say *that* is to say that I take myself to speak neutrally, objectively about you, and even, if need be, about myself. I am *burdened by consciousness;* I am, to myself, nothing but a consciousness, a voice chattering to my body through a transparent medium. This consciousness wills my body forward into action or holds it back; in my relation to my body, I am the slavemaster of myself. My consciousness takes itself to have been made for mastery; it arrogates to itself the undoubted right of mastery, without reflection. And above all, it feels *detached* in its empowerment from my body and from my environment; it *separates* itself from the physical situation. My self is dual: word of power, recalcitrant physical material. I can oppress you because I *am* oppression, because the primordial site of my oppression is my relation to *my* body, because my *self* is hallucinated as a pure will. I can make my oppression of you invisible to myself because it is a baseline for me, a basic, ever-present condition of my being, like a white noise that becomes inaudible in its droning repetition. My oppression of you is already externalized because I as body, as beast, am ejected from myself, lost to myself, invisible to myself because my mammalian body has been erased in hallucination by my consciousness. That, in my opinion, is what it means to be a white man. Whiteness is the color of ghosts.

And of course this is not only the site of self-loathing; it is the site of *release;* it is the place where I can be relieved of my particularity, where I can take pleasure in an *a priori* apparent purity. And it is also where I find the pleasure of power: the pleasure of an identification with the empowered class of white men, whether they are rednecks or intellectuals; the place where I can reap (usually effortlessly, unconsciously) the benefits of power made in self-division. I can float free of my self, be released from sin and pain in my imagination. It is the place from which I can survey the world with the calm detachment of the white philosopher, the place where comprehension lives and yields the pleasures of technological control. And that is also, in my opinion, what it means to be a white man.

In his speeches, Malcolm often exposed the structure of the externalization/internalization of oppression to devastating effect. At the London School of Economics, for example, he said this:

> Somebody's got nerve enough, some whites have the audacity, to refer to me as a hate teacher. If I'm teaching someone to hate, I'm teaching them to hate the Ku Klux Klan. But here and in America they have taught us to hate ourselves. To hate our skin, to hate our features, to hate our blood, hate what we are. Uncle Sam is a master hate-teacher, so much so that he makes someone think he's teaching law when he's teaching hate. When you've made a man hate himself, you've really got it and gone.[9]

This passage cuts to the core of the American racial dilemma. First, it tries to reveal African-Americans to themselves, both by displaying the possibility of their self-loathing, and by reaching under that self-loathing to show its source in oppression. Second, it tries to show European-Americans to themselves as persons who have shunted their hate into the "objective" realm of laws and institutions (and "values" and "sciences") and then failed to experience themselves as haters. This movement into the objective displays the ghost-white self writ large.

The state, the law, the institution, as construed in the European tradition, is the will bloated imaginatively to the collective scale; the state is the *text* that *commands* the social body forward, that reshapes by the sorcery of the word the recalcitrant physical situation: bodies and their material conditions. The state is what dominates nature. So the white state, like the white self, is a hallucinated self-division, a body/mind, nature/culture dualized fantasy. Just as the white self hides its material origins and effects from itself, the white law hides its violence from itself; it is a codification and systematization of violence that proceeds as though with regal majesty and neutrality. Thus, to repeat, blackness is constructed as a sheer transgression, as a specific body, as crime, as anarchy. Making Malcolm visible as a "hate teacher" is part of the self-construction by which we disguise to ourselves the awesome material machinery of our own hatred.

Malcolm goes so far as to assert that the explicit racism of the "white Southerner" is preferable to the implicit racism of the "northern liberal":

> The white Southerner, you can say one thing—he is honest. He bares his teeth to the black man; he tells the black man, to his face, that Southern whites never will accept phony "integration." . . . The advantage of this is that the Southern black man has never been under any illusions about the opposition he is dealing with. (*Autobiography*, p. 312)

It is worth pointing out that the white Southerner, too, has by now for the most part learned to externalize oppression, has learned to produce the right signs, learned not to say "nigger," not to segregate universities by armed force, and so forth. The racism that describes itself as neutrality, even tolerance, is more obnoxious and in some ways more dangerous than overt hate. The end of such practices produces the bizarre spectacle of a culture in which almost no one is a racist in one traditional sense of the term, but which is also segregated, economically divided along racial lines, and so forth. The culture is racist, but no individual in it is racist; here ideology and reality have come apart completely, and no one is doing the things that everyone is doing. This is the final, crystalline construction of whiteness: a perfect amnesia of the material situation, an apotheosis to the realm of pure spirit. The civil rights movement taught us white folks how not to appear to be racists, even to ourselves. In that sense, it represented the perfection of a certain form of oppression, and a form of oppression that is unbelievably difficult to resist because it is invisible, above all to itself. There is then no one to blame for your oppression, except perhaps yourselves. White people look on in amazement at the "black underclass" so beloved by the press. It certainly can't be the result of racism, because there are no more racists! So it must be a result of distorted values in that very underclass. Meanwhile, the people maundering on in this fashion continue to participate in the racist machinery of oppression, and continue to reap its benefits (start with cheap labor).

It is paradigmatically this latter fact—that the white population reaps the benefits of racism and is unconscious of so doing—that forms the structure of racial exploitation in America. Just as the "black underclass" must be responsible for its predicament, we white folks must be responsible for our success: Hard work and solid values have brought us our stuff. Malcolm has a rather different view:

> The only reason that the present generation of white Americans are in the position of economic strength that they are is because their fathers worked our fathers for over 400 years with no pay. . . . All of that money that piled up from the sale of my mother and my grandmother and my great-grandmother is what gives the present generation of American whites the ability to walk around the earth with their chest out; you know, like they have some kind of economic ingenuity. Your father isn't here to pay his debts. My father isn't here to collect. But I'm here to collect and you're here to pay. (*By Any Means*, 123)

And he could have added, and did assert elsewhere, that structural inequalities continue to benefit white people economically and in many other ways (psychically, for example). So, also, does the regime of appearance that defines and enforces a notion of the "normal," acceptable person; white people simply recognize other white people as more appropriate for, say, good jobs. (I have noticed this in academic job searches: Everyone wants to hire a black candidate. But get me into the interview with senior white professor guys and there will be an immediate mutual recognition that will help me get the job.) The very self-image of American white culture as industrious, entrepreneurial, ingenious, and so forth, makes use of various stereotypes of black people. But we are and must remain blissfully ignorant that our image of our industriousness depends on our image of your laziness, that our image of our goodness depends on our image of your criminality, and so forth.

It is, therefore, a condition of the possibility of the oppressive machine in its current configuration that it *has nothing to do* with race. The images of our culture circulate either by inscribing and then erasing beauty, for example, as something with a specific racial content and function, or else deploy a racial even-handedness which is perfectly and self-consciously maintained, but wherein the various "normalizing" functions are only subtilized (there are "black" models, for instance, but they have "white" features, or the models have vaguely "ethnic" features, but are identifiably white; the dualism is endangered or subtilized or elaborated but ultimately reinstated in the erotics of the exotic). That these images always have a precise location in power relations *cannot* be acknowledged in a situation in which oppression is externalized.

Malcolm, revealingly, calls this the "science" of image-making; he discusses the circulation of images in our culture that coalesce around stereotypes and that relentlessly emphasize black animality and embodiment:

> It's a science that they use, very skillfully, to make the criminal look like the victim, and to make the victim look like the criminal. Example: In the United States during the summer [of 1964] they had riots. I was in Africa, fortunately. During these riots, or because of these riots, or after these riots, again the press, very skillfully, depicted the rioters as hoodlums, criminals, thieves, because they were busting up property. . . . And instead of sociologists analyzing it as it actually is, trying to understand it as it actually is, again they cover up the real issue, and they use the press to make it appear that these people are thieves, hoodlums. No! They are the victims of organized thievery, organized landlords who are nothing but thieves, politicians who sit in city hall and who are nothing but thieves in cahoots with the landlords and merchants.[10]

This passage raises many of the issues that have appeared before or will appear later in this book. I will mention just a couple. First, it describes the use of the science of sociology as a political instrument of oppression. The "neutral" knowledge in sociology proceeds and enforces certain social constructions of animalistic criminality. Second, this passage seeks to make white people visible to themselves; they have attributed their own criminality to someone else. As Malcolm points out, the people who rioted did not own their own dwellings or the stores they shopped in, and when they lashed out at the white power structure, they lashed out at its direct ownership of their environment. This is as true of the riots of 1992 as it is of the riots of 1964. That *you* are the *particular* criminals, that you commit the particular, small-scale transgressions, allows us to hide from ourselves (though not necessarily from you, or rather, necessarily not from you) that we are the general criminals, committing robbery and murder on a global scale.

In fact, "philosophical" notions such as that beauty is universal, that it is the subject of a disinterested aesthetic regard conceived as general—these are externalizations of oppression writ large, ejected into an objective realm where they are nobody's standards in particular. The same might be said of the articulation of ethical values in universal guise: that to act ethically is to act according to a principle on which anyone could act in similar circumstances, or to create the greatest good of the greatest number. Such values insist on their independence from actual relationships, for example, and rely on the shadowy assumption that there could *be* values that are no one's values, that is, that are "everyone's" values.

And the same must be said, and repeated, about epistemic values such as truth and knowledge. The educational power structure, with its economic consequences, "offers" these values even to recalcitrant cultures. Thus black families "don't value education," and so forth, a claim which is not only false but focuses the whole of Western epistemology into a single "neutral" act of cultural destruction. Cultural destruction through education is not only not thematized as racist in this country; it is held to display white commitment to equality. The content of the education itself, which is by and large a catechism in Western culture, is thought of as entirely culturally neutral. And note that power in education is still raw; education is *compulsory*. If you don't send your kids, we'll come and get the little truants, and we'll remove them from your custody if we have to do that too often. And what we are "offering" you is precisely that from which we are in a thousand ways excluding you: our comprehension.

At any rate, we have mirrored self-divisions. The oppressed person embraces the values of the oppressor, while the oppressor loses track of himself as an oppressor and believes the most sentimental claptrap about himself. But these divisions quickly become something different, if it is right to point to a moment of division at all. For in all these cases, the self is not simply dividing—it is disintegrating. One no longer knows what one wants, what one thinks, what one is. One's desires, one's opinions become concealed to oneself, so that one experiences oneself as something elusive, something that has been "lost." This is a prototypically American variety of lostness: where one does not in fact believe what one has always taken oneself to believe, where one is not doing what one takes oneself to be doing. Do I (an African-American) believe that whites are beautiful and blacks ugly? No! Am I straightening my hair? Yes. Why, exactly? I (a European-American) am not a racist. I'm just more comfortable in a white neighborhood, with white schools. Why, exactly? And so on.

As the self-divisions mirror one another, so do the yearnings. What the oppressor lacks, necessarily, is self-knowledge: The oppressor does not know what he actually desires. Above all he does not know that he desires to oppress, but the whole range of his desires is hidden from him in the process by which his body and its actions become invisible. (And then he can only desire *to desire*, to appropriate the mark of desire, to dominate the other.) The oppressor is departicularized; he becomes to himself something universal, necessary, objective; he makes a scientist of himself. On the other hand, the oppressed person is relentlessly driven toward the particular, driven inward, made idiosyncratic. The oppressed may be the object of scientific study, but cannot, *qua* oppressed person, be its subject: cannot be a subject eradicating his own embodiment, detaching his voice from his position. Thus the oppressed person becomes, for the oppressor, the embodiment and sign of desire per se. The oppressed person (think of women here, as well) is "spontaneous," "natural," "irrational," "passionate," and "embodied." And though these are stereotypes, they are stereotypes that are capable of transforming persons when they take up a place within disciplinary regimes. Oppression as we practice it in the West must always be oppression of bodies by minds, oppression of emotions by reason, oppression of subjectivity by objectivity, oppression of spontaneity by consciousness, oppression of the particular by the general, because oppression as we practice it continually makes itself neutral as among particular facts, continually desituates itself. The self-divisions that allow us or constrain us white folks to practice these forms of oppression, and the divisions from the other that allow us or constrain us to practice these forms of self-division are, as I have repeatedly insisted, imaginary. No matter how importunate my will, the little chattering consciousness I take, or mistake, for myself, *I am* a body. No matter how powerfully I try to machine you into a pure, spontaneous, anarchic, natural body, you are also a consciousness, a culture. But the dualism that formulates oppression in the West supposes a dualized self, and the dualized self as it appears in modernity crystallizes the conditions under which oppression operates.

These conditions are embodied through and through in this book, for example. The material I'm interested in is African-American *autobiography,* and I am interested in this material as formulating by its very existence and character an attack on the Western tradition. While I want to read the white Western philosophical tradition as a tradition of *comprehension,* of subsumption of the particular to the general, I want to read the African-American response to this tradition as an explosion of particularity back into the general (though I also simultaneously inscribe my resolve not to read it in this way only, to take seriously its theoretical aspects). Thus I am pitting particular lives against general theories. This certainly distorts and simplifies both traditions, but it also says something true about what has emerged in persons through their participation in the oppressive structure. So in choosing to work with just these materials, I both historicize (denaturalize) and reinforce the entire apparatus of stereotypes in which the black is the embodied and the particular, and the white is the disembodied and the general.

Here we enter dangerous territory. For I cannot myself absolve myself of the stereotype. I romanticize black people precisely as embodied, particularized, and so forth, and both yearn toward and fear them as I so construct them. My encounter with Malcolm's voice was formative in this regard, and though I have perhaps left Malcolm behind as an author in this discussion, I have not left behind my experience of his authorship. Malcolm's was the first voice of black militancy that I heard (as it emerged from Mr. Singleton, my teacher), and I was immediately fascinated and repelled. That voice was confronting *me,* showing me to myself, giving me, to some extent for the first time, a sense of *my own* racial position. Even as I sat in a classroom, in a school, in a city, full of black folks and tortured by the confrontation of the races, it took this material to bring me to a confrontation with *myself.* My response to Malcolm's voice is simultaneously a confrontation and an identification; I would like to speak the way Malcolm does: out of anger, and rebellion, and clear analysis, but also with great humor and ease. I recognize Malcolm as the kind of truth-teller I would like to be.[11] But I *do* recognize him under the auspices of a certain range of stereotyped qualities, whether they are lauded or despised; he speaks, to me, with the voice of particularity, embodiment, passion. So I speak here out of the simultaneous ejection and desire I have been describing. My *identification* with Malcolm is a kind of desire; among other things, it eroticizes transgression. And yet, rebel as I may, or immerse myself in blackness, I will never be able to speak from Malcolm's position; I can transgress, but I cannot be the sign of transgression and speak myself as such a sign. My identification with Malcolm subverts the racial dichotomy, but it absolutely presupposes that same dichotomy.

One question that arises is this: are the racial constructions that configure desire mere myths, or are they truths; and if they have any purchase at all in reality, is the reality antecedent or subsequent to the myth; is it the myth that makes the reality, or vice versa? Hurston, as we are going to see, mounts a celebration of the passion and embodiment of African-American culture. By contrast, Wright dismisses all such talk as racism:

> After I had outlived the shocks of childhood, after the habit of reflection had been born in me, I used to mull over the strange absence of real kindness in Negroes, how unstable was our tenderness, how lacking in genuine passion we were, how void of great hope, how timid our joy, how bare our traditions, how hollow our memories, how lacking we were in those intangible sentiments that bind man to man, and how shallow even our despair. After I had learned other ways of life I used to brood upon the unconscious irony of those who felt that Negroes led so passional an existence! I saw that what had been taken for our emotional strength was our negative confusions, our flights, our fears, our frenzy under pressure. (*Black Boy,* 37)

Notice that in whatever direction one turns on this issue, self-loathing lurks for blacks, and racism for whites. If I were simply to dismiss black culture in the way Wright does here, I would be a racist. On the other hand, if I simply celebrate it, out of my desire, as embodied and passionate, I am also a racist. When Wright attacks his own culture, he endangers himself, but if he remarks on his own naturalness, say, he dismisses himself in a certain way as an author, for example.

I am not, I am afraid, going to negotiate this thicket in a very satisfactory way. My goal is to display and even to heighten this tension, not to resolve it. But I want to try this: Whether the notion of white folks as disembodied intellects and black folks as natural bodies has any purchase in reality or not, it is central to the cultural imaginary. The notion has been expressed from the time of slavery to the present and, if anything, is more intense now than it was a hundred years ago. It is both a racist construction and, as I will suggest especially in the chapter on rap, an instrument or a locus of resistance to racism. And *if* it has any purchase in reality, it is because it calls into its service a gigantic machinery of trainings, a technology for remaking people in its image and then revealing or studying them as confirmation of its reality.

The white side of this construction is usefully understood in relation to the asceticism that in some ways dominates European thought. In an ascetic expression of objective values, the particular, the emotional—the body—must be annihilated. The division of races yields a very convenient arena for this ascetic discipline, which can now be expressed by inflicting pain on or destroying other persons rather than by inflicting pain on or destroying oneself. The privileged white American transcends embodiment, and particularity, and passion not by a discipline of self-overcoming, but by a discipline of oppression. This is a much more satisfactory technique than traditional self-denial, self-abasement, and so forth, because it affirms that one is *already* a pure soul, one is *already* fully rational, and so forth. Instead of engaging in the complicated, difficult business of overcoming oneself, one attains the life of the spirit—a pure, white, light-filled life—by overcoming others.

Segregation, then, has a philosophical and spiritual significance: It is an ascetic discipline, a purifying of the mind by an ejection of the body. Genocide would be the final victory of spirit over matter, reason over emotion, will over desire. Death is the final victory of the ascetic over his own body, the mortification of his own flesh.

Nevertheless, it goes without saying, or ought to, that too much consciousness is burdensome, that too much mind is tiresome (and dangerous), that too much reason is boring, that too much objectivity is painful to a creature fated to be subjective. Wherever one finds ascetic discipline, one finds it already in the process of being breached. What is denied in ascetic discipline is not eliminable short of death. In the long run, ejecting or destroying one's own desires are very unpromising strategies. In fact, they have the effect of strengthening the desires that are attacked. Once you have told yourself not to desire something, you will never forget it again.

When self-division comes to be expressed in social division and vice versa, longings are created that can only be satisfied by intercultural unifications of various kinds. Thus privileged white people in our culture yearn (at moments, anyway) to be black, that is, to be "spontaneous," "sexual," "physical," "violent." But ejected ascetics, in a racially stratified society, can "get" their spontaneity by controlled contact with the ejected, without danger of having to *stay* there. Malcolm writes,

> When it got late, Sophia and I would go to some of the after-hours places and speakeasies. When the downtown nightclubs had closed, most of these Harlem places crawled with white people. These whites were just mad for Negro "atmosphere," especially some of the places which had what you might call Negro *soul*. Sometimes Negroes would talk about how a lot of whites seemed unable to have enough of being close around us, and among us—in groups. Both white men and women, it seemed, would get mesmerized by Negroes. (*Autobiography*, 108–9)

The use of the word *soul* as applied to white and black people is an interesting inscription and ambiguation of the raced dualism. For the "soul" of white folk is the ruler of the body, whereas the "soul" of black folk is immanent in the body, is a redoubled embodiment, is a commitment to embodiment. That accounts, in part, for the power over white people of "soul music" and the religious tradition from which it emerges. Black Christianity displays the possibility of a reembodiment of Christianity, a relocation of the soul in and as the body; this is also a reinstitution of some of the primordial content of Christianity, which called for the resurrection *of the body* and described God's *incarnation* in a particular human body. When we slum, we attempt to buy our own reunification, the beautiful sign of which is, for example, the voice of Aretha Franklin.

Malcolm describes the prostitution business in Harlem as being dominated by white men looking for black women ("the blacker the better" [*Autobiography*, 138]), and by white men who wanted to watch white women having sex with black men. In sexuality, ejected asceticism becomes literalized: Ejection is ejaculation. "Jungle fever" of this variety, of course, plays on the erotic cachet inherent in taboo, but the reasons for the taboo and the intensity of the desires that coalesce around it are remarkable. Sex always contains the possibility of interpersonal fusion, of two people literally becoming one organism, or trying to. Heterosexual erotics deploys various metaphors of partial persons being made whole by sex. In the case of interracial sex in the West, such themes emerge with total intensity. A mind merges with a body, reason with passion, sexual strategy with sexual spontaneity. Interracial sex is a way that fragmented persons try to make themselves whole. White people want not only black bodies but black music, black religion, black food, black culture (all of which are sexualized in one way or another in the white imaginary), as a way to rediscover what in themselves has been lost to themselves by their oppression.

Western heterosexual erotics, however, deploys another and related use of desire: domination. Women, who are embodied, emotional, spontaneous (but *not* violent, dangerous, or animalistic, in the case of upper-class white women, as against the comparable stereotype of the African), are subjugated by sex. They are to be made available as sexual resources in certain ways; they are raw material in the technology of sexuality. Thus the dominance which men sometimes seek to impose directly in the sex act (most "emphatically" in cases of rape) informs the construction of gender. This situation is redoubled in the relations of white men to black women. First, there is a legacy of rape and a history of the legitimation or trivialization of rape in cases where the victim is black and the perpetrator white (see, for example, Du Bois, "Of the Coming of John," in *The Souls of Black Folk*, not to mention Jacobs's *Incidents in the Life of a Slave Girl*). There is the double subjugation: sexual resource and black person. And then there is the use of black women as a way to humiliate black men, as a demonstration of power.

I say that the desires for fusion and for domination are related because domination might, at least in certain cases, be thought of as a mode of fusion: One *ingests* the dominated person. The individuality of the dominated person is (at least imaginatively) liquidated into the dominant person (more clearly, it is rendered "invisible"). We can desire to dominate; we can desire that which we dominate; we can desire it by virtue of our domination of it. Domination makes fusion "safe" in the sense that it seems to offer the possibility of fusion with retention of individuality, without danger to ourselves. In the interracial case, it offers sex with the retention of asceticism, full-fledged embodiment with the preservation of the commanding will. Of course, domination and fusion may also be experienced as being in tension with one another; after all, no true fusion can take place where one of the terms of that fusion is expunged. The white people who were "mad for Negro atmosphere" no doubt thought of themselves as enlightened resistors of racism. It does not follow, however, that domination is not experienced as fusion, or even in part engaged in out of a need for fusion. And of course, domination has an ambiguous relation to desire: One can desire to dominate; one can desire to be dominated; the prospect of domination can enhance or inhibit desire. In the case of interracial sex, it seems to me, any or all of these relations may be in place, and the potential for their intensification is very great indeed. And of course all of these possibilities play across the possible sexual situations: black man and white woman, black woman and white man, black man and white man, black woman and white woman. Even this little catalogue leaves aside the fact that whiteness and blackness (and perhaps the gender categories as well) are always a matter of degree, and that fine distinctions of skin color are fraught with erotic significance ("the blacker the better").

Furthermore, a taboo is always an erotic node, a place where desire coalesces. To be seduced is to tumble into the violation of a taboo. Now we white folks construct black folks as pure particulars, and hence as that which by definition resists our ethics. Thus black people are thought of as criminals, as transgressors. To transgress into the very sign of transgression is to violate not this or that taboo, but taboo in general. Thus interracial sex has a very intense and particular erotic/specular power, an erotic power that draws the white men described by Malcolm to stare obsessively at black men fucking white women.

"Slumming" is a technology of the self. A need for embodiment arises in people who feel endangered by the loss of their own bodies, who threaten to float free into the abstract, or into the role (accountant, lawyer, businessman). In a situation in which the body has been ejected racially, interracial contact is a strategy for reembodiment. Thus, slumming *utilizes* the black body, seeks to bring it within a technological framework. This utilization connects slumming to slavery, in which black bodies were also used technologically, though what we intend to produce is ourselves rather than cotton. So this is a mode both of fusion and of domination, both of incorporation and ejection of the other. Hortense Spillers puts it this way:

First of all, [the African-American's] New-World, diasporic plight marked a *theft of the body*—a willful and violent (and unimaginable from this distance) severing of the captive body from its motive will, its active desire. . . . But this body, at least from the point of view of the captive community, focuses a private and particular space, at which point of convergence biological, sexual, social, cultural, linguistic, ritualistic, and psychological fortunes join. This profound intimacy of interlocking detail is disrupted, however, by externally imposed meanings and uses: (1) the captive body becomes the source of an irresistible, destructive sensuality; (2) at the same time—in stunning contradiction—the captive body reduces to a thing, becoming *being for* the captor; (3) in this absence *from* a subject position, the captured sexualities provide a physical and biological expression of "otherness"; (4) as a category of "otherness," the captive body translates into a potential for pornotroping and embodies sheer physical powerlessness that slides into a more general "powerlessness," resonating through various centers of human and social meaning.[12]

This is an astonishing series of insights, and I will content myself with a couple of elucidations from the "white subject position." First of all, perhaps the dirtiest secret of white racism is its eroticization of dominance: its sexual sadism. If we cannot acknowledge the fact that we get off on brutalization, and that our ancestors associated orgasm with the whip and the threat of the whip, then we cannot penetrate to the heart of whiteness. Very few people will acknowledge to themselves, much less to others, still less to their victims, that cruelty is pleasurable, but the whole history of American race relations is incomprehensible without that acknowledgment. The "pornotroping" here is specifically sadistic, and sadism involves both a reduction, in Spillers's sense, of the body to flesh, and the hope or wish that this reduction is a form of sensuality in what is so reduced. (And here is another dirty secret, even within the "contradiction": it may be.)

It is worth saying that *as* a mode of domination, this constantly removes that which is desired. It sets the black body up as a device or a technological resource, which works for producing cotton, perhaps, but does not work terribly well for producing selves, because that which one seeks to bring into the closest proximity is constantly distanced by the technological relation. What is utilized technologically must remain an object; it cannot collapse into an identity with the subject. But that too is in play: The person who is slumming both desires to "become" a body and desires to keep bodies at a distance. At most, the desire to become a body is to be satisfied intermittently, so that it doesn't directly interfere with being an accountant. Thus, slumming simultaneously tantalizes with the possibility of unification and insulates the possibility of unification in the slum. That is one reason we seek to hold black people in ghettos: so that our own encounter with ourselves can be controlled, limited spatially and temporally, set up as an object for use.

White people, then, desire black people and black culture in a variety of ways, for a variety of purposes; all I will insist upon is that we do desire them. By the same token, black people may romanticize white culture, adopt white aesthetics, and so forth, because they want what white people have: intellectual development, or "mind" as it appears in the European tradition, but above all money and power. For example, consumer goods become central to self-image. Money and power flow in this culture from certain forms of self-division, and so these too may be taken up as strategies of empowerment. In a journal entry from her girlhood, dated summer 1952, Evelyn Rosser, who grew up in rural Georgia, writes as follows:

> I had fun today. My best friends, Shirlie and Alice, came to play with me. . . . We played a game of make-believe. Shirlie was Elaine Stewart. Alice was Jane Russell. I was Marilyn Monroe! I live in a beautiful house on the beach. Every evening I took my French poodle for a walk. . . . Shirlie made me mad. She said I am chocolate, and everybody knows only white ladies have poodles and live on beaches. She said she could live on the beach, because she looks like Lena Horne. I started to cry. That's when Alice made Shirlie shut up. Alice said it didn't matter what color I was when I was born. I could bleach my skin. She knew it for a fact. Her cousin Betty did it. She used something called Black and White Ointment. . . . I trembled at the idea. I'll miss playing with Shirlie and Alice, but I want to live in a fine house someday like the white ladies do. I'll ask God to speed up my bleaching.[13]

The "trembling" here may be similar to a trembling in Malcolm's slumming whites, born of intense desire and the awareness of the transgressive implications of racial mobility.

There is a strikingly similar passage in Maya Angelou's *I Know Why the Caged Bird Sings*:

> Wouldn't they be surprised when one day I woke out of my black ugly dream, and my real hair, which was long and blond, would take the place of the kinky mass that Momma wouldn't let me straighten? My light-blue eyes were going to hypnotize them. . . . Then they would understand why I never picked up a Southern accent, or spoke the common slang, and why I had to be forced to eat pigs' tails and snouts. Because I was really white. . . . [14]

(Anyone who has seen Maya Angelou speak knows that she overcame this loathing of her own blackness, and came to regard herself as in her own way beautiful, graceful, and powerful.) Later in the book, she speaks of the community where she grew up (Stamps, Arkansas):

> A light shade had been pulled down between the Black community and all things white, but one could see through it enough to develop a fear-

admiration-contempt for the white "things"—white folks's cars and white glistening houses and their children and their women. But above all, their wealth that allowed them to waste was the most enviable. (40)

If white people may desire black bodies—black dance, black violence, black sex—as what they have excluded from themselves, black people may desire white power—white wealth, white prestige, white mind—as that from which they have been excluded. The "fear-admiration-contempt" of which Angelou writes is a desperately conflicted and complicated want, and it runs both ways. But notice that Rosser and Angelou do not want to get into that fine house and then *leave*. White slumming takes place in a situation of domination that enables whites to "play" at, or with, black people or black codes, without having to endure actually *being* black in our culture, living as black people. I may want to tell the truth like Malcolm. But I don't want to end up shot, and I can probably avoid it.

And so we end up with a great spectacle: two cultures separated by oppression and exploitation but yearning for each other, united, by exactly the same factors. Each culture approaches the other in a posture of simultaneous loathing and need, driven by different exigencies to a similar desire. This both pushes forward integration—since it piques the interest of the peoples in one another and pulls them into proximity—and preserves segregation, insofar as the entire structure of racial difference inscribed in these needs props up our racial thinking. The assumption of separateness, of difference, undergirds the drive for identification and completeness. That is, each culture both requires the other's proximity and requires its distance. For distance and difference to be eradicated—an event that some liberals blithely claimed was on the horizon after emancipation, or after *Brown v. Board of Education*—would require mind-bending feats of self-unification. We white folks would have to fully acknowledge and experience our particularity. We are very far from such an event, and whatever we say, we find it almost insurmountably difficult to want it, though we yearn toward it all the time. For to experience our particularity fully would be, first, to experience ourselves as oppressors and sadists: a frightful confrontation. Second, fully to experience our particularity would make it impossible to continue to be oppressors, so that we would cease to cash in on and enjoy our privilege. Few people indeed will do that voluntarily. And third, fully to experience our particularity would force us back into our bodies, would compromise our religious, and philosophical, and physical sense of ourselves.

The text that broaches all of these themes in an exemplary way is Wright's *Native Son*. Bigger Thomas is a big, uneducated, physically oriented black man of the underclass who gets a job chauffeuring for a rich liberal family (who also happen to own the tenement in which Bigger's family miserably lives). The family supports the NAACP and hires blacks as servants as an expression of their commitment to racial equality. The daughter, Mary, however, leans further to the left and has a communist lover, Jan. Bigger drives Mary and Jan around town one night, and writhes at every profession of respect and equality that they show him. He describes Jan's shaking hands with him as "an awful moment of hate and shame."[15] Here is Mary, speaking as Bigger drives through his own neighborhood:

> "You know, Bigger, I've long wanted to go into these houses," she said, pointing to the tall, dark apartment buildings looming on either side of them, "and just *see* how your people live. You know what I mean? I've been to England, France, and Mexico, but I don't know how people live ten blocks from me. We know so *little* about each other. I just want to *see.* I want to *know* these people."

Here is the response:

> There was silence. The car sped through the Black Belt, past tall buildings holding black life. Bigger knew that they were thinking of his life and the life of his people. Suddenly he wanted to seize some heavy object in his hand and grip it with all the strength of his body and in some strange way rise up and stand in naked space above the speeding car and with one final blow blot it out—with himself and them in it. (510)

As the evening progresses, the mirrored desires and annihilations reach incredible intensity: Bigger and a drunk Mary begin to have sex; when Mary's blind mother enters her room, Bigger accidentally smothers Mary to death with a pillow to keep her quiet, then beheads her body and incinerates it. He subsequently experiences moments of total exhilaration and liberation (he also quite intentionally kills his black girlfriend). He has overcome his race, his culture, his self-division, and the division that surrounds him. In the ritual manner, he is eventually executed. To the American ear, *Native Son* has the perfect inexorability of Greek tragedy.

Later, awaiting trial, Bigger reconstructs the transaction of desire and loathing between Mary and himself:

> "She acted and talked in a way that made me hate her. She made me feel like a dog. I was so mad I wanted to cry. . . ." His voice trailed off in a plaintive whimper. He licked his lips. He was caught in a net of vague, associative memory: he saw an image of his little sister, Vera, sitting on the edge of a chair crying because he had shamed her by "looking" at her. (772)

Here, the power and desire of the oppressor are focused into the gaze, so that being looked at is experienced as intolerable. The gaze, which is maintained with obsessive intensity, pulls Bigger into proximity and makes him aware of himself in his difference. The gaze of the oppressor and the desire both to possess and to annihilate that motivates that gaze become instruments of oppression, but the very existence of the desire is experienced by the one who gazes as an overcoming of oppression; that she *looks* shows Mary's commitment to improving the lot of the Negro. Indeed, the gaze has subversive and transgressive implications; it compels the invisible to make themselves available as objects. But that very fact swallows the gaze back into the machinery of oppression. The gaze makes Bigger visible to Mary, not as Bigger, but as a black man. It departicularizes him into the generalized particular even as it departicularizes Mary into a pure eye.

The yearning for the other by virtue of its otherness, which is the initial explosive impulse of *Native Son,* emerges out of and quickly intensifies a self-loathing born of intrapersonal fragmentation. Thus, to be an African-American yearning to look like Claudia Schiffer is to be divided against oneself and to turn against oneself by yearning to be the other. And it brings the crisis of selfhood to ever-greater intensities, brings the consciousnesses closer and closer to one another in a tension in which they can easily start to leak into one another, especially when the forms of self-division are themselves thematized in the culture by folks like Malcolm and Spike Lee.

Likewise, "white guilt" of the kind so conspicuous in Mary follows on a certain sort of consciousness of oneself as an oppressor. The odd thing about that, however, is that it appears most frequently and deeply precisely in those who deny or seek to negate, even by deed, their status as oppressors: leftists, in particular, such as Jan and Mary. Mary at one point asks Bigger to sing some spirituals, in blissful unawareness of her deployment of stereotypes. But it is not at all necessary to the point that there be a racial *faux pas;* in fact, the situation is even more thoroughly compromised where one would never say such a thing.

It is, at a minimum, not necessary consciously to cooperate with oppression to be an oppressor. Whether one embraces one's status as an oppressor or tries to destroy it, or even to destroy oneself, one is an oppressor, as it were, structurally. Being an oppressor is not a state of consciousness, but a feature of a person in a situation. Mary experiences her gaze as an instrument that can liberate Bigger; Bigger experiences it as a doubling of his oppression.

Malcolm seemed to condemn all white persons (as The Devil, in his

Nation of Islam incarnation) or expressed suspicion of us *en masse*. That was certainly the most maddening thing to white people about Malcolm's approach. He didn't seem to give us white folks credit for our good intentions or the depth with which we felt our guilt. For example, he refused to allow whites to join the Organization for African-American Unity (OAAU) on the following grounds: "Whites can't join us. Everything that whites join that Negroes have they end up out-joining the Negroes. The whites control all Negro organizations that they can join—they end up in control of those organizations" (*By Any Means,* 7). This dominance of African-American organizations by whites (a topic that obviously requires careful research and a series of distinctions) shows both the yearning of whites toward blacks and the fact that racism is inherent in structures or situations and not (only) in individuals. It is, in other words, an expression of "white guilt." Once such organizations are dominated by whites, their potential use as instruments of black resistance is vitiated, no matter what the intentions of the individuals involved.

But Malcolm's seemingly blanket condemnation of whites also shows that this yearning and this guilt actually serve the purposes of racism, actually make the oppressive system more pervasive, for it drives "co-optation" of black organizations, and it drives integration of the sort that Malcolm spent his career deploring: integration that brings the races together on exclusively white terms, integration that quite blithely and unconsciously assumes that white culture is superior, and also yearns to bring blacks into proximity. This sort of integration is expressed most intensely in American education, which, not coincidentally, has been the site of the most intense battles. The white liberal never doubts the fundamental superiority of mind over body, calculation over spontaneity, French cuisine over soul food, Mozart over Muddy Waters, but is "charmed" or perhaps obsessed by the "black" bit of each comparison. (There is also a yearning that runs much more deeply and cuts much more deeply into selves: Some white folks really seek to become black, really value what is [supposedly] black over what is white. That is also not, however, ultimately a liberatory instrument. I speak from first-hand knowledge.) This shows, as well, why segregation gets reinstituted at the micro level (within schools rather than among them, for example): because the white integrationist yearns toward the blackness of the black, even as he seeks to make it white, so that blackness must be both preserved and eradicated, segregated and integrated, and all without reference to the actual desires, aspirations, or ideas of those people termed "black."

Malcolm's "blanket statements" about whites and his exclusion of them from his movement are easily, and have been repeatedly, condemned as reverse racism. But Malcolm does not deny that some white people mean well, that they are sincere in their opposition to oppression:

> We don't question their sincerity, we don't question their motives, we don't question their integrity. We just encourage them to use it somewhere else—in the white community. . . . They don't have to come around us showing all their teeth like white Uncle Toms, to try and make themselves acceptable to us. (*By Any Means, 58*)

This notion of the "white Uncle Tom" is incisive. Du Boisian double consciousness is at its most extreme in the Uncle Tom. White double consciousness is most extreme in the liberal. Malcolm points out that even as liberals condemn racism in American society, they reap the benefits of it. And he points to the breakdown of self-consciousness that renders white people incapable of seeing their own racism. Such a breakdown is most obvious in the (sincere!) denial that one is a racist, which may even be true in some cases, but which, given the situation, is the most suspicious possible assertion.

Here, too, double consciousness has "leaked," so that one is aware both of one's status and use as an oppressor and of one's belief that oppression is wrong. Thus one is both guilty and sure that one is not a racist: a strange combination indeed, and one that exists under continual internal instability. Further, though, this self-loathing is brought on precisely by fragmentation, by a yearning for blackness. I know this structure of consciousness very well from the inside, and I am instantiating it even as I describe it. The situation is one of mirrored self-loathings and corresponding forms of self-destruction. (Every form of self-loathing is or corresponds to a particular mode of self-destruction.) Black self-loathing issues in the abuse of one's body to make it white, violence trained on other black people, and so forth. White self-loathing issues in the attempt to strip oneself of power as an oppressor: to try to join the OAAU, for instance, to condemn one's own culture. (It ought to be obvious that I cannot exclude myself from this criticism.) One seeks to shed power, or to eliminate oneself by voluntary acts from the structure of oppression in which one finds oneself.

The absorption of each side into this self-destruction or self-negation, however, is precisely what drives racial difference in America. It literally makes a "mixed" society impossible in certain respects (though in others it is inevitable). For the atmosphere of black-on-black violence and other expressions of personal fragmentation are, by their nature, confined to a ghetto (though various sorts of ghettos are possible here). More clearly, every attempt by whites to shed their whiteness (their status as oppressors) and help blacks, much less to become black, becomes a form of co-optation, an occasion precisely for the subtilization and increased pervasion of power. Few people voluntarily shed power, and power that I have given you is still mine in a sense, at least within certain limits. Power that you owe to me is a debt, and being in debt is being disempowered. Thus, my attempts to empower you are, above all, reminders of my own power. When we tolerate you, or improve you, we do not share our power but bring you more fully within it.

This is a fact that Malcolm understood perhaps better than any American public figure of this century. He says, for example,

> Negroes don't realize this, that they are within their constitutional rights to own a rifle, to own a shotgun. When the bigoted white supremists realize that they are dealing with Negroes who are ready to give their lives in defense of life and property, then these bigoted whites will change their whole strategy and their whole attitude. . . . There can be no worker solidarity until there's first some black solidarity. There can be no white-black solidarity until there's first some black solidarity. (*By Any Means*, 11, 13)

That was interpreted as a call to violence; rather, it is a call for self-empowerment. That is precisely what Malcolm meant when he defined his position as "black nationalism." The charter of the OAAU spells out how African-Americans can take control of their own education, their own economy, their own polity, their own media and forms of cultural expression, and so on, not by the tolerance or good will of whites, but by internal organization.[16] Many parts of this agenda are being explored today: for example, Afrocentric education and cultural construction. Malcolm says, with the simplicity of the profound: "You've got to get some power before you can be yourself. Do you understand that? You've got to get some power before you can be yourself" (*By Any Means*, 64).

Now the transactional loss of selfhood in the situation of cultural contact and confrontation throws into question, among other things, the epistemic values that drive it from the oppressor's viewpoint. Notice that, for Descartes for example, access to the self is supposed to be unmediated, incorrigibly accurate, and so forth.[17] We who have known the disintegration of consciousness as a cultural condition or as a personal crisis, or both, know how naive, how suspicious, and how culturally particular such claims are. We have been in situations in which epistemic access to almost anything is less problematic than access to the truth about ourselves, in which our desires and beliefs are the most elusive, compromised, ephemeral, and questionable data of all. Malcolm makes the following stunning remark:

> I'll tell you something. The whole stream of Western philosophy has now wound up in a cul-de-sac. The white man has perpetrated upon himself, as well as upon the black man, so gigantic a fraud that he has put himself into a crack. He did it through his elaborate, neurotic necessity to hide the black man's role in history. (*Autobiography*, 208)

Notice that the Enlightenment (as has often been observed) coincided with European expansionism; it is correlated precisely with new forms of oppression. The two pivotal figures that began the great philosophical ages of the Western tradition, Plato and Descartes, both built their epistemologies *expressly* to deal with the pressures on local belief brought to bear by contact with other cultures—to find permanent, objective truths that would counteract the influx of truths from alien cultures. The fragmentation of the self that is required to institute and sustain oppression has very particular epistemological expressions. It hides the black from visibility, which means (for it) that it hides the body, the emotions; that it privileges reason over spontaneity, composed as against improvised music; that it excludes itself from transgression precisely by the means by which it makes transgression available to itself. It asserts incorrigible access to itself precisely by the means it uses to divide itself from itself. This series of conceptual decisions marks the construction of a culture, emerges out of a situation of unequal privilege, and legitimates oppressions. It is no accident that the epistemology of Descartes, which restricts real knowledge to those minds sharing Descartes's conception of God, emerges from a fairly cosmopolitan member of a culture beginning its colonial expansion.

Indeed, in the last year of his life, during which he traveled extensively in Europe and in Africa, Malcolm placed white racism and its self-divisions directly in a historical context with regard to European colonialism in Africa, the history of the slave trade, and so forth:

> Having complete control over Africa, the colonial powers of Europe projected the image of Africa negatively. They always project Africa in a negative light: jungle savages, cannibals, nothing civilized. Why then naturally . . . you and I began to hate it. . . . In hating Africa and in hating Africans, we ended up hating ourselves, without even realizing it. Because you can't hate the roots of a tree and not hate the tree. You can't hate your origin and not hate yourself. . . . You know yourself that we have been a people who hated our black characteristics. . . . We wanted one of those long,

dog-like noses. . . . Our color became to us like a prison which we felt was keeping us confined. . . . It made us feel inferior; it made us feel inadequate; it made us feel helpless. (*Final Speeches*, 93–94)

"Civilization" is the social expression of "mind," and the attribution of civilization to Europe and its denial to Africa is ejected asceticism practiced at the collective level. The savagery of the African was a European construction in which Europeans practiced an ejected dualism: We are mind (state, text, etc.), and they are body (animal, heathen, without language). (Booker Washington, again: "We went into slavery without a language; we came out speaking the proud Anglo-Saxon tongue.") Of course, that requires of Europeans a subjugation of Africa and Africans, as we are required to subjugate the animal and the savage and the transgressor within ourselves to enter into the "social contract." In fact, it makes the subjugation and enslavement of Africans into an act of charity: something *they* need from *us*. The self-righteousness, and in fact the savagery, of such a position is too obvious to need emphasizing; we show ourselves to be precisely what we take ourselves to be subjugating in our very subjugation of it. But that self-righteousness motivates the bizarre claims that slavery is charity, that oppression is uplift, that acts of cultural destruction are sciences.

When we oppressors want unmediated access to the self, we do not introspect, we slum. Perhaps if I listen to enough rap music, I can become a self capable of showing itself to itself. My desire to sleep with black women, a tripled transgression made necessary by my intolerable hiddenness from myself as an intellectual white man, becomes my attempt to discover myself or to make myself whole, to reinsert myself (as it were) into the body of the physical, the earth. Malcolm suggests that white men who wanted to see white women have sex with black men wanted to see the enactment of their deepest fear. No doubt. Explicating the erotics of such an event would require serious consideration of the mutual construction of gender and race; white men have several axes of ejection in play with regard to white women and black women and men. But though the self is thrown into question, is penetrated and ambiguated by transgression of its boundaries, it can also, in imagination, be made whole. In fact, selves can only be made whole by being multiplied, by being compromised or shattered, when those selves have constructed themselves out of imaginary ejections. Wholeness in this situation requires ceasing to police the boundaries one has erected precisely in order to *impose* wholeness on oneself, in order to make of oneself a single homogeneous substance, to bar the transgression of oneself by life. In fact, if Zora Neale Hurston is right, wholeness *is* letting go, is allowing oneself to be incoherent, is the realization that the self is the most fundamental fiction. For such reasons, one's deepest fear always has the potential to mutate into one's deepest desire. Black and white cultures in America fear each other in ways that range from the banal to the elemental, but they desire one another too, desire one another so deeply that they are in fact merging, and have been since there was an America.

4

FREEDOM AND FRAGMENTATION
THE ART OF
ZORA NEALE HURSTON

Malcolm X mounts one response to the disintegration of the self in the face of racism, poverty, segregation, and violence; he seeks to retrieve a self out of the materials of his culture, to retrieve a self by concerted acts of reverse purification through cultural identification. This response is compelling, and has been put into practice with success. Afrocentric education, for example, which is inconceivable in its current form without Malcolm's influence, seeks precisely to bring into being coherent selves out of traditional cultural materials. The "rediscoveries" in contemporary historiography and anthropology of the profundity and elaborateness of African cultures on the continent and in the diaspora yield materials out of which selves can be rearticulated. African-American artistic and political materials provide rich possibilities for transforming conditions by reanimating traditions. And Afrocentric education is a compelling alternative to education as cultural destruction through integration; it is not surprising that it has been advocated almost exclusively by black people, and resisted by whites.

There are, nevertheless, difficulties with the attempt to construct coherent African-American selves by reverse purification. First of all, this strategy conceives of the disintegration of selves as undesirable, which implies that selves are or ought to be unitary in the first place, that selves are atoms that can only be split with disastrous results. This picture of personhood arises precisely out of Western intellectual traditions. It is in play, for example, in the Cartesian ego and the Kantian noumenal will. But we ought surely to regard the claim as problematic. It is not so clear, after all, that the natural or desirable state of human subjectivity is coherence. All people turn against themselves in a variety of ways; all people experience intrapersonal conflicts, doxastic dissonances. Each person's access to himself is impaired in numerous respects. The task of making doubled or splintered consciousnesses whole, conceived as a general project of human engineering, is not self-evidently possible or desirable, though some particular splinterings are horrendous and require treatment for the misery they produce. (That is particularly true of self-divisions that are *induced* by oppressive technologies of appearance.)

Furthermore, the raising of racial consciousness has its dangers as a strategy for self-unification and self-mobilization. Notice that, as we have seen, racism proceeds by the application of templates or stereotypes; each such template is a strategy for vision, an attempt to control modes of visibility. Their application introduces particular sorts of intrapersonal fragmentation that impair one's capacity for direct action to transform conditions. But the application of a template is also the strategy of Malcolm's program of reverse purification, though here it yields the possibility of individual pride and readies one for collective action. The content of what ought to be seen varies with the norms, so that here the defiant, proud, African-American aware of her "roots" is allowed or even constrained to make herself visible; nevertheless, the epistemic strategy remains the same. In fact "the rising tide of racial consciousness" sweeps persons and cultures before it; blues music is condemned as subservient, for example, or Southern blacks are condemned for taking too long to conform to the new paradigm. (A similar problem has been encountered in feminism conceived as the application of a new, "correct" picture of the emancipated woman, a picture to which actual women are subjected precisely as their *liberation*.)

I should hasten to add that the templates that white people impose on black people should not be equated with those that black people may impose on one another in seeking to empower themselves. The former are directly oppressive and embedded in forms of economic exploitation. They attempt to inculcate a self-loathing that rises to the level of violence. They are premonitions of genocide. On the other hand, the "Afrocentric" or "black pride" template seeks to resist oppression by empowerment; it tries to overturn precisely those strategies of oppression, seeks to make what was invisible visible. And it is effective as a mode of resistance; I would say that, at a minimum, it is a necessary moment in the history of resistance, because it provides the basis for a collective mobilization. Nevertheless, it is perfectly possible for individual persons to experience some of the same difficulties with respect to "racial consciousness" that they experience with respect to stereotypes. Such consciousness has the potential to exist in tension with aspects of the self and force them into invisibility. It can force selves into concealment in such a way that new forms of multiplied consciousness arise.

"The rising tide of racial consciousness" creates particular difficulties in situations of racial mixing. Here, ironically, through a celebration of one's heritage, one may come to hate precisely one's heritage. This could not be clearer than in Malcolm's treatment of the whiteness in himself as if it were a separate entity inhabiting his body, a pollution in his blood. It is hard, in the racial situation of America, not to conceive the races *in oneself* as separate or segregated selves, not to feel both the rapist and the victim of rape in one's own blood. Then, if one feels the need to *give an account of oneself,* or to make a coherent self out of the mass of racially inflected materials, one can do this only by an ever more intense and precise internal segregation, by an assertion of inner purity that must take the form of disavowal of part of oneself.

Most generally, these forms of resistance seek again to make a unified self out of fragments, and they seek to do this precisely by a racial construction. In our situation, this can amount only to an ejection, here practiced in reverse, and again obvious in Malcolm. In the ejection of the white in oneself, and the rejection of the white culture in which one is embedded and which is bent on one's destruction, one reinstitutes and revalues the segregation of the dominant culture; one takes on its taxonomy and uses it as a means of resistance. I am going to explore this structure—which, to repeat, is a powerful strategy of counterattack—in the next chapter. Here I want to point out that it relies to some extent on the same *means* as racism; it constructs a racial taxonomy, circulates templates for visibility that emerge from that taxonomy, and uses those templates as ways of making and understanding selves.[1]

Zora Neale Hurston's work stands as a monument of resistance to all impositions of specific forms of visibility. That she existed and wrote in resistance to white stereotypes of the black woman is obvious. But she also existed and worked in resistance to black stereotypes of the black woman. She existed and worked, in short, in resistance to all forms of epistemic domination, against every attempt to control the ways she made herself and her people visible. Her work, in the last analysis, is a tribute to the power of fragmentation; it displays an astounding ease in the lack of a unitary subject. And Hurston goes beyond ease into joyous celebration, into a dance that insists simultaneously that it is absolutely her own and that she is unconcerned with *what it means* to be herself.

This is evident in what is usually taken to be her masterwork, *Their Eyes Were Watching God.* The book has been subjected to a variety of directly feminist readings, but as consonant as it is with such readings in many respects, it is jagged to them as well, fragmented before them, as is evident in the discomfort of some feminist critics with regard to Hurston's politics, or opposition to politics, as these find expression in her writings.[2] The main character of the book, Janie, is continually being forced by people—first by her grandmother and then by her first two husbands—into constraints of visibility. The first set of these constraints is directly related to white oppression; her grandmother seeks to impose on her a series of folk norms learned in slavery that are related, moreover, to gender roles; in seeking what is best for Janie, her grandmother more or less sells her to the highest bidder. (The implication is surely that marriage may be a form of slavery.) Janie's marriage to Logan Killicks is a "good match" because Killicks owns land and the only organ in a colored home in the area.

But Janie is unable to make the reality of her emotional life fit her role as Killicks's wife. She *waits* for love to follow marriage; it never does. She says: "Ah wants things sweet wid my marriage lak when you sit under a pear tree and think. Ah . . . " Her grandmother responds:

> "'Taint no use in you cryin, Janie. Grandma done been long uh few roads herself. But folks is meant to cry 'bout somethin' or other. Better leave things de way dey is. Youse young yet. No tellin' what mout happen befo' you die. Wait awhile, baby. Yo' mind will change."[3]

The ideal that her grandmother puts forward is to reach the point at which the appearance is so thoroughly produced that it expunges the inner life, expunges the possibility of desire, expunges the possibility of love or creates love as a hideous caricature. Janie tries, but is unable to accomplish this self-destruction. She remains herself, not because she learns conscious resistance, not by manufacturing a true atomic self that she holds on to, but simply because she is unable to do otherwise.

Janie is puzzled by the fact that appearance and reality have been severed but, characteristically, she accepts that this has taken place, and she leaves Killicks for Joe Starks. Starks has money, and uses it to become the mayor, postmaster, and store-owner of Eatonville, the all-black town in which Hurston grew up. Starks regards Janie as an ornament; having a beautiful wife is appropriate to his position—it creates the right appearance. He consistently undercuts or seeks to destroy anything in Janie that resists her ceremonial and ornamental function. When Starks is appointed mayor, the townspeople ask Janie to say a few words. Starks says,

> "Thank yuh fuh yo' compliments, but mah wife don't know nothin' 'bout no speech-makin'. Ah never married her for nothin' lak that. She's uh woman and her place is in de home."
>
> Janie made her face laugh after a short pause. She had never thought of making a speech, and didn't know if she cared to make one at all. It must have been the way Joe spoke without giving her a chance to say anything one way or another that took the bloom off things. But anyway, she went down the road behind him that night feeling cold. (*Their Eyes*, 41)

Starks is obsessed with the appearances of wealth and power; he paints his huge house a "gloaty, sparkly white" (44), for instance. Joe seeks to place himself over the life of the town, and seeks to place Janie outside it entirely. He doesn't allow her to participate in events such as the "draggin'-out" of a dead mule (the tale is based on Hurston's folklore collecting), or to learn to play checkers. He is embarrassed by her enjoyment of the "lyin' sessions" that take place on the porch of his store (sessions that were particularly loved by Hurston). And he incessantly seeks to control the way she appears and the roles she assumes; he makes her hide her hair, of which she is proud.

The marriage finally devolves utterly into appearance:

> So gradually, she pressed her teeth together and learned to hush. The spirit of the marriage left the bedroom and took to living in the parlor. It was there to shake hands whenever company came to visit, but it never went back inside the bedroom. . . . She wasn't petal-open to him anymore. (67)

Janie is to be the subservient black girl, she is to be the hard-laboring farm wife, she is to be Mrs. Mayor of Eatonville. All of these roles carry with them very fine-grained forms of permitted visibility.

After Joe Starks dies, Janie works her way free of her role and into the liberating arms of Tea Cake, whom the world takes for an irresponsible freeloader, but who simply allows Janie to assume whatever form the moment may call forth. The first thing he does is teach her to play checkers, for the reason that she wants to learn: "He set it up and began to show her and she found herself glowing inside. Somebody wanted her to play. Somebody thought it natural for her to play. That was even nice." (91–92). Janie's marriage to Tea Cake is itself best described as play. In play, as in art (and Tea Cake is a gambler and a musician, among other things), one *forgets* oneself in an absorption in activity: The joy of play is a joy of self-forgetting. And Janie has a massive talent for play in that sense: a talent for letting herself become absorbed in people and things, a flowing-along that is a self-forgetting and hence a self-recovery, that is, a release from the disciplines by which one tries to make oneself into oneself. Janie's relationship with Tea Cake brings with it no overdetermined role which she is expected to perform; since her former social circle already disapproved of him, Janie feels freed from being any kind of woman in particular, and begins to do what she feels like doing. Tea Cake's great virtue is to participate in this process without trying to direct it. Janie becomes a part of a social life *with* Tea Cake, and becomes absorbed in her life with him without the painful submersions that characterized her earlier situations, in which only parts of Janie were allowed, or required, to appear.

Hurston loved Spinoza and Eastern mysticism. Her philosophy is characterized precisely by absorption, by a world-oneness that recalls Emerson and Thoreau. In her autobiography, *Dust Tracks on a Road,* she writes,

> Life, as it is, does not frighten me, since I have made my peace with the universe as I find it, and bow to its laws. The ever-sleepless sea in its bed, crying out "How long?" to Time; million-formed and never motionless flame; the contemplation of these two aspects alone, affords me sufficient food for ten spans of my expected lifetime.[4]

Hurston's sense of herself is precisely as a "million-formed and never motionless flame," a thing of constant change, consumed by and consuming her part of the world. Like Thoreau, but with very different inflections, Hurston maintained a deep connection to nature throughout her life. For example, she lived on a houseboat for some years, and took deep delight in her relation to rivers. The pear tree in *Their Eyes Were Watching God* is a central image of sexuality and love, and is used in ways that are anything but superficial. This image may have been taken from her own early experiences. She writes that, in childhood,

> I was only happy in the woods, and when the ecstatic Florida springtime came strolling from the sea, trance-glorifying the world with its aura. Then I hid out in the tall wild oats that waved like a glinty veil. I nibbled sweet oak stalks and listened to wind soughing and sighing through the crowns of the lofty pines. I made particular friendship with one huge tree and always played about its roots. I named it "the loving pine," and my chums came to know it by that name. (*Dust Tacks,* 41)

Such expressions of identity with nature—which, as I say, recall the American transcendentalists—are highly unusual (though not unique: there are similar expressions in Wright's *Black Boy* and Era Bell Thompson's *American Daughter,* among others) in the history of African-American writing. And though such passages resemble Thoreau's writing quite closely, for example, they can hardly be read outside of an extremely vexed context of racial signifiers that were not thematized by Thoreau.

In the dualism of American race, the white man is culture, the black woman nature. So when Thoreau engages in the project of a reunification of himself with nature, he is seeking his other. Or to put it in terms that Thoreau might authorize more comfortably, he is seeking to show that he *is* his other, that the ejection of nature from culture was imaginary in the first place. I do not doubt the profundity and also the subtlety of Thoreau's years at Walden, his river explorations, his naturalism. But these activities have, as well, an element of slumming. That is, they betray an anxiety of distance between the self and the environment in their attempt to bring nature into proximity to oneself. Thoreau goes out seeking himself, or trying to restore to integrity what has been divided by his implication in civilization. It is no coincidence that Thoreau was also an anti-slavery activist.

On the other hand, Hurston stands in the imaginary as a *representative* of nature itself, or as a "natural phenomenon." That is, perhaps, one reason why one does *not* often find identification with nature thematized in African-American writing; it would lend itself all too easily to an appropriation by stereotype. But as we shall see, Hurston not only did not hesitate to confirm stereotypes (though she also resisted them in many respects), she took great glee in doing so. Indeed, she was often described in precisely such terms in her own time (as a "force of nature," for example), and even reviled for *allowing* herself to be read that way. And as we shall also see, she described African-American art as "natural" and celebrated it on that basis. Furthermore, her experience, in contrast to that of Thoreau (who is standing in here for an entire white, male, American tradition), does not, as she describes it, *originate* in a separation by culture from nature along which desire is configured and coherence of the self reinstituted through identification. On the contrary, Hurston presents herself as primordially unified with nature (as she also presents Janie; Janie's first moment of adult selfhood and desire is her moment beneath the pear tree). That is, Hurston presents herself, writes herself, as precisely the other that Thoreau desires, that Thoreau requires to make himself whole.

But then Hurston's presentation of this other is the presentation of a

never-arrested flow, a continual change. This is the other not as the reverse side of the white self, not as a coherent antiself, but as a self in identity with a flamelike change. Unlike Thoreau, Hurston is no naturalist;
there is not a trace of the distanced, taxonomic consciousness present in
her appreciation of nature. For to approach nature as a naturalist is precisely to disambiguate it and arrest it temporally. Thoreau, conceiving the
project of a reunification with nature out of the intense desire that seeks
a reunification with the ejected self, cannot escape the Western technological approach to nature even as he resists it. For to make nature at
Walden the site of his reunification is to hold nature in readiness as an object, as a resource by which he can satisfy his desire for a rapprochement
with the parts of himself that have been ejected in his cultural location.
To *try* to get back to nature is precisely to conceive oneself as separate
from it. Thoreau, in short, approaches nature as a white man; he could
hardly do otherwise, and it would be senseless to say that he should have.

But Hurston, by identifying herself with nature as a black woman,
seeks not a reunification of the divided self, but the redoubling of a flowing self. To *confirm* one's "naturalness" as a black woman is to confirm
various stereotypes, to elicit certain desires (desires that were perhaps expressed with Hurston as their object through white patronage). That is a
very dangerous thing, because it can easily be sucked into the racist discourse, and because it leaves intact (for the moment!) the nature/culture
dichotomy, at least insofar as one's identification with nature seems to pre-
clude one's cultural accomplishments. But it is also subversive in that, by
confirming a certain expectation, it subverts another ("race consciousness") and because it intensifies the very desire by which the races are segregated and by which they are also pulled toward unification. Yet in
Hurston's aesthetics the nature/culture dichotomy *is* concertedly attacked,
precisely from the "underside," as Hurston strives to display and con-
tribute to a *culture of nature,* a culture that emerges in part from its own
"naturalization."

In the service of this strategy, there is, in Hurston as well as in the great
Eastern and Native American traditions, and in the American transcendentalists, a rejection of an atomic self for a self in identity with all things:

> Somebody else may have my rapturous glance at the archangels. The
> springing of the yellow line of morning out of the misty deep of dawn, is
> glory enough for me. I know that nothing is destructible; things merely
> change forms. When the consciousness we know as life ceases, I know I
> shall still be part and parcel of the world. I was part before the sun rolled
> into shape and burst forth in the glory of change. I was, when the earth

was hurled out from its fiery rim. I shall return with the earth to Father Sun, and still exist in substance when the sun has lost its fire, and disintegrated in infinity to perhaps become a part of the whirling rubble in space. Why fear? The stuff of my being is matter, ever changing, ever moving, but never lost; so what need of denominations and creeds to deny myself the comfort of all my fellow men? The wide belt of the universe has no need for finger-rings. I am one with the infinite and need no other assurance. (*Dust Tracks*, 202–3)

Again, this recalls various mystical traditions. And its rejection of denominations and creeds—"finger-rings" for the universe—is a rejection of the structures that make Western scientific, and philosophical, and religious knowledge possible. What is perhaps unusual about this passage is its emphasis on materiality and flux. The oneness in question is oneness with a continuous change, oneness with a flow. This throws the unitary, unchanging self into the realm of complete illusion. Hurston's power, like Janie's, is a power to let herself flow, a power to fail to define herself. Both the Christian tradition from which, in part, Hurston emerged (her father was a preacher) and Malcolm's Islam put forward an ensouled body, a body inhabited by a unitary self; Hurston's cosmology postulates a self in joyful identity with shifting matter. This is a celebration of embodiment and the body's flow: Hurston loved and performed dance. And, to repeat, it matters that this is the writing of a black woman, so that if it resembles the discourse of romanticism, for example, it does so *through* difference, or from the position of difference to which the romantics yearned to be reconciled.

Hurston celebrated African-American art in part for its sheer movement, its participation by change in change. She describes a service at the Zion Hope Baptist Church as follows:

The congregation just got hold of the tune and arranged as they went along as the spirit moved them. And any musician, I don't care if he stayed at a conservatory until his teeth were gone and he smelled like old-folks, could never approach what those untrained singers could do. LET THE PEOPLE SING, was and is my motto. (*Dust Tracks*, 152)

As a dramatist, director, and theatrical entrepreneur, Hurston pitted herself against the representation of African-American art that relied on "trained" voices and bodies. She resisted, that is, the attempt to appropriate black folk material into white performance styles, styles which, for her, seemed dead. If my (self-loathing) diagnosis of Western culture is correct, this is exactly the right way to put it. What we eject when we eject body, nature, and particularity is precisely life, and this is as visible in our arts as anywhere else (compare, say, Little Richard to Pat Boone, or Aaron Douglas to Piet Mondrian). In the performing arts, we mortify the body in our *use* of the body (Hegel: "The sensuous is *spiritualized* in art").

Hurston wanted the volatility that she associated with life to be embodied in her art, and she achieved that consistently. *Mules and Men*, for example, delightedly contextualizes African-American "lying" and storytelling as part of an unfolding cultural scene. As one of her informants puts it in that book, "God said, 'A world is somethin' ain't never finished. Soon's you make one thing you got to make somethin' else to go wid it.'"[5]

Another example of this temporalized oneness and wonder is found in Hurston's description of Caribbean voodoo dancers in *Tell My Horse:*

> The dancing begins in earnest now. The Governess is like an intoxicating spirit that whips up the crowd. Those rackling men become fiends from hell. The shuckers do a magnificent muscle dance which they tell me is African. The drums and the movements of the people draw so close together that the drums become people and the people become drums. The pulse of the drums is in their shoulders and belly. Truly the drum is inside their bodies.[6]

For Hurston, the engagement, temporality, and identification achieved with and through art is what characterizes African as opposed to European artistic traditions. Now Western arts may *seek* such unifications through art, and they often have (though they have just as often resisted this), but for Hurston this unification is already present in African arts of the diaspora *before* any dualism of nature and culture is formulated. Of course, Hurston's own descriptions of this unity can appear only in the tropes that inscribe the dualism she wants to get underneath or before. Thus she *struggles* for a language in which to express these notions, and thus she winds up precisely with a dualism of Western and African arts. But Hurston's aesthetics brings into this discourse what stands outside this discourse, and what she finds *there* is also discursive. (Recall the passage from Joanne Braxton quoted in the first chapter: "Her tools of liberation include sass and invective as well as biblical invocation; language is her first line of defense." Sass is Hurston's art form: I daresay she is the greatest literary exponent of sass in history.) African peoples, whatever Washington may have believed (or at least said), were not without language. What stands previous to or outside of the European tradition is *not* unspeakable, even within the languages of that tradition, which have also absorbed many non-European elements and, indeed, have non-European origins. When Baldwin says that white people have tried to deprive black people of their names, he asserts among other things that black people do have their own names and thus their own languages, their own cultures. Hurston writes an African-American vernacular which speaks the other in its previousness to our construction of the same, as does Maya Angelou in her autobiographical writings.

Hurston herself constantly moved into the oneness of which she wrote, for example, in her own initiation as a voodoo priestess as described in *Mules and Men*. Art and religion are one. Art and sociality are one. Rhythm and person are one. Human being and world are one, are taken up in art into a single flow. Such things *can* be spoken in a dualized English, where they always appear as a collapse and reinstitution of the supposedly primordial dualisms. But Hurston spoke them in an African-American vernacular in which these dualisms are *not* primordial, or not simply and non-problematically primordial.

The world's flow was, then, constantly expressed for Hurston in her art, which she regarded as her participation in the work of the world's becoming:

> I don't know any more about the future than you do. I hope that it will be full of work, because I have come to know by experience that work is the nearest thing to happiness that I can find. No matter what else I have among the things humans want, I go to pieces in a short while if I do not work. What all my work shall be, I don't know that either, every hour being a stranger to you until you live it. I want a busy life, a just mind, and a timely death. (*Dust Tracks*, 208)

Hurston continued to work long after the usual rewards had ceased; she worked for a decade on a life of Herod the Great, for example, with no prospect of publication. And she was fearless in the pursuit of experience that could be worked, pursuing voodoo (a belief system that is, by white standards, *beneath* our dualized metaphysics, *beneath* speakability, or "unspeakable," but which Hurston spoke), for example, in New Orleans and Haiti.

For Hurston, *no* aspect of the flow of the human in nature was isolatable from the rest. Art, religion, food, work, sex, and struggle run together. Here is Hurston on love:

> Under the spell of moonlight, I sometimes feel the divine urge for an hour, a day, or maybe a week. Then it is gone and my interest returns to corn pone and mustard greens, or rubbing a paragraph with a soft cloth. Then my ex-sharer of a mood calls up in a fevered voice and reminds me of every silly thing I said, and eggs me on to say them all over again. It is the third pre-

sentation of turkey hash after Christmas. It is asking me to be a seven-sided liar. Accuses me of being faithless and inconsistent if I don't. There is no inconsistency here. I was sincere for the moment in which I said those things. It is strictly a matter of time. It was true for the moment, but the next day or the next week, is not that moment. . . . Each moment has its own task and capacity. . . . So the great difficulty lies in trying to transpose last night's moment to a day that has no knowledge of it. (*Dust Tracks*, 191)

Though one may easily imagine how maddening Hurston was as a lover, this passage should not be taken to mean that she lacked deep commitments. Indeed, she herself says that she wrote *Their Eyes Were Watching God* as a way to try to work out for herself a relationship that had gone on for years. And in a passage from *Dust Tracks* that recalls a pivotal moment in *Their Eyes*, Hurston describes coming to jealous blows with that lover (though Hurston, unlike Janie, hits first). The violent passage in the novel, in which Tea Cake strikes Janie, has given some interpreters a great deal of trouble; Hurston *does not condemn* these blows as abuse in the way some commentators wish that she had.[7] But Hurston's treatment of this incident refuses to assign permanent, coherent, acontextual meanings to any event or action. Meanings in human society depend on a variety of contexts, and in the relationship of Janie and Tea Cake, his blows are *interpreted* by their friends, and possibly by themselves, as expressing their commitment to one another. Hurston has created a good deal of consternation in subsequent readers by treating violence as a part of human processes, as lacking a fixed meaning. It is not as though, for instance, *any* violence directed at Janie would have meant this to her; when her previous husband hit her, it *was* abuse. Violence, like love, changes its meaning in temporal and social processes.

Hurston's commitment is always to process, to love as a flow of the self toward the other that happens moment by moment if it happens at all:

I have a strong suspicion, but I can't be sure, that much that passes for constant love is golded-up moment walking in its sleep. Some people know that it is the walk of the dead, but in desperation and desolation, they have staked everything on life after death and the resurrection, so they haunt the graveyard. They build an altar on the tomb and wait there like faithful Mary for the stone to roll away. So the moment has the authority over all of their lives. They pray constantly for the miracle of the moment to burst its bonds and spread out over time. (*Dust Tracks*, 191–92)

For Hurston, every template, whether it is the template of race, of gender, of abuse, or of romantic love, is a premonition of death, of stasis. Every such template is a suicide, an attempt to arrest the flow of life. Hurston's life and work are a continual testimony to her resistance to death in this sense and to her celebration of life. This, as we have seen, informs her account of nature and of art, and of art as nature, of culture as natural, of nature as cultural: it establishes her place before dualisms.

Janie's marriage to Tea Cake is a flowing through moments, a continuous letting go and a continuous self-discovery. She is as surprised as anyone by some of the things she learns about herself: that she can shoot a rifle with dead-eye accuracy, that she can work in the fields, that she can party all night. Now the jaggedness to some feminist readings lies in this: first, that Janie's transformation, though profoundly self-motivated, is made possible by her husband. Much more deeply, however, Janie is wholly unconcerned with thematizing her liberation as a new template: she simply flows forward, living with what comes. That *is* Janie's liberation: not freedom from degrading labor (again, she works in the fields), or freedom from patriarchy, or even freedom from violence. She does not make herself over into a free woman; she finds freedom simply in allowing herself to be.

And though Janie is read by other people through a system of raced and gendered signifiers, she never reads herself that way, and Tea Cake does not read her that way, either. This is simply an example of the fact that Janie does not "read" herself *at all*. She is a good match for Killicks and for Starks in part because of the lightness of her skin and her "good" hair. When she is living in the Everglades with Tea Cake, she encounters Mrs. Turner, a woman who is obsessed with small differences in skin tone. Mrs. Turner thinks that Janie has made a bad marriage because Tea Cake is dark, and tries to pry her loose to marry Mrs. Turner's brother. Janie is surprised by the whole line of thought, and says, "Ah never thought about it too much." What she does assert is just that "we'se uh mingled people" (135), a line which also appears in Hurston's first novel, *Jonah's Gourd Vine*.[8] Janie is a mingled person (the product of rape, in fact), a person whose position with regard to racial signifiers is always equivocal. Janie is also equivocally placed with regard to gender signifiers; she half agrees with the wifely expectations of her first two husbands, but finds them impossible, finally, to inhabit.

Here, as in many other places in her writings, Hurston thematizes the stereotypes of black people deployed within black communities, just as Malcolm did. These stereotypes are parasitic on white stereotypes and work to the same effect. But Hurston puts a politically suspect spin on this material; where the stereotype is still in place, the empowerment offered by "racial consciousness" threatens always to remain a mere form of words, a temptation to hypocrisy. In *Dust Tracks,* Hurston describes, in witheringly sarcastic terms, "uplifting" speeches she heard that included such things as this:

> (a) The Negro had made the greatest progress in fifty years of any race on the face of the globe. (b) Negroes composed the most *beautiful* race on earth, being just like a flower garden with every color and kind. (c) Negroes were the bravest men on earth, facing every danger like lions, and fighting with demons. (160)

Such speeches built on the work of both Washington and Du Bois, who are explicitly credited with such ideas in *Jonah's Gourd Vine* (148), for example. The problem for Hurston is not that these claims were false (in fact I think Hurston believed such claims much more deeply than did the people she heard mouthing them), but that the people who spoke them, and the people who cheered when they heard them, did not believe them. The same people could be heard distinguishing black women by their color:

> I found the Negro, and always the blackest Negro, being made the butt of all the jokes—particularly black women.
>
> They brought bad luck if they came to your house of a Monday morning. They were evil. They slept with their fists balled up ready to fight and squabble even when they were asleep. They even had evil dreams. White, yellow, and brown girls dreamed about roses and perfume and kisses. Black girls dreamed about guns, razors, ice-picks, hatchets, and hot lye. (*Dust Tracks,* 164)

The truth here, as always for Zora, is a mixed bag, and any simple account by which people try to understand themselves becomes a problem. Her refusal of such accounts, as in her "denaturalized" relation to nature, her refusal of "naturalism," is a refusal of technologies of the self, an attempt to find a place before technology. Hurston is simply not *interested,* as Du Bois was interested, in generalizations about black people, or white people either; she shrugs them off as though such pronouncements could not possibly be true, at least not in the way they purport to be. Du Bois's early talk of racial destinies becomes a location in a problematic taxonomy (and for Hurston, *all* taxonomies are problematic) just as much as do white stereotypes of black persons, though these templates have differential political effects. And for Hurston, even while black folks mouth the template's demands, they remain mixed, and so the template degenerates into the flimsiest of appearances. The reversed purification inscribed in the value-inverted template is inadequate to the irremediably mixed, chaotic racial situation. Hurston's attitude throws into relief the *anxiety* with which "black spokesmen" such as Washington and Du Bois regarded the question, "What is the Negro?" Why, really, does anyone think there *could* be a general answer to that question?

Janie's radicalness, like Hurston's, is that she makes no attempt to render herself comprehensible to herself or to others by the standards of these signifiers, or by any others. Janie is an elusive character; it would be very hard to describe her inner life in a few broad strokes, and Hurston never seeks to do so. She is of mixed race and mixed attitude. And her awakening is an awakening simply into allowing these things to be true of her, and, finally, allowing all the world to proceed whither it may. Janie's liberation is a very simple act of letting go. And what she lets go of most deeply is any particular sense or definition of herself: She allows herself to fragment and coalesce, and simply watches herself do so. And in this letting go she finds an inordinate, overflowing joy, a joy which she identifies with her love for Tea Cake, who also displays a great talent for letting things and himself be.

Janie's love for Tea Cake is a pure and perfect love because it interrupts any particular account of love; it is a love that resists every explanation, every mode of comprehension. After Janie kills Tea Cake (in a harrowing series of scenes, he contracts rabies and attacks her), she returns to Eatonville, and says this to her friend Pheoby:

> "Ah know all dem sitters-and-talkers gointuh worry they guts into fiddle strings till dey find out whut we been talkin' 'bout. Dat's all right, Pheoby, tell'em. Dey gointuh make 'miration 'cause mah love didn't work lak they love, if dey ever had any. Then you must tell 'em dat love ain't somethin' lak uh grindstone dat's de same thing everywhere and do de same thing tuh everything it touch. Love is lak de sea. It's uh movin' thing, but still and all, it takes its shape from de shore it meets, and it's different with every shore." (*Their Eyes*, 182)

This is an insistence that love is always irremediably particular, that it resists every fixed definition, every move to force it into a particular comprehensible form. Love is what exceeds form, what allows itself to be continuously and fluidly reformed. That is an observation not only about love, but about Janie's entire comportment toward life; it is the source of her power, her beauty, and her joy. And here again, as with the nature/culture dualism, Hurston simply makes herself the champion of particularity, which seems to reinstitute the dualism it attacks and also to confirm the stereotype. But here again, the attempt is to find a love that collapses the dualism by showing that it need not have been formulated, or rather that its formulation was an *act,* that love stands beyond this formulation, and that this ineffability is itself speakable if we can speak another language, or speak from a different site in the same language.

Their Eyes Were Watching God is not "about" race; in fact, it is pointedly not about race. But Hurston's resistance to "racial consciousness" was perfectly explicit. In a chapter of *Dust Tracks on a Road*—a chapter that she conceived as the book's ending, but which the publisher repressed as too controversial—she addresses the theme explicitly:

> The solace of easy generalization was taken from me, but I received the richer gift of individualism. When I have been made to suffer or when I have been made happy by others, I have known that individuals were responsible for that, and not races. . . .
>
> This has called for a huge cutting of dead wood on my part. From my earliest remembrance, I heard the phrases "Race Problem," "Race Pride," "Race Man or Woman," "Race Solidarity," "Race Consciousness," "Race Leader," and the like. It was a point of pride to be pointed out as a "Race Man." And to say to one, "Why, you are not a Race Man," was low rating a person. Of course these phrases were merely sounding syllables to me as a child. Then the time came when I thought they meant something. I cannot say that they ever really came clear to my mind, but probably they were as clear to me as they were to the great multitude who uttered them. Now they mean nothing to me again. At least nothing that I want to feel. (*Dust Tracks,* 338)

First of all, this is an assertion of individualism that is classically American. I hold, however, that Hurston's individualism is very different than, say, Thoreau's, because again in Hurston there is a resistance not only to fitting the self into comprehensible forms, but to the notion that there is an atomic self at all.

She writes,

> I do not say that my conclusions about anything are true for the Universe, but I have lived in many ways, sweet and bitter, and they feel right for me. I have seen and heard. I have sat in judgment upon the ways of others, and in the voiceless quiet of the night I have also called myself to judgment. I cannot have the joy of knowing that I found always a shining reflection of honor and wisdom in the mirror of my soul on these occasions. I have given myself more harrowing pain than anyone else has ever been capable of giving me. No one else can inflict the hurt of faith unkept. I have had the corroding insight at times, of recognizing that I am a bundle of sham and tinsel, honest metal and sincerity that cannot be untangled. (*Dust Tracks,* 254)

This passage was written by someone who knows about internal conflicts, who knows in the deepest way that selves are not coherent. But it was written by someone who does not respond to this "corroding insight" by an obsessive attempt to force herself into coherent shape. The most remarkable thing about Hurston's response to her own fragmentation is that she is able to accept the fact that she "cannot be untangled," made whole, or that her fragments form a whole that is beyond her comprehension but in which she trusts. She does not attempt to redescribe her past, for example, in a way that makes "sense" in her present, unless the "sense" is simply that the woman who writes is the woman who has that particular past. This passage was written by a person who, out of pain, has learned to allow herself to be.

Second, however, Hurston's resistance to conceptualizing herself by race is compatible with the "scientific" facts. Like Du Bois, she saw perfectly clearly that the races were socially constructed rather than biological categories:

> I know that I cannot accept responsibility for thirteen million people. Every tub must sit on its own bottom regardless. So "Race Pride" in me had to go. And, anyway, why should I be proud to be Negro? Why should anybody be proud to be white? Or yellow? Or red? After all, the word "race" is a loose classification of physical characteristics. It tells us nothing about the insides of people. (*Dust Tracks*, 239)

And she adds with precise self-understanding,

> Many people have pointed out to me that I am a Negro, and that I am poor. Why then have I not joined a party of protest? I will tell you why. I see many good points in, let us say, the Communist Party. Any one would be a liar and a fool to claim that there is no good in it. But I am so put together that I do not have much of a herd instinct. Or if I must be connected with a flock, let *me* be the shepherd my ownself. That is just the way I am made. (*Dust Tracks*, 252)

Hurston constantly struggled with figures such as Richard Wright, whose work was focused on direct collective political action, though in his way Wright also found "race consciousness" tiresome, or rather, provincial.

Hurston's political views have caused consternation in many of her most enthusiastic readers, including Maya Angelou and Alice Walker (who has the distinction of having spearheaded the dramatic revival of Hurston's literary reputation). Deborah Plant's book *Every Tub Must Sit on Its Own Bottom: The Philosophy and Politics of Zora Neale Hurston* even takes the ultimate, desperate expedient of reading *Dust Tracks on a*

Road, all of it, against itself.[9] Plant argues that Hurston's political and personal identity, as expressed in that book, is a sham that conceals the pain she experienced as an oppressed black woman. This is a desperate expedient because it systematically deauthorizes Hurston as the speaker of her own experience; it is desperate because it requires an incredibly strained undermining of the text, sentence by sentence; and it is desperate because it misses or rather attacks everything in Hurston that is most characteristic and most interesting by seeking to impose a template on her work and her identity. But it is also an understandable expedient, because it would be an understatement to say that Hurston's politics are hard to hear from a revered, black, female author. Toward the end of her life, Hurston evidently considered herself to be a conservative, and she repudiated *Brown v. Board of Education.*

One factor in her life that is used to explain a variety of difficulties in her authorship is that she was raised in Eatonville, Florida, one of the few incorporated, all-black towns in the country. The influence of this situation can easily be overrated: Eatonville was very near Maitland, a white town, and Hurston was exposed to white racism from an early age, including the activities of the Ku Klux Klan. But in Eatonville, and later at Morgan College in Baltimore, at Howard University, and in Harlem, Hurston's community was to a large extent a black community. Thus it is not surprising that it was black expectations that she experienced as most immediately constraining. She constantly flouted these restraints, and did so, we may well imagine, with a gleam in her eye. Her political views were above all a determination not to be forced into being a Negro first, and Zora second.

The reasons for her opposition to forced integration, however, bring us into the center of Hurston's work. Notice that Malcolm, too, opposed integration. As we have seen, integration can be a mode of uplift and also a mode of cultural destruction. It defuses white stereotypes of black people as incapable of white culture, but it attempts to "bring them into American culture," that is, to make them over into dark-skinned white people. (Of course, and as I have said, this is based on a fundamental misunderstanding of American culture as being European; our culture—our language, for example—is also deeply African.) Hurston no doubt saw integration as a threat to communities such as Eatonville and to the institutions and folkways that African-Americans had developed in order to survive and sometimes to flourish. That is, it appears that Hurston's opposition to integration was motivated precisely by "race consciousness."

In fact, in the light of Hurston's work, her own claim to ignore race appears bizarre. Hurston the anthropologist and folklorist was utterly immersed in Southern black culture: she tried almost single-handedly to preserve and present this culture in written form. She studied the black church, hoodoo, folktales, and black vernacular language with total dedication, and all of her novels (except *Seraph of the Suwanee*) center around the use of this same material. She dedicated her life to celebrating African-American art and religion. She certainly believed that this material was culturally distinctive, that it was of the highest quality, and that it ought to be taken seriously and enjoyed. She was much more immersed in the details of African-American culture than, say, Du Bois or Richard Wright. And she lived a compendium of that culture, entertaining the Harlem Renaissance and her white friends and employers with a constant stream of vernacular tales. She was a folk artist and a work of folk art.

This conflict—her simultaneous immersion in and rejection of race—is typical of Hurston's conflicted personality, though it seems that only other people experienced the tension. But there is an underlying unity here as well. For Hurston was *open* to the voices of "the folk" in a way that Wright, for example, could never let himself be. Wright had a certain *picture* of what it was like to be black in America, and he spent his career elucidating it. Hurston had no picture (or at least no theory-driven picture, no picture universalized from her own case), which was why she was perfectly suited to a career as a folklorist. Again, she sought to discover a place anterior to the dualized racial taxonomies. (Whether there *is* such a place, and a language with which to speak about it, is not a question to be answered *a priori,* but by *listening.* That was Hurston's point, and she also allowed *us* to listen to her material.) Malcolm tried to reconstruct what it was to be black, to formulate a normative black experience; Hurston sought only to *discover* what was black, what experiences black people were having. (In addition, whereas Malcolm's experience was predominantly of Northern, urban African America, Hurston, while also hanging out in Harlem, emphasized the Southern, rural African America in which she was raised.) And to begin with, whatever Zora already was counted for her as black; whatever the folks at Joe Clarke's store in Eatonville already were counted as black. Hurston did not look for the defining characteristics by which the "true" black experiences could be winnowed out, and the "false" excluded. Malcolm and Wright proceeded from template to data and art; Hurston had quite a different method. She always started in and wound up in the particular. She didn't need to repress the "bad English," the aspects of "subservience," the "primitive" or African "superstitions" that she found: She was capable of seeing and enjoying it all. Indeed, what are called from the dominant position the vernacular tongue and the primitive way of life are precisely where Hurston *needed to look,* away from the dualisms. When "the primitive" as a category is used as a mode of ejection and hence of insulation, what is happening in the *interior* of the zones thus marked off is expunged from the language; but *something* is still happening there, and people are still speaking.

Race pride can blind. It can blind one to people of other races, but it can blind one as well to one's own people. The most conspicuous aspect of Janie is her openness to experience once she has shucked off her various roles; Hurston's most conspicuous characteristic is her openness to herself. And it is this characteristic that makes it possible for her to celebrate the artistic and spiritual achievements of her race, not as reconstructed into a narrative of progress or a narrative of degradation, not as a tradition that ultimately sustains itself by European-American standards, but simply for itself.

Race consciousness is *imposed* on black people in America; we will simply not let you forget that you are black. This has become more rather than less intense as the century has lingered on and as racism has been subtilized and inflected in the ways we have observed. For one thing, integration has the effect both of drawing (some) black people into the "mainstream" culture and of shattering black communities, or of segregating such communities by class: There are the folks who are making it in the "white" world, and the folks abandoned by the white world into the deep ghetto. Now if you are operating in the white world and you are black, I do not have to tell you that all the white folks are intensely aware of your race at all times. They watch what they say around you (so that it won't be "misinterpreted" as racist); they use your presence as a little badge of their goodness; they seek also to ghettoize you again, maybe by putting you in charge of black issues or something. Now you're left wondering in almost every little interaction: Are they doing this because I'm black? Thus, by the very means used to bring the races together, black race consciousness is intensified as explicit references to race are forbidden. It's one thing to hear the race words and know, "*Now* they're thinking about it"; it's another never to hear the words and thus to wonder *constantly.*

On the other hand, it would not be too much to say that white race consciousness *is* race unconsciousness, or that our white race consciousness is not a consciousness of ourselves, but precisely of *you.* I've actually tried asking white people *what it means to them to be white,* only to met with blank stares. It means nothing, phenomenologically, to be white; to be white is to be whited out; white race consciousness is the erasure of itself. White people will say there is no content to whiteness, even as they are able to produce amazingly detailed knowledge of what is not-white, that is, what they must avoid to stay white.[10] This erasure is precisely the phenomenological form of white authority, its formation of itself as the position of no position: the position of objectivity to which epistemic and economic mastery accrues.

Now we could talk about two interwoven possibilities for liberation. If black folks could *forget* their race consciousness, and if white folks could become conscious of theirs, that would demonstrate that the machinery driving race for centuries in this country had broken down. That possibility, of course, has only to be articulated to be shown to be almost laughably utopian, as well as, on the other hand, potentially disastrous. After all, the *Nazis* were conscious of their race in a certain way, and black race consciousness in the present situation is absolutely needed to mount or preserve the only forms of resistance that have had any power. Furthermore, we white folks cannot possibly *become* conscious of our race *except* in a situation in which black folks are conscious of their race, and hence are able to *give voice* to the racial constructions current in our culture. In virtue of our construction of ourselves, a construction that entails the erasure of that very construction, we are precisely the people who *could not* become conscious of our race on our own.

Hurston explores the possibility of *letting go* of race consciousness, and finally of letting go of or attacking all technologies of the self. To explore that is to explore the final possibility of liberation. Yet I assert again, and this is in a certain sense compatible with Hurston's art, that the letting go of race consciousness *can only proceed through its intensification.* This is because, first, we white people cannot let go of the racial technology by which our selves are manufactured if we exist in blissful unawareness of it. We have to be *made visible to ourselves,* which is only possible by our disempowerment, by the raising of voices that shatter our regime of silence about ourselves, or by the disempowerment of the technological conception the self altogether. Second—and this is now *deeply* compatible with Hurston's art—the best strategy to show the contingency of these identities is to *play* with them, to take up various spots in the taxonomy *consciously,* or from time to time, or as a performance. Hurston was precisely a performer of this kind, as are many rap artists. Now if such performances could bring us to the point where white folks could self-consciously perform and parody and pantomime *whiteness,* we would be somewhere close to the end of race. For though race is not something that will end anytime soon, and though it may again and soon and thoroughly be soaked in blood, it is something that *could* end; there could be different and incompatible human taxonomies, or there could be less power *in taxonomy;* there could be a post-scientific, post-technological age. I want to be *forgiven* this utopian moment.

Hurston, I think, attempts in a certain way to bring black people to visibility in a post-technological celebration. For of course, both the templates deployed by white racism and the resistance templates of race pride are technologies not only (and perhaps not primarily) of visibility, but of concealment. Folklore could be construed here as an alternative to sociology, and Hurston's folklore seeks *immersion* in ways of life in all their complexity and interior tensions. For example, in *Moses, Man of the Mountain* (and also in *Jonah's Gourd Vine* [147]), Hurston describes Moses as a hoodoo man. In his excellent biography of Hurston, Robert Hemenway criticizes *Moses, Man of the Mountain* for failing to come up with a coherent account of Moses's power: Moses is treated as the greatest scientific mind of his day, as a conjurer, and as an instrument of God.[11] But the power of Moses comes from his deep identification with nature, which is also God's creation. For Hurston, speaking among other things as a hoodoo adept, no distinction is available, or needed, between these functions. Hoodoo is based on the empirical; it does not float free of sensible reality, else it would have no power. It yields power and connects the adept to God. Here, Hurston uses what she has found about power in the African-American tradition rather than forcing the material into a form comprehensible by European-American standards.

To return to another example, Hurston resisted the presentation of Negro spirituals in concert settings by trained voices such as Paul Robeson and many others. She took her white supporters to a storefront church in Harlem to see what black song was like in its context. It is significant that to hear such music in context required white listeners to leave their familiar concert halls, move into someone else's neighborhood, and deal with being, and being seen as, interlopers. To hear this music, you can't have it brought to you. Hurston also staged musicals that were based on the folklore she had collected, and that were performed by "folk" performers, including her friends from Eatonville, rather than professionals. Robeson in a sense celebrated the African-American tradition by elevating it to "high art." For Hurston, however, such an elevation was a betrayal. First, the elevation immediately admits the dominant model of art—art of the concert hall and the museum, and of the dualisms that mark those zones off as the "aesthetic" sites of white culture—to be of paramount validity. Second, it yanks the art out of the context in which its transformative power is manifest. It "integrates" African-American art into white culture, but precisely by making it over into European art, safe for European consumers, sanitized for your protection.

Hurston might have applied some of the same criticisms to much of the literary production of the Harlem Renaissance and other black artists. Wright's works, for example, bring black experience to bear precisely within the traditional European form of the novel. Hurston wrote novels, but she wrote them in vernacular, and in resistance to traditional novelistic technique, using "folk" models of construction. (When I taught *Their Eyes Were Watching God* in an ethics course, the white students were initially confused, and indignant, that the language was not *already* comprehensible to them, that they would have to *work* to understand it; it was not pre-chewed for easy reading by white audiences.) Hurston's technique is, it seems to me, ultimately more powerful, more deeply subversive, and more enjoyable. But it eschews "race consciousness" (while teaching you something about race) in favor of openness and celebration; it is a letting go of restraints on self-presentation. It seeks to show that what has been ejected conceptually from European languages is sayable, at any rate, or partly sayable, in black English, that there is already a culture, and a speech, and an inscription in which the logos has not taken up a hegemonic place. This is instantiated in the amazingly nuanced relation of oral and written forms in Hurston. She tried, throughout her career, to develop a written form that would adequately embody black oral traditions: that, I think, is the central project of her authorship. With regard to *Their Eyes Were Watching God,* Nellie McCay incisively describes one expression of this nuance: as Hurston narrates Janie narrating her story, "In the mingling of their complementary voices reading themselves into the canon, Hurston gains immortality in the literary tradition, whereas Janie inserts her voice into the Afro-American oral tradition."[12] And we might add that Hurston seeks to insert Janie's insertion into the oral tradition into the written canon. This is also the problematic within which Henry Louis Gates locates Hurston's authorship. He says she negotiated between "a profoundly lyrical, densely metaphorical, quasi-musical, privileged black oral tradition, and a received but not yet fully appropriated standard literary tradition." He adds that "the quandary for the writer was to find some third term, a bold and novel signifier, informed by these two related yet distinct literary languages. This is what Hurston tried to do in *Their Eyes.*"[13] This is a difficult move, and of course it is not unprecedented (black poets such as Paul Laurence Dunbar had written in the vernacular). But it is a project to which Hurston dedicated her career as a writer: she made a black logos, or maybe compromised or polluted the logos with a dark contagion.

Hurston worked out an African-American aesthetic, and she did it not by asserting that African-American art was defensible by European standards, but by attempting to understand it on its own terms and as an alternative to a European tradition that she viewed (rightly) as impoverished in certain respects by its own systematic exclusions. Her synoptic essay "Characteristics of Negro Expression," published in 1934, gives an introduction to an entire artistic orientation in integration with the wider lives of individuals and cultures. It is typical of Hurston in several respects, including its political problematicity; she refers to Negro expression as "primitive," for example. But what she celebrates in African-American tradition is precisely what she celebrates in Janie and in herself.

Negro art of the South, she asserts, is oriented around flux.

> The Negro's universal mimicry is not so much a thing in itself as an evidence of something that permeates his entire self. And that thing is drama.
>
> His very words are action words. His interpretation of the English language is in terms of pictures. One act described in terms of another. . . . Every phase of Negro life is highly dramatized. No matter how joyful or sad the case, there is sufficient poise for drama. Everything is acted out. Unconsciously for the most part of course. There is an impromptu ceremony always ready for every hour of life. No little moment passes unadorned.[14]

For Hurston, the deepest function of art was precisely the adornment of moments: a dance and a poise that connected persons with the changes of nature and culture, or rather, showed that they were already so connected, or showed that the "connection" doesn't even need to be conceptualized. "The prayer of the white man is considered humorous in its bleakness," she says. And by comparison, she points out, in black prayer, "the supplication is forgotten in the frenzy of creation" ("Characteristics," 54).

The fundamental features of Negro expression that Hurston identifies—angularity and asymmetry, for example—emphasize resistance to formulas. She writes,

> It is the lack of symmetry which makes Negro dancing so difficult for white dancers to learn. The abrupt and unexpected changes. The frequent changes of key and time are evidences of this quality in music (Note the St. Louis Blues).
>
> The dancing of the justly famous Bo-Jangles and Snake Hips are excellent examples.
>
> The presence of rhythm and lack of symmetry are paradoxical, but there they are. Both are present to a marked degree. There is always rhythm, but it is the rhythm of segments. Each unit has a rhythm of its own, but when

the whole is assembled it is lacking in symmetry. But easily workable to the Negro who is accustomed to the break in going from one part to another, so that he adjusts himself to the new tempo. ("Characteristics," 55)

Hurston compared Negro to white dance, and found the latter distinctly inferior:

Negro dancing is dynamic suggestion. No matter how violent it may appear to the beholder, every posture gives the impression that the dancer will do much more. For example, the performer flexes one knee sharply, assumes a ferocious face mask, thrusts the upper part of the body forward with clenched fists, elbows taut as in hard running or grasping a thrusting blade. That is all. But the spectator himself adds the picture of ferocious assault, hears the drums, and finds himself keeping time with the music and tensing himself for the struggle. . . . The white dancer attempts to express fully; the Negro is restrained, but succeeds in gripping the beholder by forcing him to finish the action the performer suggests. Since no art can ever express all the variations conceivable, the Negro must be considered the greater artist; his dancing is realistic suggestion, and that is about all a great artist can do. (55–56)

Hurston asserts that the communal and communicative function of art is different for black and white Americans.

These functions are freighted with the content of the racial ejection by which white culture is constituted. Our neutral, neutralized, neutralizing, and neutered standards of beauty parade around in the robes of the universal. The calm, static, arid, Western beauty that arises in the Renaissance, the ideal of a perfect balance and composure that makes possible a Kantian universalization of the judgment of taste is, again, characteristic of our construction of ourselves. That is the *concealed* function of *our* arts in *our* construction of whiteness (a construction humorous in its bleakness), and it has, because it is white, to conceal itself *as* a communal construction. To be sure, this construction has only to be articulated and instantiated to be already breaking down; it is the impossible position of no position, and the impossible detachment of beauty from desire. Western art history, thus, is an oscillation of the objective and the subjective, composure and perturbation, objectivity and subjectivity, classicism and the baroque, neoclassicism and romanticism, inscription of the same and slumming appropriation of the other. The classical (perfectly white) moment has to be imposed, break down, be recomposed.

The attempt in Hurston is to *show* the art of the other not as an inverse construction of the same which makes the same possible, on which the

same depends, but as something with *its own* history and its own standards. One might simply assert that there could be no discussion in "Western" languages of arts that fall outside of these conceptualities. But that
would just be an *a priori* mourning, or wish. Hurston went, and looked,
and noticed that people were producing semiosis in lumber camps in
Florida, or whatever. Then she set about making a language in which that
language could be spoken again to a wider public, a language that took
up the signs made in the lumber camp and inserted them into the sign system of the novel or the work of anthropology. One thing that this project
demonstrated was that these sign systems were not distinct to begin with,
that our culture is much more complicated than we white folks might
think it is. *Simplification* is a key function of asceticism, ejected or otherwise, so that we take the very conceptualities we are deploying to be
without vexed histories, multiple origins, elaborately negotiated contradictions. Hurston seeks to recomplicate our signs. That this is *possible* is
the utopian assertion. But whether it is possible or not, Hurston stakes
her artistic life on it.

What Hurston celebrates in African-American art is, first, its internal
organization, which is more dynamic and volatile than that of comparable
European productions. Second, she celebrates the use of art in, or rather
its identity with, the life of the culture; she does not attempt to distinguish
the sermon or the lie from literature: There is no distinction in Hurston's
aesthetics between beauty and use. Among the arts of African-American
culture, she includes insults, threats, and love-making, all of which are
performed artfully in public space, as she describes beautifully in her accounts of Florida labor camps in *Mules and Men,* where she finds herself
at the center of various conflicts involving tongues or knives, all of them
artful. She appears simply to ignore the Western taxonomies and consequent valuations of artistic forms. She also explicitly criticizes Western art
practices, in which art is isolated in hallucination from everyday cultural
interchange, set apart in separate buildings, to visit which is a marker of
class. I am going to discuss rap music in the next chapter, but here I will
remark that much of it falls squarely into the tradition Hurston celebrates.

Third, she celebrates the adjustment by art to the flow of nature, to the
world and to the gods: "We merely go with nature rather than against it"
("Characteristics," 60). This again employs the nature/culture dichotomy;
Hurston in this essay is trying to make Negro expression comprehensible
to people who try to live in that dualism. But the essay, finally, opens the
space from which this dualism is possible, shows the process out of which
it is abstracted.

That African-American artistic traditions are distinguished in these ways from the Western tradition (a fact that was also celebrated by Malcolm X) has implications that are subversive not only to the Western tradition, but to black politics. For Hurston, integration constituted the threat of cultural destruction: The "gift" of education in the Western classics, for example (many of which, including *Paradise Lost,* Hurston loved), threatened the African-American aesthetic with destruction. When the attempt is made to integrate works of African-American art into Western aesthetic contexts such as the concert hall, the theater, or the museum, there is the constant possibility that they will fail by Western standards. Even if they succeed, however, they are marginalized as "quaint" and distorted by Western aesthetic presumptions and presentational practices. What is expunged is whatever stands beyond the dualisms within which Western aesthetic production is articulated, whatever does not appear in the already delimited space of Western art consumption. Though the performance of the blues by an opera singer does have bizarre capacities to disturb the structure (what in the world is the natural doing in the tortured, spiritualized world of the operatic voice?), the introduction of a *communal* art, an art that does not depend on the separation of "performers" from "viewers," into a space that does so divide the participants must denature that art. Nevertheless, the appropriation of African-American art into Western practice makes it comprehensible to us and also allows us the comfort of finding it inferior; it ghettoizes it and makes it available for slumming. Hurston insists that African-American aesthetic products be judged by their own standards (and perhaps most radically, she asserts that there *are* such standards, that there are non-European cultures), and she insists furthermore that these standards provide interesting alternatives to the Western standards, and that they yield great works of art. Hurston set herself the task of *demonstrating* these facts by adducing concrete examples. The sense one gets of African-American art through Hurston's eyes and ears is one of delighted openness to experience and delighted resistance to Western standards of comprehension. Such resistance was demonstrated synchronically in the angularity and asymmetry of the visual arts, and diachronically in the movement of dance, speech, song, and story. There *are* standards of quality here, but they are standards that emphasize precisely the possibility of shifts in standards, of flow.

Hurston's celebration of African-American culture and art as superior in a variety of ways to European-American culture placed her into an interesting relation to African-American discourse. For example, Hurston had absolutely no time for Du Bois's "double consciousness"; she felt that it was an artifact of integration, of the attempt of black people to find a place for themselves in the white world. In part, this difference was related to the difference between North and South: Malcolm's self-loathing and Du Bois's double consciousness arose in part because white and black cultures were in closer juxtaposition in some ways in Massachusetts and Michigan than in Florida and Alabama. What produced both double consciousness and cultural destruction, for Hurston, was the economic undertow of white culture: the ambition on the part of blacks to enter white culture and reap its financial rewards. She says, in what is a thinly veiled attack on Du Bois's reading of black life,

> The average Negro glories in his ways. The highly educated Negro the same. The self-despisement lies in the middle class who scorns to do or be anything Negro. "That's just like a Nigger" is the most terrible rebuke one can lay upon this kind. He wears drab clothing, sits through a boresome church service, pretends to have no interest in the community, holds beauty contests, and otherwise apes all the mediocrities of his white brother. The truly cultured Negro scorns him, and the Negro "farthest down" is too busy "spreading his junk" in his own way to see or care. ("Characteristics," 59)

One suspects that when people said of Zora as she was spreading her junk (she was famous for it), "That's just like a nigger," she wore it as a badge of honor. As we will see, today's rappers also wear it as a badge of honor. Black folks said such things of Hurston publicly. She rejected double consciousness as an accurate picture of the psychology of most African-Americans, and sought in her work to re-embed herself in an aesthetics and, inseparably, in a cultural scene that she regarded as among the world's richest. That the "Negro farthest down" spreads his junk in his own way marks the existence of a cultural zone outside of the construction of the Negro as other.

For just such reasons, and as we have seen, Hurston's work always had an ambiguous and problematic relation to stereotype. She was unafraid to present Southern blacks in ways that seemed to confirm white stereotypes, though the flash of intelligence and creativity that is constantly manifest in *Mules and Men*, for instance, is incompatible with racist estimations of black intelligence. Her work, however, was extremely problematic to the African-American literary community. In an astoundingly obtuse review of *Their Eyes Were Watching God*, for example, Richard Wright says that the novel has no "basic idea or theme which lends itself to significant interpretation. Miss Hurston seems to have no desire whatever to move in the direction of serious fiction." He continues,

> Miss Hurston can write; but her prose is cloaked in that facile sensuality that has dogged Negro expression since the days of Phyllis Wheatley. Her dialogue manages to catch the psychological movements of the Negro folkmind in their pure simplicity, but that's as far as it goes.
>
> Miss Hurston *voluntarily* continues in her novel the tradition that was *forced* upon the Negro in the theater, that is, the minstrel technique that makes the "white folks" laugh. Her characters eat and laugh and cry and work and kill; they swing like a pendulum eternally in that safe and narrow orbit in which America likes to see the Negro live: between laughter and tears.[15]

First of all, Wright is certainly correct that Hurston approaches the confirmation of stereotype and seems unconcerned or even gleeful about it. But he is utterly wrong that the novel is not "serious" (it is one of the most serious novels I have ever read). And he is wrong, too, about the "simplicity" of Hurston's characters, who are no more simple than say, George Eliot's, though they speak in the vernacular; they are certainly no simpler than Wright's. And where Wright is most deeply wrong, it seems to me, is in his implication that Hurston's playfulness and joy are not themselves serious. One of the most important developments in Janie's self-exploration is precisely her discovery of her ability to play, an ability that Hurston possessed prodigiously. A life without play is a disaster; thus, play is serious. And I must remark that Wright's own writings, as great as they are, are among the most humorless produced in this century.

Nevertheless, it should be obvious that my own relation to stereotype here is problematic.[16] If Hurston presents black women, for example, as playful and sexually unpredictable, I can hardly absolve myself of Wright's charge that I am enjoying watching my stereotypes confirmed. I love Zora Neale Hurston; she is an absolutely central intellectual figure for me. But it would be silly for me to deny that part of what I like about Hurston is the opportunity for scholarly slumming in the privacy of my own home. Indeed, as will emerge more fully in the next chapter, I am sympathetic to some extent to "strategic essentialism": the attack on stereotype that comes precisely from the materials of stereotype, from the confirmation of stereotype. For Hurston, stereotype is a weapon with which to deal a blow to the philosophical and artistic pretensions both of European-American and of African-American authors. Nevertheless, if there is an essentialist moment in Hurston, it remains merely and self-consciously strategic; as we have seen and are going to see, her conception of personhood is anti-essentialist to an extreme degree.

Hurston's voice is intensely particularized; where those of Du Bois and even Malcolm shift from one mode to another, Hurston's is a "pure black" authorship in the sense I have been developing throughout; there is never a moment in her folklore of calm white detachment. This both confirms and attacks stereotypes, because it celebrates the stereotype in a certain way. But the stereotype is precisely meant not for celebration but rather for degradation. And, as I have been arguing, the confirmation of the stereotype is one strategy for bringing what stands outside of racial construction into the whitened realm of "public" discourse. For to present characters who seem at first comprehensible by the standards of the stereotype and then go on to show them as wits, as artists, as individuals who live deeply, is precisely to threaten the white construction of ourselves as the bearers of culture.

But as I watch this use of stereotype as a liberatory instrument, I am, as well, often in the position of the white men who watched the spectacle of Bibb and company fighting, gambling, drinking, and so forth—precisely the sort of events Hurston describes both in her fiction and in her folklore. I stare obsessively at the spectacle and urge it on. It is a treatment for my asceticism and a cure for the disease that is my authorial voice. It is a seeking after reunification, as my love for Hurston is accompanied by a certain erotic *frisson*. So though I reject Wright's criticism of Hurston, and am perfectly sincere in doing so, I simultaneously confirm the grounds of that very criticism. The predicament of the black artist, which I will describe in a moment, is parallelled by the predicament of the white critic of her art: I am a racist if I agree with Wright, and I am a racist if I do not.

Hurston's self-presentation crystallized the difficulty; she entertained everyone—including her white patrons, such as Mrs. Osgood Mason—with her vernacular tales. Langston Hughes, with whom Hurston had a close friendship and then a very difficult relationship after they tussled over their coauthorship of the play *Mule Bone,* went so far as to say in his autobiography,

> In her youth she was always getting scholarships and things from wealthy white people, some of whom paid her just to sit around and represent the Negro race for them, she did it in such a racy fashion. . . . To many of her white friends, no doubt, she was a perfect "darkie."[17]

That is surely meant as a devastating attack on Hurston's character, though Hughes adds that Hurston was "very clever" and that "she had a great scorn of all pretensions, academic or otherwise." (Indeed, if there is one thing I love Hurston for above all else, it is her scorn of pretension.) And it is obvious that she behaved in precisely the same "racy" way with her black friends, some of whom evidently found this acutely embarrassing (while of course it delighted others). Hurston's blackness was not the cultivated race pride of the Harlem Renaissance "New Negro."

It is worth noting that Hughes himself, who was also dedicated to making a vernacular art out of folk materials (he wrote poems in blues forms, for instance), faced very similar attacks from black critics. He was practically driven from the country by the reception of his book *Fine Clothes to the Jew*. In his autobiography, Hughes quotes a review by Eustace Gay: "It does not matter to me whether every poem in the book is true to life. . . . Our aim ought to be to present to the general [white?] public . . . our higher aims and aspirations, and our better selves" (*Big Sea,* 267). The odd thing about this review is that it acknowledges that stereotypes could be confirmed by art that is "true to life." Hughes replies:

> I sympathized deeply with those critics. . . . [But] I felt that the masses of our people had as much in their lives to put into books as did those more fortunate ones who had been born with some means and ability to work up to a master's degree at a northern college. Anyway, I didn't know upper-class Negroes well enough to write much about them. I knew only the people I grew up with, and they weren't people whose shoes were always shined, who had been to Harvard, or who had heard of Bach. But they seemed to me good people, too. (*Big Sea,* 267–68)

This illustrates the deep dilemma facing the making of African-American art out of African-American cultural materials, a dilemma faced by Hurston and Hughes, but also faced, for example, by today's rappers. It is a dilemma discussed by Amiri Baraka in 1966:

> As one of my professors at Howard University protested one day, "It's amazing how much bad taste the blues display." Suffice it to say, it is in part exactly this "bad taste" that has continued to keep Negro music as vital as it is. The abandonment of one's local (i.e., place or group) emotional attachments in favor of the abstract emotional response of what is called "the general public" (which is notoriously white and middle class) has always been the great diluter of Negro culture. "You're acting like a nigger," was the standard disparagement. I remember being chastised severely for daring to eat a piece of watermelon on the Howard campus. "Do you realize you're sitting near the highway?" is what the man said, "This is the capstone of Negro education."[18]

(Of course, Howard University had, by the 1980s and 1990s, become a much different sort of place.) The dilemma is between the confirmation of the stereotype and the erasure of cultural difference, between a "Negro literature" that is a pale ambition to enter white culture and a "Negro literature" that eats watermelon ("That's just like a nigger"; "You're acting like a nigger"). To display black vernacular life, particularly life of the lower classes, is to use material that has already been taken up into the structure of racism (though if I am right, it is also to make available materials that remain beyond that structure). Thus the artist may find herself—uncomfortably—celebrated by white patrons precisely, though implicitly, for a confirmation of stereotype. And she may find herself, simultaneously, and for the same reason, reviled by critics of her own race, as Wright (and Hughes) reviled Hurston, and as Gay reviled Hughes. But, of course, these criticisms also take up a place in the racial transaction I am elaborating here. They assume that the purpose of black art is to show "better" black selves to an evaluating public that does not, to say the obvious, include the residents of Eatonville. The eyes that Gay and Baraka's interlocutor are worried about, the eyes that black art and education are "for," are white eyes watching black selves.

This retraces the line of thought we explored earlier with regard to integration: To make oneself and one's culture visible in white social space is to liberate oneself in a certain way from the oppression that drops a veil over one's culture. It may be an explosive, defiant, or joyous assertion of cultural legitimacy. In Hurston, it is more than that; it is the assembling of materials for a liberation from the accounts that cultures give of themselves. But it is also to make oneself vulnerable to white power in ways that can be swept up into oppression. Here, as in so many places, the oppression might even take the form of patronage: We might buy your books, see your shows, commission your folklore collecting, write about your autobiography. But though we do this to support you, we do it also to amuse ourselves in an effort at self-unification; that is, we do it in such a way that our stereotypes are confirmed. So that if your poems are "racy," say—sexually charged, in black English, violent, and so forth—we slum as we buy them, we slum as we celebrate them. We reinscribe our power as we judge them. Thus we have incorporated your attempt at cultural celebration and solidarity into a reinforcement of our own cultural solidarity; we use your revelation of blackness in our own further construction of whiteness, and, finally, for your continued exclusion from the signs of whiteness: especially stuff (Hurston died broke) and authority (Du Bois is studied in African-American Studies classes, not "general" social philosophy classes, since he is taken to be talking only about black people).

It is for just such reasons that Wright was uncomfortable with Hurston's art, for just such reasons that Hughes's own art was attacked by black critics, and for just such reasons that Hughes, in sympathizing with his critics, displays a discomfort with his own art. But the alternative, as Hughes argues in *The Big Sea,* is intolerable: that the black artist be constrained to show only the "acceptable" aspects of his own culture (acceptable to black critics of Gay's stripe, anxious to display to white folks the progress of the race). This will take the rather horrid form of an erasure of cultural difference, so that black folks come out sounding just like white folks. Hughes criticizes the novels of Jessie Fauset on just such grounds. That strategy simply reinforces double consciousness, acquiesces in invisibility. Caught in this dilemma, it is little wonder that Hurston tried to check out of the politics and the aesthetics of identity entirely; she simply wanted to be left alone to do what she did.

Hurston's life and her authorship implicate her in the dynamic of hiddenness and revelation as modes of oppression and as means of resistance. In one sense *Dust Tracks on a Road* is one of the oddest autobiographies ever written; it starts as a standard recounting of her story, but by the time Hurston arrives in Harlem, it omits virtually her entire life. For such reasons, Maya Angelou calls the book "puzzling" and remarks on its "strange distance,"[19] and Alice Walker calls it "the oddly false-sounding autobiography of that freest of all black women writers."[20] For such reasons, Plant is able to read the book against itself, and Braxton can imply, with some justice, that the book is a failure because its narrative form is unsatisfactory. Hurston systematically concealed herself (though by her own standards she had nothing to conceal, no coherent self). And she also retired personally into obscurity as a partly voluntary exile, preferring to live where no one knew "who she was." On the other hand, Hurston's personality and her life are vividly present in all her writings. *Jonah's Gourd Vine,* like *Their Eyes,* is set in Eatonville, and is roughly autobiographical (she appears as the character Isis). And Hurston the folklorist and ethnologist performs herself vividly as a participant in the activities she describes in *Mules and Men* and *Tell My Horse.* There she makes the move that Du Bois made in *Souls of Black Folk;* she qualifies or undermines the scientific stance by showing herself to be a full-fledged, fully interested participant, and does anthropology in a much more engaged way than did her mentors at Columbia, Franz Boas and Ruth Benedict. Zora is at once the most and least reticent author I have ever read. In the sense of oneness in her art and her philosophy, in her self-assertion and self-fragmentation, in her openness and hiddenness, Hurston continually problematizes the self.

Hurston's lovely essay "How It Feels to Be Colored Me" has been widely attacked precisely for its rejection of any race-based definition of herself and for her seeming unconcern with racial uplift. It contains expressions of patriotism that seem highly problematic, and includes a sentence that is virtually a quotation from the horrible line of Booker T. Washington quoted in the first chapter: "Slavery is the price I paid for civilization."[21] Hurston, I think, takes herself to be trying to point out the opportunities that arise precisely from pain, the joy that is available only in struggle, a constant theme of her writings from *Jonah's Gourd Vine* forward.

> No one on earth ever had a greater chance for glory. The world to be won and nothing to be lost. It is thrilling to think—to know that for any act of mine, I shall get twice as much praise or twice as much blame. It is quite thrilling to hold the center of the national stage, with the spectators not knowing whether to laugh or to weep.
>
> The position of my white neighbor is much more difficult. No brown specter pulls up a chair beside me when I sit down to eat. No dark ghost thrusts its leg against mine in bed. The game of keeping what one has is never so exciting as the game of getting. ("How It Feels," 827–28)

Hurston's fascinating insight here is that, by the constant attempt of white people to marginalize them, black people have been centralized in the life of the culture. They are the objects of a certain sort of rapt and anxious gaze that freights their every public action with added significance. This gaze is our construction of you, but it is above all our construction of ourselves as that-which-gazes, whether our gaze predicts your death or your uplift. Thus, this passage displays the structure of ejected asceticism: Our attempt to make you into pure bodies and shunt you away only centralizes you, shows the dependence of our constructions of ourselves on you the specular object.

For such reasons, Hurston resists every attempt to make of her a martyr to her color; she tries to view her marginality as an opportunity. And the essay concludes with a perfect statement of Hurston's sense of herself. First, she says this:

> At certain times I have no race, I am *me*. When I set my hat at a certain angle and saunter down Second Avenue, Harlem City, feeling as snooty as the lions in front of the Forty-Second Street Library, for instance. . . . The cosmic Zora emerges. ("How It Feels," 154–55)

But what it means to be "the cosmic Zora" is the key to understanding Hurston's life and work:

> In the main, I feel like a brown bag of miscellany propped against a wall. Against a wall in company with other bags, white, red, and yellow. Pour out the contents, and there is discovered a jumble of small things priceless and worthless. A first-water diamond, an empty spool, bits of broken glass, lengths of string, a key to a door long since crumbled, a rusty knife-blade, old shoes saved for a road that never was and never will be, a nail bent under the weight of things too heavy for any nail, a dried flower or two still a little fragrant. In your hand is the brown bag. On the ground before you is the jumble it held—so much like the jumble in the bags, could they be emptied, that all might be dumped in a single heap and the bags refilled without altering the content of any greatly. A bit of colored glass more or less would not matter. Perhaps that is how the Great Stuffer of Bags filled them in the first place—who knows? ("How It Feels," 829)

This passage—which is at once modest and shattering—amounts to no less than a theory of the human self. It is a theory of the self that is precisely poised opposite the Cartesian ego or even the Humean "bundle of ideas." For here the self is simply a miscellany, a "jumble" of memories, objects, hopes, souvenirs, jewels. What lends these things their apparent "coherence" is the bag that contains them: In America, it is race. The "coherent" self is thus a surface, an appearance, rather than a deep truth. The "authentic" self we hope to discover is in fact an artifact of the disciplines that, among other things, make race. This is Hurston's response to the problem I isolated at the end of the chapter on Du Bois. For Hurston, it is specularization and the machinery for its enforcement which create the *demand* for a coherent self. The black coherent self is a zone of concealment and resistance; the white coherent self is a purification by ejection. But these are not things that we discover about ourselves; they are things we impose on one another. And since what demands that the black self be a zone of resistance is precisely a black template for black people, Hurston *must* reject this template in rejecting the claim that selves, including her self, could be or already are coherent.

What the bag contains is not the true, hidden self that must be brought to light, but fragments, bits of broken glass. The fragments have no internal or necessary relation to one another; they are not pieces of one thing that has been broken; what relates them is that they are in the same bag. If the self could see itself whole, it would let go of itself as whole; liberation would be found in an acknowledgement of irremediable fragmentation, and in a sharing of fragments with other fragmented selves. That is

Janie's liberation; that is Tea Cake's liberation; that is Moses's liberation; and that is Hurston's liberation. The "coherent" self is a bag, a trap, an appearance; the "true" self, the internal self, does not exist at all.

Or rather, again, the coherent, true self is an *artifact* that must be *manufactured* technologically. And it *has* been manufactured by a thousand invisible disciplines, a thousand fables that account for themselves as objective pieces of knowledge, themselves organized into a coherent structure for comprehending the world. The selves described by Descartes or Kant are not discovered by a serial stripping away of the detritus of lives until a core is revealed; such selves are *achieved* by a refusal to allow oneself, and by technologies for refusing to allow others, to be anything else—a refusal that is required, for example, for the psychological remanufacturing of distorted, or disoriented, or incoherent selves. A fragmented self of the sort that Hurston celebrates comes very close to the Western tradition's conception of *madness,* of the other of the coherent subject. And of course, one way the coherent self is made is by the ejection of its madness and fragmentation. But another way it is made is in the racial ejection: What gives the white self whatever coherence it seems to possess is the ejection into the other of whatever shows the self in its fragmentation. Now one result of this is the power of the reversed stereotype, because to say that the ejected selves, the selves of black folk, *are,* after all, coherent, is to say that the material on which the ejection is practiced stands outside of what has been made of it by that ejection, that it constructs *itself* as coherent. But the power that Hurston explores is that of an excess of every self beyond every form of coherence. To display *that* would be to display the *failure* of *all* technologies of the self to subdue and transform the raw material on which they are practiced.

Derrida has argued that Western languages are the languages of logos, of reason, the dominating word, of power as truth. If that were right, then Hurston's miscellaneous self, or nonself self, would be precisely the self that *could not be spoken.* The other, or madness, cannot be spoken without reinstituting the same; black pride reinstitutes the language of racism (that is true, in some sense, but also has a potential for the subversion of logos that Derrida does not, I think, sufficiently appreciate). But what is radically other to the whole complementary structure of ejection, what simply stands there in excess of any construction—*that,* we might surely agree, cannot be spoken, supposing that the notion makes any sense at all (well, it cannot be spoken). But what we have to take seriously is this: Hurston speaks. Hurston says herself as a miscellany. And when she does, she shows forth not only the excess of selves beyond the technologies by which they are shaped, but the excess of language beyond logos. American English is Greek. But American English is a glorious mess; American English is African; American English speaks in and out of a multiplicity of isolated and interlocking communities. And, for God's sake, Greek is a mess, not a shining logos in the sky. Greek is African, and so forth. The point is not to delineate the limits of what can be said but to listen to what *is* being said.

There are two aspects to Hurston's questioning of the self. First, there is the identification of self with culture and with nature that is the great theme of Hurston's art. This oneness with people and things in love is a theme that puts Hurston's work into relation with some of the great spiritual traditions of the world. Hurston's magnificent addition to this theme is temporality: the notion that the ecstatic identity of persons with one another and with things is a matter of the ever-unfolding moment; it is never still. And yet this very identification reflects and depends on something internal, on an allowance of oneself to be fragmented, a gentle resistance to coherence and internal stasis. It is *acceptance* as resistance. Here, Hurston resists every attempt at self-explanation, and every attempt by others to make her comprehensible by race, gender, or by any other means whatever. She tries to *show,* I think, that coherent raced or reasoned selves have been *machined.*

Hurston is absolutely explicit in her rejection of the project of making people over into coherent objects:

> People are prone to build a statue of the kind of person it pleases them to be. And few people want to be forced to ask themselves, "What if there is no me like my statue?" The thing to do is grab the broom of anger and drive off the beast of fear. (*Dust Tracks,* 26)

Few people indeed have the guts to ask the question, "What if there is no me?" And fewer still have the guts to find art and joy in living that question as a question; the question is *fearsome,* mad. Hurston had the guts. People will try to make you into a statue: the statue of the black woman, for example. They will try to freeze the life out of you in order to comprehend you. But the fate to be abhorred above all others is to try to do that to yourself, whether it is through race consciousness, marriage, or education. Hurston could live with being a statue for other people, but she insisted on being alive to herself.

Being alive to oneself is, finally, freedom. As she says in her famous remark about Moses in *Moses, Man of the Mountain,* "He had found out that no man may make another free. Freedom was something internal."[22] If my reading of Hurston has been anything like right, this internal freedom is not a freedom of the self to think whatever it likes, for example, or secretly to will what it cannot accomplish; it is a freedom to let oneself go, to allow oneself to experience one's own fragmentation, or to allow one's experience to be fragmented. And Moses says,

> Freedom looks like the biggest thing that God ever made to me, and being a little hungry for the sake of it ought not to stop you. . . . I lift your eyes to the hills. I have been hungry a lot of times in places just like this, but I felt that getting what I was after was worth it, so I made myself satisfied. I found out that want won't kill you half as quick as worry will."
>
> "Where you get that good word from?" Aaron asked Moses in quick admiration.
>
> "Oh, I don't know, exactly. Just from living, I reckon, Aaron." (*Moses,* 205)

Hurston went hungry for the sake of freedom as she construed it. She could not make herself over into the statue of a black author. She sank into obscurity, sabotaged by the reception of her work, yet continued to write for many years after all hope of publication was gone. Her grave was unmarked until Alice Walker found it, and her reputation was dead until Walker, among others, revived it.

Thus Hurston's assertions of selfhood, a constant theme of her auto-biographical writings, are much more radical than is usually supposed. For she does not, like Du Bois and Malcolm, call on herself or other people to show themselves by bringing the deeply buried authentic self to the surface. Du Bois's and Malcolm's resistance takes the form of locating the self in culture, and thus locating hope in cultural overcoming. But the self Hurston asserts is not a racial self, and it is not exactly "culturally constructed" because at the deepest level it exceeds or is incomprehensible to *any* construction. That is because it is bits and pieces; the self Hurston asserts is in a sense not anything in particular. To repeat, Hurston's account takes up an American tradition of individualism, but it also deeply repudiates even the possibility of individualism; there are no selves to show out in public space, only fragments to be shared. This allows, for one thing, that the cultural location of any particular individual is always multiple, ambiguous, mixed, a fact which was as difficult for Malcolm X to countenance as it was for Lester Maddox. That Hurston loves such selves while holding fast to their fragmentation is a magnificent achievement, and one that makes her life and work consistently problematic across all the discourses by which they are engaged.

5

RAP MUSIC AND
THE USES OF STEREOTYPE

Zora Neale Hurston resisted epistemic power by rejecting all cultural constructions of herself, by refusing to allow herself to be made comprehensible through the technology of race and its representational regimes. She resisted the constructions imposed by the black community as much as those imposed on it. This resistance is both problematized and intensified by her celebration of black Southern culture. One transgressive aspect of Hurston's work and self-presentation is a strategic deployment of stereotype; her work alternately deconstructs and reconstructs the architecture of race; it is a rhythmic coalescing and fragmentation of racial signifiers as the materials of the self. Some rap music, I will suggest, represents a similar move, one that synthesizes Hurston and Malcolm X: it uses the materials of the representational regimes that manufacture race as nodes of resistance.[1]

Even the very use of music here, and my own focus on it as a locus of black expressivity, is in a problematic but also potentially subversive relation to stereotype. For of course black folks are supposed to be musical, and the aesthetic products of black culture that have been known best and appropriated most by white culture have been black musical forms. For such reasons, Michele Wallace, in emphasizing black visual culture, writes,

> There is by now too vast an array of compelling narratives in which African-American music is the founding discourse of the African-

American experience. Indeed, African music is the founding discourse of the diaspora, and that is probably as it should be. But, for my part, I am at war with music, to the extent that it completely defines the parameters of intellectual discourse in the African-American community.[2]

One senses from this passage that Wallace is just sick of hearing about it; she wants to talk about something else. And certainly African-American visual culture is an incredibly rich field for investigation that is still largely unexplored, especially given the vexed history of visuality in relation to race, which we have discussed at length already. For the emphasis on music in this chapter, then, I cannot exculpate myself, and as I say, I, like a lot of white folks, have been fascinated or even obsessed with black music since I was a child. It should be noted, however, that rap also, in the era of the music video, is to some extent a visual form. And it is an incredibly dense semiotic textual form. In fact, the first criticism of rap by those who hate it (mostly white people, in my experience) is that it isn't music at all, because it is not sufficiently melodic. Rather, it is held to be a style of declamation or speechifying. That criticism is wrong—much rap is intensely melodic—but it contains a grain of truth: In rap, the text (which must be understood as a spoken and recorded form, not as a written form) is the thing. And if what I am saying about the use of the stereotype as a weapon is right, then all of this must be factored in about rap: that it is music, that it is spoken, and so on.

Where Hurston simply professes disregard for whether she is confirming stereotypes, rap often seizes the stereotype and wields it directly, self-consciously, as a weapon. Rap transforms oppression into resistance, and it does so in a way that makes the conceptual structure of that oppression (the structure I have described as ejected asceticism) absolutely clear. This is an extremely hopeful moment, it seems to me, because in order for the dichotomy of race to be overcome, it must first be made visible. And it must be made visible not once or twice, or here or there, or in general; it must be made visible over and over again in as many locations as possible and with total specificity.

Rap is, among other things, music, poetry, fiction, autobiography, advertising, philosophy, commodified spectacle. As philosophy, rap is simultaneously assertion and demonstration, theory and enactment. As autobiography, it is description, but also performative self-creation; it remakes the life that is described, as the rapper tells us what she is doing right now as she raps (smokin suckaz wit logic, perhaps). Rap as autobiography and as fiction takes up experience into narrative, but it also transforms the life that is being narrated. And it interrupts or transgresses narrative with what exceeds narrative. As spectacle, it both participates in and alters the racializing transaction of ejected asceticism by seizing power at key points in the structure of exchange and the circulation of commodities.

The music that underlies rap—hip hop—is a quintessential postmodern form; it consists of snatches of appropriated songs. This point is developed in some detail by Houston Baker, who says that "by *postmodern* I mean the nonauthoritative collaging or archiving of sound and styles that bespeaks a deconstructive hybridity. Linearity and progress yield to a dizzying synchronicity."[3] Hip hop takes up the songs it samples and uses them, but also transfigures them, or reduces them to single, essential gesture, or ridicules them, or turns them against themselves. The entire history of recorded sound is available to be sampled; the instrument of hip hop is the history of recorded sound. Rap as poetry drives rhythm into speech, investing the act of speaking with a very pure power. One thing that is inevitably missing from a written discussion of rap is that recorded or performed rap is presented as spoken (usually) by the voice that composes it; it is not primarily a written form. Thus it relies on, indeed is inconceivable without, the dissemination of sound on the vinyl record, the audio tape, the compact disk. Any written discussion of rap needs to acknowledge that the form must be heard as recorded, or rather that the form is itself recording, and that transcriptions of rap inevitably lose much of its artistic power.

Rap does not speak with one voice. It is tenaciously multivocal, often within the same song. The early rappers—The Furious Five, The Sugarhill Gang, and later Run DMC and Whodini, for example—rapped in crews or tag teams, each voice as identifiable by its preoccupations as by its timbre. Albums such as Dr. Dre's *The Chronic* or the Notorious B.I.G.'s *Ready to Die* are sprawling collaborations of voices: male and female, tough and tender, violent and mellow. The musical styles appropriated on these disks—soul, jazz, advertising jingles, funk, rock—reflect a similar diversity, as do the lyric themes in rap generally: everything from the politically charged philosophy of Public Enemy to the evocations of sex and violence by the Los Angeles Gangsters, the out-front feminism of Queen Latifah, and the celebratory bawdiness of Salt 'n Pepa or Positive K. There are regional differences and identifications: from the staccato attack of New York to the slow melodic groove of LA, the Southern rural orientation of Arrested Development, and Fesu's tales of Houston housing projects. Thus if there are generalizations in what follows, I warn you in advance to take them with a grain of salt.

I think it is fair to say that all of the themes of the earlier chapters—

truth, double consciousness, self-loathing, self-assertion, fragmentation, and the desire born of fragmentation—are explored in rap from a variety of angles. But there is a further element in rap that I want particularly to develop by the end of the chapter. Some rap *plays* with race in a way that betrays both awareness of the power of race in the American experience and an ability to wield that power, an empowerment over that power.

Rap is, often enough, precisely about power (one of the defining moments for the form was Spike Lee's use of the Public Enemy song "Fight the Power" at the opening of *Do the Right Thing*). But the content of that "about" is of interest. Rap often asserts superiority: the superiority of black over white, man over woman (or woman over man), or the personal superiority of the rapper over other rappers, or other people in general. But as a rapper describes the superiority of her skills, she does so by displaying those very skills. Rap, then, becomes a very particular sort of speech act; it has a ceremonial force. It effects power by incantation. The fact that my voice is coming out of your speakers shows that there is a particular power in what I am doing, and that very voice as it comes out of your speakers is telling you that there's a particular power in what I am doing. If rap asserts the superiority of black over white culture, it mounts a demonstration precisely within that assertion. Another common assertion of power is the rapper's claim to move the bodies of the audience, to produce words and rhythms that *possess* the listeners' bodies, making them dance. The creativity of the slang and word play, the profundity of the poetry, the engagement of the body by the beat: these are aspects of this particular African-American cultural production that show you, as they tell you, that black culture has power. (And these are, by the way, precisely the aspects of African-American art that Hurston celebrated.)

Thus, the rap speech act aspires to, asserts, but also enacts a reversal of cultural and personal domination. Here's a typical enactment of personal power by MC Lyte:

> Moonroof open in the BM,
> Windows tinted they can't see in.
> They know it's me though.
> MC Lyte she's bigger than bolo.
> . . . .
> So act like you know.
> The things that I do just ain't for show.
> This is my livin, so I am givin
> Everything I got if not a lot more
> For the people, for the buyers,
> For all of those that seem to try a

MC Lyte tape in your Benzi box.
What can I say. Hey thanks a lot.
Cause I flip and trip and do all that good shit.
That's why the brothers they can't get off my tip.
They know whose show this is.
Whose show is this?
This is MC Lyte; act like you know.[4]

This passage displays, as many rap songs do, a reversal of the power/knowledge relations that have characterized the history of African-American speech. Knowledge here is not something MC Lyte wants, or wants to use to explain herself; it is *fame*. She demands that you know her, bases her claims to superiority on how well known she is (Biggie Smalls: "And if you don't know, now you know, you know"). The assertion of fame in rap, repeated over and over, requires that to *know*, listeners must take those rappers on their own terms. Being known as a rapper precisely inverts the relations between agency, power, and knowledge present in, say, case histories of prisoners. This knowledge is not supposed to be extracted from bodies or lives, but rather bubbles up through word of mouth and radio play. Being "known" in rap terms means having your neighborhood's attention and loyalty, means having fame and fans, means *setting the terms* of representation through the power to be heard. MC Lyte *makes* you know what she *wants* you to know, and in the process takes your twenty bucks. And if you *don't* know, you better *act like* you know; if you're ignorant, you're going to be roundly abused.

Likewise, there is a constant cultural aggression in rap, an assertion of the *reality* or *truth* of black culture in the face of white domination. This aspect connects rap with the African-American response to oppression that stretches back to the slave narratives. As do Baker and Henry Louis Gates, Ice T, in his book *The Ice Opinion*, connects rap to African-American traditions:

> The main misinterpretation and misunderstanding of rap is in the dialogue—in the ghetto talk and machismo, even in the basic body language. From the nasty tales of Stagolee in the 1800s to H. Rap Brown in the '60s, most of rap is nothing more than straight-up black bravado. . . . In the ghetto, a black man will say, "I'll take my dick and wrap it around this room three times and fuck yo' mama." Now this man cannot wrap his dick around the room three times and probably doesn't want to fuck your mother, but this is how he's gonna talk to another brother.[5]

Notice that this both confirms and contextualizes the material of stereotype; aggressiveness and sexuality are put *in play* here in a way that is typical of rap. We have a celebration of black traditions (playing the dozens, for example) that is related to an Afrocentric self-construction of the sort that Malcolm put forward and to the African-American aesthetic enunciated and enacted by Hurston. African-American linguistic codes and cultural traditions are centralized and their meanings explained without excuse. But here it is precisely the elements of African-American culture that are despised and feared by white culture (also by some elements of black culture: the Reverend Calvin Butts springs to mind) that are simultaneously thematized and enacted. That was Hurston's strategy in, for example, *Mules and Men* and "Characteristics of Negro Expression." Rather than asserting that African-American culture is a "high" culture by European standards, there is here an expression and demonstration of a power whelming from below.

As expressed in rap, this aesthetic has one criterion of quality: reality. An alternate formulation of the same standard is this: blackness. KRS One (Knowledge Reigns Supreme Over Nearly Everyone), for example, raps, "Let me show whose ass is the blackest." To assert that his ass is the blackest is for him to assert precisely that his stuff is real, authentic, hard-core rap. The association of reality with blackness should resonate out of everything I have argued thus far: that whiteness is constructed out of an imaginary ejection of the concrete, the embodied, the real, that white culture is a deathbound culture, a culture aiming toward or making a supreme value out of unreality. "Let me show whose ass is the blackest" turns that construction around on a dime. A "real," hard-core rap is an extremely black rap, and that means bass-heavy, gritty, completely embodied, completely intrinsic in its own enactment.

Here, to take another example, is the introduction to Guru's album *Jazzmatazz*:

> Peace, yo, and welcome to Jazzmatazz, an experimental fusion of hip hop and live jazz. I'm your host the Guru. That stands for gifted, unlimited rhymes universal. . . . Hip hop, rap music, it's real. It's musical, cultural expression based on reality. And at the same time jazz is real, and based on reality. . . . I got Donald Byrd, Roy Ayers, Lonnie Liston Smith, Branford Marsalis, Ronny Jordan, N'Dea Davenport, Courtney Pine, and MC Solaar, all in the house.[6]

The disk then becomes an exploration and celebration of black musical traditions, and an attempt to focus them into a single coherent synthesis that demonstrates their reality and power. It is a use and embodiment of truth as an agent of resistance. And it gives this truth a poetic turn, as in the song "Transit Ride," which uses the recording that blares from subway trains as a figure of urban entrapment: "Watch the closing doors." Thus, much rap is a form of literary "realism," a slice of life and so forth; it is "based on reality." But the typical movement in Guru's introduction shows the distinctiveness of rap as a form (though the same thing is attributed to jazz by the Guru): it is both based on reality and itself real. It is no mere reflection of reality, but also a real thing that takes up the antecedent reality, both the realities of black life and the manufactured realities of stereotype, into its own real enactment. This is not the realism of Dickens or Flaubert, which attempts "description" while concealing the author. Imagine Dickens interrupting his tales constantly to *tell* you that Oliver is real, and detail his authority so to tell you (by, say, claiming that he *is* Oliver, all grown up, with a record contract and an AK). Rap enters and transforms the context that it also reflects; it yields no distance between art object and motif. It is the human voice speaking out of the circumstances it sets out, and speaking (at its best) with grit, power, and immediacy.

Notice that, in the construction of whiteness, we white folks make of ourselves the truth: We associate knowledge, and science, and comprehension with ourselves and expel you from them. But notice too that comprehension also *falsifies,* that in ranging the particular fact under the general category, we must erase the jagged edges of that fact, its massed idiosyncracies. As we have seen with regard to Du Bois, this abandons by ejection an entire realm of truths to those who are left in the particular (behind the veil). To speak of *reality* is a powerful way of reasserting these truths; one might say that all that is left out in a Theory of Everything is . . . reality: grit, jaggedness, immediacy, violence. Du Bois moved in some of his writings to a relocation of the site of knowledge. Rappers enact this relocation, claim this site, as an aesthetic and an epistemic strategy for an attack on the initial ejection. If rappers know what they're talking about, then (white) sociologists haven't a clue. If rap is real, white culture has got to be "unreal."

Ice T puts it this way: "I rap about my life, and I rap about it in the hardest, most blatant sense. I consider what I say as real. This is the way the world I come from is. This is the way I talk and live. This is the only way I can be" (*Ice Opinion*, 97). In rap, then, discourse materializes, becomes a hard, solid thing. The discourse of white science, of ejected asceticism, is material as well, but systematically hides that materiality and denies its effects; in rap the materiality of discourse is explicitly thematized. Whereas in Du Bois the description of the particular truth is used as a mode of resistance to the general truth, rap brings the particular truth in a particular embodiment to bear directly on the racial situation.

Du Bois recounted the particular truth. Rap enacts it and slaps you with it. The particular truth of rap is put forward by and in a particular voice. The truth is transformed into art, but the reality of the art itself becomes a mode of resistance. The slave narrative made the slave's truth a possession and a weapon; it asserted the slave's ownership of his truth (recall Pennington). Rap, too, is an assertion of ownership of the truth or of the reality; the predominant mode of aesthetic evaluation of rap is not, say, beauty, but precisely reality (blackness) and the authority to present it.

A directly related theme is the rapper's claim to be "representing," in both the descriptive and political senses, some constituency. (A Tribe Called Quest: "Lincoln Boulevard represent represent. A Tribe Called Quest represent, represent.") But whereas the slave narrative authorized black truth by white testimony, and was aimed at white readers, rap refers its authority to represent back to the hood, gang, or crew, and makes an issue of whether the rapper has stayed true to the members of that constituency or turned her back on them. Rap authorizes itself in its own embodiment; its truth can be *heard*, is inherent in its expression and the power of that expression. But that power is constantly assigned to the rapper's particular history and location, and to his authorization to represent friends, family, and listeners; that authorization depends on the rapper's staying real, and staying connected (and "staying black"). Thus the individual rapper's assertion of authority supports itself through both the rapper's own skills and his connections to a specific background community, which are closely connected in an aesthetics in which the central evaluative categories are reality and blackness. Part of the power of the assertion is also the iteration and reiteration of the rapper's ability to speak about and for his reality, authorized by those who share it, with no reference needed to the epistemic structure of white authorization of the representation. In fact, such authorization immediately casts suspicion on the reality and authority of the representation.

The mode of dissemination is relevant here as well, because whereas most speech acts (giving a promise, say) are ephemeral, once-and-for-all events, the rap act as it appears on disk or tape is endlessly repeatable and reproducible. It exists as a constant potential assertion or claim; the rap speech act is indefatigable and is produced in a never-ending spiral of recycled recorded sound. It leaves you with its own evidence, reasserts itself whenever you press the right button. It can be heard anywhere, everywhere, by anybody. Rap commodifies the racial signifier with absolute precision; it sells, both to blacks and to whites, the preacher, the freedom fighter, the threatening druggie, the earthy black sex bomb, the independent and powerful mama, the black man armed to the teeth and hung like a horse, and so forth. It does this with great directness, but also, I think, often with great irony, and often with a crystalline self-awareness. The assertion of real, particular experience becomes both a *commercial strategy* (thus it *must* be accomplished in self-awareness) and an aesthetic and epistemological subversion.

That rap is a commodity, however, does not compromise it as an art; indeed, rap is inconceivable without commodification; as I say, it presupposes the current modes of dissemination and exploits them better than any other art form. Rap's *medium* is, finally, commodity, and while country music, for example, exists in an uneasy tension with its own commodification, rap revels in it, constantly makes of it an advantage. The play with race in rap, as I hope to show, both intensifies the discourse of race in our culture and violates it. The nastier the rap, the greater the hope. But rap places the nastiness directly into the marketplace; it circulates a racial enactment through the network of commodity exchange; it permeates the white-dominated world of market economics and mass media. It is to some extent co-opted and reduced in power by its location, but its market penetration also signals a significant entrance of black economic power into the economy of commodity.

Rap lends itself extremely smoothly to slumming, which can now be accomplished as suburban white boys watch "Yo, MTV Raps" (we don't even have to go to Harlem). But by the same token and by the same means, rap also subverts the structures surrounding commodity and image in contemporary capitalism as the locations of racial construction. The notion of commodity has particular resonance in African-American discourse; black folks, after all, came here as commodities. It has a wide resonance as well in black American artistic traditions; the white world has appropriated black music through the whole century and used it to make countless fortunes, while the "authentic" black artist was often left destitute. (Though the notion is abroad that this results from conspiracy, and though there certainly have been concerted efforts to buy, say, "folk" songs at the cheapest possible rates, I prefer to give this a different twist: White performers appropriate black musical styles because those styles are incredibly compelling aesthetically, but white listeners are often more comfortable hearing them from white performers—Pat Boone, for example, or Vanilla Ice.) But the only possibility of subversion within consumer capitalism is to seize control of oneself and one's race as a commodity, and that, I propose, is what many rappers accomplish, though they may line white pockets as well. I suspect that rap record labels, for example, make some people nervous the way all-black juries do;

they both signal and further the actual status of black persons as full citizens. (Consider the way that Warner Brothers, for example, insulates itself from Death Row Records through a series of embedded companies.
Yet Death Row, as I write, has released four disks, each of which has gone
at least double platinum.) In our capitalist system, buying power *is* economic citizenship. For records and movies to be made for black consumption by black people (and the core audience for rap remains black,
though it is widely marketed among whites as well) means that their economic citizenship is now beginning to count in real terms, that their tastes
and standards will more and more influence the production of public culture. This cultural shift causes consternation among white people to the
extent that such production is less and less controllable by the filter of
white epistemic and economic control. All-black juries get to make legal
decisions based on the way *they* perceive social and political reality; rap
musicians get to say how *they* see the world, including white people, with
less and less monitoring by white sensibilities. In rap, all the monitoring
that matters—at least as far as the lyrics reproduce it—is from the authorizing community of one's neighborhood or audience constituency.
Any other attempt to guide or edit what is said is explicitly rejected as il-
legitimate.

Consider this lyric, "Burn, Hollywood, Burn," from *Fear of a Black
Planet,* the classic 1989 album by Public Enemy:

Chuck D:

. . . . . .
Yeah I'll check out a movie,
But it'll take a black one to move me.

. . . .
Hollywood or would they not
Make us all look bad like I know they had
But some things I'll never forget yeah
So step and fetch this shit.
For all the years we looked like clowns
The joke is over. Smell the smoke from all around.
Burn, Hollywood, burn . . .

Big Daddy Kane:
As I walk the streets of Hollywood Boulevard
Thinkin how hard it was to those that starred
In the movies portrayin the roles
Of butlers and maids, slaves and hos.
Many intelligent Black men seemed

To look uncivilized when on the screen.
Like I guess I figure you to play some jigaboo
On the plantation, what else can a nigger do?
And black women in this profession
As for playin a lawyer, out of the question.
For what they play Aunt Jemima is the perfect term
Even if now she got a perm.
So let's make our own movies like Spike Lee
Cause the roles being offered don't strike me.
There's nothing that the Black man could use to earn.
Burn, Hollywood, burn.[7]

This rap both describes the use of black people as stereotypical commodities in media and presents the simple solution: to "make our own movies."

The thrust recalls Langston Hughes's poem "Note on Commercial Theatre":

You've taken my blues and gone—
You sing 'em on Broadway
. . . And you fixed 'em
So they don't sound like me.
Yes you done taken my blues and gone.
You also took my spirituals and gone.
. . . But someday somebody'll
Stand up and talk about me,
And write about me—
Black and Beautiful—
And sing about me,
And put on plays about me!
I reckon it'll be
Me myself!

Yes, it'll be me.[8]

This poem and the preceding rap throw the present project into deep question. There certainly are attempts by white people to "appropriate" rap; certainly some white fortunes have been made out of it (although mine won't be). Perhaps more thoroughly, and again as this chapter shows, there are white attempts to dominate the discourse *about* rap.

In the early 1980s I was working as a freelance music critic for several different newspapers and magazines. I was, as I have indicated, interested in black musical forms and had written about them, and as rap began to get popular, I started writing about it. I reviewed early records by Run DMC and the Fat Boys, among others, and also concerts by rap stars such as Grandmaster Flash, LL Cool J, and Whodini. Now, first of all, I knew nothing about rap when this started other than that I liked listening to it; for example, I did not know how hip hop was *made,* and I didn't understand why there was no band at the concerts. I thought they were saving money by rapping over the instrumental tracks from their own records. I am sure I committed a variety of howlers, both in describing the music and in evaluating it. Whatever those howlers were, there was no way for me to be notified of them. Nevertheless, and despite the fact that there were black writers dealing with rap (Greg Tate, for instance, who wrote for some of the same magazines I did), rap's ascension as a widespread pop form coincided with its recognition in the white rock press, especially the *Rolling Stone* combine (I was working, among others, for *Record* magazine, published by the *RS* people). My white voice *authorized* an appreciation of rap, inserted it into a taxonomy of popular forms, declared and hence defused its subversive potential (again here, recall the authorizing documents appended to slave narratives). There would be two or three white guys in an audience of thousands; it wasn't hard to figure out that we were the critics. I remember sitting at the Laurel Super Music Fest in 1983, in a crowd of ten thousand people, and the only three white guys were in the press box. And if I was any indication, we were probably at that point the people in that audience who knew the *least* about the music we were evaluating.

But it must be said that the creation and reception of rap has also resisted such means of authorization, much more explicitly and successfully, I suspect, than any other black musical form. More of the people who make rap records and, at this point, review them are black than has been the case with the blues, gospel, soul, and so forth. And the *criticisms* of rap that flow from institutionally accredited locations are taken, frequently with pride, as proofs that the rap or rapper has affronted the white power structure. (Ice T: "You shoulda killed me *last* year.") What better proof could there be than such criticism that a rapper has said what he isn't supposed to say?

Furthermore, the role of white performers and producers in rap seems to me quite different than their role in previous black music. Though there has often been successful black/white collaboration in black pop forms (think of Leiber and Stoller's work with the Coasters, or Jerry Wexler's with the Memphis and Muscle Shoals scenes), there has also been a rough division of labor between those who authorize the art and those whose art is authorized to enter public space. But a group like the Beastie Boys, which is a great white rap act, is authorized precisely *out of* a black discourse of authenticity, just as Vanilla Ice is extruded by it, and finally discredited by it. Still, Vanilla Ice sought recognition in this discourse, and hence made up a blackened autobiography out of whole cloth. One point of a good rap is, again, that it *be* black, and producers such as Rick Rubin learn what that means and how to make the records come out dark. There is an inversion of authorizing power here that corresponds to the inversion of the stereotype; the reversal of the stereotype or its revaluing, the attack by the stereotyped on the dominant power that uses stereotype itself, has actually reconfigured the distribution of power in the music industry to some extent. Houston Baker points out that "Unlike rock and roll, rap cannot be hastily and prolifically appropriated or "covered" by white artists. For the black urbanity of the form seems to demand not only a style most readily accessible to black urban youngsters, but also a representational black urban *authenticity* of performance" (*Black Studies*, 82). This seems fundamentally right to me, though it must be pointed out that rap has entered much more widely into pop music vocabularies since Baker wrote, and is more and more part of the common language out of which pop songs can be made by anyone. But even in that case, the authorizing function has been reversed, and it is obvious that white performers hope to glean an aura of authenticity through these borrowings, even where the vocabulary now comes very "naturally."

In fact, the Beastie Boys are an interesting case. I said in the last chapter that if we white folks made ourselves visible to ourselves as white to the point where we could self-consciously play with and parody our whiteness, race would be ending as a dualistic mode of domination. Our invisibility to ourselves is absolutely essential if the dualism is to be formulated and wielded as a weapon in the precise way it is in American culture. If anyone in our culture has approached this parodic deconstruction of race from the white side, it is the Beastie Boys, and they can only do it from a point within an ongoing black discourse. One of the funniest things about the Beastie Boys is that they *sound white* even when (as on their early albums) they rap over black beats, and it seems to me that they *try* to sound *extremely* white. Vanilla Ice and even better white rap acts, such as House of Pain or Snow, try to sound black; the move is appropriative; it is slumming. But the Beastie Boys *show themselves as white* to (among others) black audiences, and parody whiteness. This is an extremely transgressive stance, but they take it up with such light-hearted enthusiasm that it is irresistible.

That such critiques and reversals of the circulation of racial signifiers take place precisely through the media which are criticized doubles their power. Public Enemy's rap does not simply set out a criticism of the construction of stereotype in mass media, it enacts an alternative. It is itself a seizing of the means of representation and the market in images for the purpose of criticizing those means and that market. It embodies what it asserts; it is both a program for subversion and an act of revolution.

Consider, for example, Kool Moe Dee's song "Funke Wisdom," which is typical of his output and indeed of a whole style of rap:

> Mathematically, it all adds up.
> All people are equal, but equal to what? . . .
> Twenty four, seven, three sixty five,
> Cause nine to five ain't alive
> We're in overdrive.
> Take the first power, elevate to the third.
> Manifest the power of the spoken word. . . .
>
> Knowledge ain't enough, you need funky, funky wisdom.[9]

Notice, however, that while Kool Moe extols wisdom, he remains situated in African-American traditions, which he connects here to the power of the spoken word, the same power that Hurston revealed in her folklore and fiction. Rap takes up and pushes forward an oral tradition, a tradition in which the spoken word is a vehicle of wisdom, as against the European culture of comprehension which (Derrida's bizarre argument notwithstanding) privileges the written text—abstract, enduring, comprehensive, authoritative—above the act of speaking. Further, Kool Moe doesn't just recommend wisdom; he recommends funky, funky wisdom. That is, he recommends wisdom that emerges from and transforms the African-American context, that has funk to it, bass. This is not a recommendation that black people learn Western traditions (though it does not exclude that) but that they locate their own sources of wisdom, among other places, in spoken and musical communication. Socrates had wisdom, perhaps, but Kool Moe Dee has funky, funky wisdom.

This participates in a reversal of stereotype. Like Hurston, however, Kool Moe also shows in that very reversal what stands outside the stereotype: the fact that there was a real culture there with practices of wisdom that antedated the imposition of dualisms upon it by European colonialism and American slavery. Further, the antecedent culture bears within itself the possibility of a reassertion both within and outside of stereotyped materials. That wisdom can be "funky" is a delightful notion, and one that is designed to expose the impoverishment both of white constructions of African-Americans (the exclusion of African-Americans from the space of wisdom, of mind, of civilization) and of white constructions of them-selves (*we* don't have a smell, much less a funk; one of the first things I was taught about race as a child in D.C. was that black folks *smell funny*). Wisdom since Plato has been associated with a process of disembodiment that locates the wise man in the realm of pure concepts. If wisdom in that sense were possible, it would be a horror, and the attempt to accomplish the impossible has been horrifying. It has turned us against the world and the ejected body with violence. But funky wisdom is *embodied* wisdom; Kool Moe does not celebrate ignorance, nor does he celebrate *our* wis-dom; he celebrates *his* wisdom, the same wisdom that Hurston located in African arts of the diaspora. In Kool Moe's work, this wisdom is explic-itly associated with an African history and an Afrocentric cultural con-struction.

It is often asserted that rap glorifies violence. That may occasionally be true (though far less frequently, I think, than is commonly supposed), and when it *is* true, one of its functions is, of course, the reassertion of what has been excluded; rap music is, among other things, a confrontation of white culture with its ejection of the body. Violence as transgression *in-terrupts* the operation of the machinery by which dualisms are enforced. But, as I say, this is occasional, and the bald general assertion that rap glo-rifies violence makes me wonder what these people have been listening to, if anything. Just a week before the release of *Doggystyle,* Snoop Doggy Dogg was arrested for murder, apparently because his bodyguard shot someone who had been threatening them with a gun. But check this lyric from "Murder Was the Case," a song that begins with Snoop getting shot:

As I look up at the sky
My mind starts trippin, a tear drops my eye.
My body temperature falls.
I'm shakin, they're breakin
Tryin to save the Dog.
Pumpin on my chest and I'm screamin.
I stop breathin.
Man I see demons.
Dear God, I wonder can you save me?
I can't die, my boohoo's bout to have my baby.

It's too late for prayin.
Hold up, a voice spoke to me
And it slowly started sayin:
"Relax your soul; let me take control.
Close your eyes my son." My eyes are closed.[10]

Anyone who thinks that glorifies violence is tripping. It certainly *describes* violence, and obviously emerges from a situation in which people are armed and in which the threat of death is often present. But Snoop, for one, is much more interested in getting mellow and partying than killing someone, not to speak of being killed. This chilling dream of his own death, which is as vivid as any such description I've ever read or heard, is a reminder of what goes on in the heads of people who live with violence on a daily basis. In fact, there is a whole genre of rap videos that depict gang funerals, or in which the dead or injured are mourned and avenged. One thing such works do *not* do is make death an entertaining game; the pain is palpable. Ice Cube raps, "Today I didn't have to use my AK./ I gotta say it was a good day." Biggie Smalls (Notorious B.I.G.) has issued an amazing disk that begins with his birth and ends with his death by suicide ("I hear death calling me," he says, shortly before the shot rings out). He, or rather the character that he constructs, gives us an incredibly detailed description of why he hates himself enough to kill himself.

These lyrics do not glorify violence, unless you take the position that to *notice* violence linguistically, to admit that it exists, is to glorify it. Rather they tell about violence, mourn it, object to it, and rage against the conditions that make violence a day-to-day reality. (Raekwon: "I can't believe in heaven cause I'm livin in hell.") This use of narrative itself in a transgressive interruption of logocentric narrative is particularly vivid in a song by Scarface, "Never Seen a Man Cry":

> Imagine life at its full peak
> Then imagine lyin dead in the arms of your enemy.
> Imagine peace on this earth when there's no grief.
> Imagine grief on this earth when there's no peace.
>
> . . . .
>
> Now the time has arrived for your final test.
> I see the fear in your eyes and hear your final breath.
> How much longer will it be till it's all done
> Total darkness, at ease, be it all one.
> I watch him die and when he dies let us celebrate.
> You took his life but his memory you'll never take.
> You'll be headed to another place
> And the life you used to live will reflect in your mother's face.
> I still gotta wonder why
> I never seen a man cry till I seen a man die.[11]

This song is about both what it is like to die and what it is like to watch someone you love die. The grief, the darkness, the oneness that death threatens and promises are centralized in experience, but they are themselves the overwhelming of that experience, the sinking of experience into the sea of the incomprehensible, where individuality is destroyed, and the story ends. This is the dark side of Hurston's oneness with a changing realm of matter: That oneness is both an expansion and an extinction of the self, a seduction, a grief, and a celebration.

Rap yields narratives, including narratives about violence and death. But narrative is also containment, and hence threat. Narrative has been a weapon of white culture. It has been used, as Derrida puts it, as "white mythology," above all in the scientific *explanation* of the object which is ejected in the self-constructions that make science possible and that set up the material world, including the human body, as an object for study. Narrative containment is how we explain you to ourselves, and thus us to ourselves, while simultaneously removing ourselves from the scene of description by our objectivity. Our story about ourselves is that our histories are not stories, but sciences. In someone like Hegel, for instance, our story of progress becomes the entire inner truth of History and Being (significantly, as Kobena Mercer points out, Africa gets left out of history, or rather is on principle excluded).[12] Of course, this is only one possible form of the narrative, even in the modern West. There are counternarratives: not only those that sweep unnarrated materials into the dominant narrative structures, but those that display different forms and possibilities for narrative. For example, there are African models of narration, some of which were employed by Hurston, that admit a plurality of narratives without trying to gather them all into a coherent structure. And rap definitely uses non-Western or not-only-Western modes of narration in constructing a discourse of resistance that asserts the other as other and is more than the assertion of the other as other.

There is, however, an even more radical excess available here, and available precisely out of the forms and concretions of oppression; for there are experiences that resist being swept into narrative altogether, and some of those experiences are signs or nodes of oppression itself. Thus what stands in excess to narrative can be gestured toward precisely in narrative. There is a white mythology that gives the sociological story, for example, of the underclass, with its substance abuse, its poverty, its violence, and its transgression of "our" values. These very experiences, however, are constant challenges to narrative in general. There can be narratives of acts of violence, but violence as it is experienced shatters narrative structures; violence might be defined precisely as what exceeds and destroys the coherence of narrative. The "slave narrative," for example, is both narrative and an interruption of narrative; the sheer intensity of the violence depicted cannot be smoothly incorporated in a story; its intensity disturbs the experience of the narrative as story. William Andrews points out that some slave narrators "lamented the inadequacy of language itself to represent the horrors of slavery or the depth of their feelings as they reflected on their sufferings. In some cases black narrators doubted their white readers' ability to translate the words necessary to a full rendering of their experience and feeling."[13]

To narrate one's own death, for example—as do Snoop and Biggie Smalls—is to make oneself impossible as a narrator in our ordinary reality. Ice T says this:

> Gangs have been able to get away with so much killing it just continues. The capability of violence in these kids is unimaginable. Last year, five of my buddies died. I don't even go to the funerals anymore. It's just so crazy. There are just so many people dying out there. Sometimes I sit up with my friends and think, "There will never be another time on earth where we'll all be together again." . . . You get hard after a while. You get hard. People on the outside say, "These kids are so stone-faced; they don't show any remorse or any emotion." It's because they are . . . conditioned, like soldiers in war, to deal with death. You just don't know what it's like until you've been around it. (*Ice Opinion*, 31)

Death exceeds story. Living with the constant threat of death and the constant capacity to kill is "unimaginable." It cannot be told; to be understood, it must be lived. And yet rap confronts you with its results, or with the situations in which life in the face of death is the only possible life. The gesture in narrative to those forms of experience is one way that rap connects with its intended audience: It gestures toward forms of experience that are not really describable, but the gestures are understood by those whose lives are punctuated by such experiences. Likewise, to shoot up heroin or to get stone drunk are ways of being sucked into oblivion, an oblivion that interrupts and attacks narrative coherence. Ultimately, in such experiences, one must *let go* of narrative; to allow oneself to sink into oblivion is to let go of one's story of oneself, and to overflow and escape from other people's stories.

White culture is obsessed with the task of constructing a narrative of black culture, an "explanation." It does this partly in various attempts at self-absolution, self-abasement, or self-accusation. But in all cases it allocates to itself the right to tell the story of African-American culture, perhaps as a preliminary step in "solving its problems" for it. Rap insists (as did Douglass and William Wells Brown) first—as we saw with regard to

"Burn, Hollywood, Burn"—that African-Americans are, and must be, telling their own stories.

Even more profoundly, rap often indicates that African-American experience (like all experience, finally) cannot be contained in stories and psychological structures. A song by Fesu, "Fallin Off the Deep End," captures this perfectly:

I don't trust a motherfucker
Or his sister or his brother or his crack-smokin uncle.
I can't stand them white folks.
How can I stress it enough?
I'll put your ass in handcuffs.
You wasn't worried till I started makin money.
But I can't be faded, motherfucker, I'm down with the twenty.
Yeah. And I'm fallin off the deep end.[14]

Substance abuse, violence, sex, death, love, and hatred are ways of falling off the deep end, tumbling into the abyss; they are calls to oblivion and ecstasy. One of the first national rap hits, Grandmaster Flash's "The Message," said, "It's like a jungle sometimes it makes me wonder / How I keep from goin under." Oblivion and ecstasy (and there is hardly a distinction), pull narrative apart by making it particular and then inserting into it a condition that abrogates it. The experience described is a "going under." This is one reason why rap is continually asserted by its practitioners to be "real" or "true": it refuses containment in the fantasy structures of narrative, insists on particularity, and pulls toward a letting go. Violence in this sense is used, first, as a weapon against white people, and second, as a weapon against white scientific and narrative structures, as an attempt at the deepest level to undermine white art, white sociology, white pathologization of blackness and African-American culture—in short every gesture of containment.

Rap constantly enacts transgression. It flouts the law; it flouts taboos about what words to use and taboos about racial signifiers; it flouts sexual mores, and drug prohibitions, and polite language. Violence is transgression *per se:* a sheer violation. No story contains or captures violence; no story expresses the oblivion out of which it emerges or the oblivion it imposes. Violence is the Kantian thing in itself about which we can say nothing positively or wholly true. Even violence that fits into the most recognizable stories of white culture does so uneasily, and there is a penumbra of excess about it. Violence is something into which we are forced, or into which we are seduced; thus violence calls to the self for its oblivion.

Often it makes this call precisely through an intensification of self to the point of collapse; shooting someone is an assertion of self, indeed the most pointed and extreme assertion of self, but it pulls the self by vertigo into a vortex. Violence is a destroyer of selves, and hence of every attempt to contain or explain the self.

Rap music has been criticized by black leaders for reinforcing racial stereotypes. The widespread use of words such as "bitch," "ho," and "nigger" is taken as an expression of self-hatred now extended (in a terrain we have traversed) into hatred of whatever resembles oneself. And rap has even been criticized for the same reason by some rappers. Sister Souljah, who is both a rapper and a community activist, writes the following in her autobiography, *No Disrespect*:

> Racism has turned our communities into war zones where we are dying every day. It is black-on-black hate, created by racism and white supremacy, that is killing us. Black people killing black people. Can African male-female relationships survive in America? Not if black-on-black love is dead. . . . Not if our young men continue to refer to young women as "bitches," or our young women refer to young men as "motherfuckers," or all of us refer to each other as "niggas." It is a sad measure of our profound contempt for each other and of our thoroughgoing self-loathing that we continue to persist in this ugly practice.[15]

Souljah's book is essentially about the difficulties of heterosexual love in a shattered community, a community, for example, where more of the young men are in jail than in college. Some rap takes that issue up in a very "positive" way. Heavy D, for example, says "black coffee, no sugar, no cream: that's the kind of girl I want down with my team." Salt 'n Pepa's "Whatta Man" is a celebration of black male beauty. Coolio's song "Mama I'm in Love with a Gangsta," by a stunning shift of view, portrays the pain of loving a man who is in jail through the eyes of his female lover, with Coolio portraying the incarcerated man. The late Tupac Shakur's "Black Pearl" is a celebration of the strength of black womanhood (though that celebration appeared more than a trifle ironic after Tupac's conviction for sexual abuse).

But the style called "gangsta rap" shows the force of Souljah's charge. Da Brat, for example, refers to herself as a "bitch" and a "ho." It is sometimes said that rap denigrates education, celebrates violence and substance abuse, and confirms white America's image of African-Americans as ignorant, threatening crackheads (or whatever the latest drug of choice happens to be). If this were offered as a general critique of rap, it would be, as we have seen, ridiculously overgeneralized. But it is not without force.

Sherley Anne Williams gives a quite typical argument:

Black people have to ask ourselves why so much [rap] has become so ve-
hemently misogynistic, violent, and sexually explicit, so soaked in black
self-hatred? Why, given that we are so ready to jump on Hollywood, the
Man, the Media, and black women writers for negative and distorted portrayals of black people, have black academics, critics, and intellectuals
been so willing to talk about the brilliant and innovative form of rap? Pro-
claiming rap's connection to traditional wells of black creativity and thus
viewing even its most pornographic levels as "art," intellectuals have been
slow to analyze and critique rap's content. We have, by and large, refused
to call that content, where appropriate, pathological, anti-social, and anti-
community. And by our silence, we have allowed what used to be permissible only in the locker room or at stag parties, among consenting adults,
to become the norm among our children.[16]

Now I have quite a hostile response to this passage, which is notable above
all for its prissiness, for its unquestioning assumption that what is art cannot be obscene, and for its assumption that *describing* the realities of some
black lives amounts to self-hatred. Williams adds that "the best rap is
characterized by . . . innocuous messages and funky beats" (216), which
is colossally wrong. But again, it is obvious that the criticism has bite in
that it refers to the actual content of many raps.

The charge of misogyny, for example, is hardly misplaced. Here is
Claude Brown on the term *bitch*:

Johnny was always telling us about bitches. To Johnny, every chick was a
bitch. Of course, there were some nice bitches, but they were still bitches.
And a man had to be a dog in order to handle a bitch.

Johnny said once, "If a bitch ever tells you she's only got a penny to buy
the baby some milk, take it. You take it, 'cause she's gon git some more.
Bitches can always git some money." He really knew about bitches.

Cats would say, "I saw your sister today, and she is a fine bitch." Nobody was offended by it. That's just the way things were. It was easy to see
all women as bitches.[17]

Here, the use of the term *bitch* is related directly to the predation of
women by men, which is a predominant theme of *Manchild in the
Promised Land*. So the last thing I want to do is simply to suggest that
such speech is not problematic.

But one question that remains is, Problematic to whom? A common bromide of some sorts of feminist discourse is that the animal metaphors used for the genders are differentially inflected: a man is "cock of the walk" or a "dog" for instance, while a woman is a "bitch," a "cow," a "shrew." It is taken as obvious that those words *must* be valorizing of men and derogatory to women. And certainly in the history of white gender discourse they are derogatory. But is it obvious that such words must always, wherever they are used, mean just that? Or do some listeners assume that the comparison of a woman to a dog *must* be a derogatory metaphor, even when those using it claim otherwise? I do not want to answer this question definitively here, but only to point out that to assume that the meanings of words are set by one particular history of meaning encodes a certain cultural assumption of superiority. No matter what you claim to mean by certain terms, or what those terms mean in your community in practice, cultural commentators are likely to dismiss your claim about meaning in the name of what the words *really* mean—that is, what they would mean in the white community and what practices they support in the white community. (Recall here Hurston's contextualization of violence between the sexes.) As I explore this, I want you to understand that I take seriously the fact that black figures such as Sister Souljah, Queen Latifah, and Sherley Anne Williams also attack such forms of words. It is worth mentioning that the term *bitch* is a particularly unstable one in the current scene of changing gender politics. A feminist friend of mine was called a bitch by a male objector to the feminist discourse in which they were speaking. Another, older feminist told her not to worry about it, but to be proud of it; "bitch," she said, is just what men call women when women don't go along with male preferences and definitions, and thus is a badge of honor. Ice T, in an interview on National Public Radio in which the interviewer sought to confront him with his "misogynistic" use of the word *bitch,* tried to show her that it could be used as a term of affection, in a talk that started out, "Say you were *my* bitch," and finished off with, "Oh baby, quit trippin. You know I love you. But you're still my bitch." This reduced the interviewer to silence, though I suspect to enraged silence. And of course, had the interviewer been a man, Ice T could not have reduced him to silence in just this way. The question of *who gets to say what words mean,* however, is central to the possibility of a discourse that resists white hegemony of the sign. And typically, in the white discourse, it is words themselves as abstract objects that are supposed to be holders of power, as if the sheer phonemes in *bitch* or *nigger* carried the same meaning whenever, or wherever, or by whomever they are uttered—as if to expunge them from the language would actually be concretely to remedy sexist or racist oppression.

I am going to try, however, to give an analysis of the sort Williams demands. Seizing upon and turning around stereotypes is a weapon of subversion. In his memoir, *Colored People,* Henry Louis Gates Jr. writes,

> I used to reserve my special scorn for those Negroes who were always being embarrassed by someone else in the race. Someone too dark, too "loud," someone too "wrong." Someone who dared to wear red in public. Loud and wrong: we used to say that to each other. Nigger is loud and wrong. "Loud" carried a triple meaning: speaking too loudly, dressing too loudly, and just *being* too loudly.
>
> I do know that, when I was a boy, many Negroes would have been the first to censure other Negroes once they were admitted into all-white neighborhoods or schools or clubs. "An embarrassment to the race"—phrases of that sort were bandied about. Accordingly, many of us in our generation engaged in strange antics to flout those strictures. Like eating watermelon in public, eating it loudly and merrily, and spitting the seeds into the middle of the street, red juice running down the sides of our cheeks, collecting under our chins.[11]

(Recall here the passage from Amiri Baraka quoted in the last chapter, in which he described chowing down on watermelon at Howard. And recall Hurston's "That's just like a nigger.") Where assimilation may be a form of cultural erasure and where a culture resists assimilation by its loudness; where integration means the production of the appearance of whiteness and hence the minting of double consciousness; where the nonassimilated culture is constructed by stereotype—there the stereotype becomes a weapon of resistance to hegemonic power. Nigger is loud and wrong, hence dangerous and recalcitrant. Gates says that he eventually tried to stop telling people how to be black. But meanwhile being *extremely* black precisely by the standards of the stereotype is a way of asserting cultural existence and cultural difference.

It is one thing for a white moviemaker to portray black men as dangerous, violent addicts; it is quite another for Spike Lee to present such characters (as he did, for example, in *Mo Better Blues* and *Clockers*). Even if the portrayals coincided precisely (and they do not), they have exactly opposite positions in the power structure. One way to try to destroy the power of stereotype is to defy it, to go get a Ph.D., for example. This has its advantages, and of course it is not only a strategy for racial empowerment but for personal development. But *as* a strategy for racial empowerment, it has its disadvantages as well. First, stereotypes stand up

remarkably well to "exceptions"; stereotypes are not really generalizations, even bad generalizations, but rather templates through which we
interpret experience. (That is, as I said in the chapter on Du Bois, the character of the generalization is *given* in the antecedent taxonomy, and the
generalization can break down even as the taxonomy remains unques-
tioned.) It is very easy for me to see a black professor as a racial anomaly; worse, the blackness of the black professor is in danger of
disappearing in my eyes; he may walk like me and talk like me, and perhaps I can make of him an honorary white guy. And notice, too, that the
Ph.D. may be seen by African-Americans as being purchased at the price
of racial identification; it may be seen as a racial betrayal; one may be told
to "stay black." I am certain that this is a maddening thing to be told, particularly in a situation such as (say) academia, which is fraught with racial
tensions and in which the color of the professor is not, ultimately, forget-
table. It is, I am sure, a maddening thing to be told to stay black when
there is really no choice in the matter. Nevertheless, the black professor at
Harvard or wherever is operating in the white-dominated world, and may
be doing so in part by creating a white surface. This compromises stereotypes, but only locally, and it also raises the threat of cultural annihilation
by assimilation (an issue that is also vividly present in the Jewish community, where it focuses around intermarriage).

Academia is one perfect node of white self-construction; we professor
types are pure minds, and we are notoriously physically inept and badly
dressed because we have forgotten our bodies. To be a professor is to be
very, very white, though there are also transgressive ways of taking up this
or any other role. This is one reason that academia resists integration, and
one reason why the forms of integration practiced in academia are particularly insistent in demanding a white surface from those by whom it is
integrated. Yet the integration of this space is particularly needful and particularly fecund; as figures such as Cornel West, bell hooks, Gates, Baker,
and Patricia Williams strive to make a black authorship in the academic
culture, they strive to operate within that culture while simultaneously
throwing into question its most basic underpinnings in race. If we could
be confronted with the minds of our pure bodies, we might watch a collapse of our own self-image. It goes without saying, however, that we
white academics take extraordinary measures, unconscious to ourselves,
to avoid that confrontation.

Another strategy is to use the stereotype in profound acts of self-
empowerment: "If you think this is what I am, I'll give it to you (so to
speak) in spades." And notice the potential of the stereotype, particularly
of the black man, as a weapon against the power that creates it: Black

guys are, according to the stereotype, animalistic, armed, violent, out of control. Rap's reply: "Hell yes we are, so get the fuck out of the way." (Consider MC Eiht's song "Niggaz That Kill," which ends up being more or less a simple list of those folks; it says, "There's a whole bunch of us out here, and we're coming.") Ice T says,

> Crime is an equal-opportunity employer. It never discriminates. Anybody can enter the field. You don't need a college education. You don't need a G.E.D. You don't have to be any special color. You don't need white people to like you. You're self-employed. As a result, criminals are very independent people. They don't like to take orders. That's why they get into this business. There are no applications to fill out, no special dress codes. In crime you need only one thing: heart. (*Ice Opinion*, 53)

This is something of an explanation. But it is also a demonstration of the power of transgression, a demonstration of how transgression becomes a form of economic and characterological resistance. It confirms the stereotype, but with a self- and other-awareness that are incompatible with the supposed neutrality of the values that make and enforce the stereotype, and with a skill and self-consciousness that are incompatible with the stereotype itself. It says, "*This* is what you have made by stereotype." People are *trapped* in a situation of violence, and the claustrophobia that accompanies the description of violence in rap is palpable.

Furthermore, it leads to a heightened romanticism of black culture by whites; every confirmation that black people are earthy, ignorant, violent, criminal, sexy, or drunk calls up both a greater fear and a greater yearning toward that culture on the part of people whose lives have been designed to omit or simply fail to acknowledge these things. So white parents find their children listening to and dressing like Snoop (and maybe sipping on gin and juice or smoking chronic [a kind of marijuana]), and they face a racial situation that has been to some extent transformed. One runs across a similar strategy in certain strands of feminism ("eco-feminism," for instance), where the image of woman as intuitive or instinctive mammalian nurturer is not derided as a stereotype but intensified into a mode of subversion. "Bitch" animalizes the person to whom it is applied. "Ho" sexualizes, or equates person with sexual body. "Nigger" carries with it the weight of the entire white cultural construction of black people as savages. There's no doubt that such terms are "degrading," and so forth. But there is, equally, no doubt of the capacity for reversal and subversion that lies in those terms when they are appropriated by black people and shoved at or sold to white people.

In the marketing of rap to white folks, we see something very like the erotics of interracial sex that I have described in bits in the earlier chapters. And let me make clear my own positioning with regard to that erotics, as I did briefly with regard to Malcolm X. I *identify* with figures such as Ice T or Snoop: they're my "ego ideal." These guys are my *heroes*. Of course, in yearning to be them, I am yearning to be what I am not, or yearning to be what I have excluded from my self; I am yearning to become my other. And yet, somewhere at the point where Ice T is on the lecture circuit and I'm at the rap show, our lives are actually running together in certain ways precisely out of the strength of our mutual exclusions and the concomitant desires. I not only *want* what I'm *not supposed to want* (black women), I want to *be* what I'm *not supposed to be* (a black man). Now this is not to say that if I actually woke up tomorrow in a black body I could remain happy about that for very long; I'd then have to deal with all the shit that goes along with that position. And yet when I'm watching a rap video, I'm identifying more intensely with the star than when I'm watching a Woody Allen or Clint Eastwood movie (to take two poles of white masculinity). This erotics of identification is of course intensified precisely by its transgressiveness, and by the fact that the black man is, for us white guys, very close to a pure sign of transgression. I yearn to be a pure body, a pure violence; but what I yearn for most of all is to *use* that status strategically, intelligently in an attack on white culture, the way Ice T does. This book (you may have noticed) is just such an attack on Western culture, but I would like it if this attack took the form of a rebellion against those who oppressed me, and hence generated a pride in myself and my culture, rather than the form of a rebellion against my apparent peers that generates only a measure of relief from self-loathing.

In rap music, by a magical reversal, the instrument of oppression, the stereotype, becomes—in the hands of those against whom it used—an instrument of resistance. My criticism of white culture is not the same as Ice T's; it would not be the same criticism even if we used the same words. The words are not the same when different voices speak them for different ends. Critics who read rap as a manifestation of self-hatred are supposing that the words and images *must* mean what they *would* mean if they proceeded from white mouths, under the auspices of white authority. But the shift in voice and authority fundamentally changes the speech act. It is not too much to say that rap, by a sort of alchemy, converts oppression itself into resistance. Like a martial art, it turns the attacker's energy against him and threatens him with his own violence.

This is appropriate to the particular mode of oppression in which we white folks are now engaged. For, as I have argued, we have become invisible as oppressors; we have learned not to say the wrong words. Our oppression has been continually subtilized until it is maddeningly elusive; as the oppressed turn their thoughts to resistance, they find it difficult to finger any particular individual as directly responsible. (There are, of course, exceptions to this, such as certain members of the LAPD.) Racism has been subtilized to the point that no *persons* seem responsible for it; it seems to be a matter of fudged vocabularies and implicit standards, a sort of linguistic log-jam of domination assignable to no body's act or control. But rap has invented a manner of resistance that employs the submerged energy of oppression that still flows palpably in the direction of African-Americans; rap hijacks the language of oppression itself and both attacks and uses the constructions of its imaginary locations. Tupac Shakur said, "I'm not a gangster; I'm a thug." He had "Thug Life" tattooed on his stomach. Then the oppressor feels threatened even if he is not aware that he *is* an oppressor.

The stereotype is, in the first place and as we have seen, a mode of ejection, an attempt to insulate the culture from aspects of its own humanity that it perceives as threatening or bizarre. The stereotype in this sense is conceptual segregation. It functions the same way in individuals: Bigotry is an attempt to eject aspects of oneself that one finds intolerable. For such reasons, bigotry has been at its most explicit in segments of white culture that are in fact closest to black culture: in poor Southern whites, for example. Here the conceptual exclusion of the other is at its most tenuous, and so extreme methods of insulation must be developed. With regard to rap, this ejection has been quite explicit and quite extreme; rap is continually censored. Many artists make one version of their songs for CD and another for radio and television. Words such as *nigger, bitch*, and *ho* are omitted, bleeped, or replaced. This has its ironies, since Queen Latifah cannot say, on the radio, that you shouldn't call women bitches. This is the problem of *equality of language* reappearing: even the oppressed cannot use the words to say, "Don't call me that." It is as though words had meanings outside purposes for which and contexts in which they are spoken. This is an important *strategy* for declaiming responsibility, and for repressing speech mechanically. The fact that you can't say "nigger" in polite white society does nothing to combat racism; it intensifies racism because it renders it invisible. (Unbelievably, during the O. J. Simpson trial, "nigger" was referred to by the white-dominated press as "the 'N' word." People, please: Let's get real.) But it is supposed to follow from that prohibition that black folks shouldn't say "nigger" either.

Tupac, who before his death in the second hail of bullets directed at his body had been consistently censored, as well as legally hounded (perhaps for good reasons), samples Dan Quayle on "Pac's Theme." Quayle says, over and over, "It has no place in society," a perfect call to cultural ejection; Tupac's equally perfect reply: "I'm a product of this society." Ice T, who was forced to remove the song "Cop Killer" from one of his CDs when prosecutors in a murder trial claimed (wrongly) that the song had motivated a young Texas man to kill a policeman, writes, "I realized a long time ago that censorship is as American a tradition as apple pie." And he adds,

> We made the album *Rhyme Pays,* and then Warner Brothers came to me at the label and said they wanted to put a sticker on the record. I asked why. They explained it was to inform the public some material on the album might offend listeners.
>
> I said, "Fine, that's cool." Then they explained to me the organization behind the stickering was called the Parent's Music Resource Center—the PMRC. I thought, "What a nice organization, what a nice name." Little did I know that it was founded and headed by this crazed bitch named Tipper Gore, who made it her job to put down nearly every artist in the music industry for saying what's on their minds. Gore and the PMRC are wholeheartedly against information exchange. Tipper Gore is the only woman I ever directly called a bitch on any of my records, and I meant that in the most negative sense of the word. (*Ice Opinion*, 98)

The modes of ejection and marginalization that white culture practices against black culture could not be clearer than they are in the case of rap. The operations of the PMRC echo the censorship of Queen Latifah's feminist anthem. Since white people don't need the word *nigger* anymore to keep the machinery of racism humming, it now becomes forbidden for anyone to say the word, even those to whom its use is essential in describing the history of their oppression. *Nigger* reminds white people too uncomfortably of their very recent past, and suggests (unthinkably!) that the situation is not so very different now just because the word is out of style.

White identity could not be more perfectly visible than in these cases of ejection and marginalization. As Tipper defends our children, she does so in the blandest, most boring way; she appears in her pure whiteness. She becomes a pale spokeslady for pale "family values," the neutral ethical centerpoint on which we are all supposed to be agreed. She even claims a kind of nice appreciation for sixties black music, nice party dance music: We normal matrons aren't racist. We like black music, as long as it stays apolitical and doesn't offend us and corrupt our children. Whereas the people she attacks are relentlessly particularized, she, in her matronly outfit, is relentlessly generalized into a defender of "our" values, "our" children, "our" culture from the bizarre forces of obscenity, transgression, and violation. She is protecting us from those who *say the wrong words* and thus compromise our culture as a *white* culture. White culture, in the person of Tipper Gore, can consume and enjoy black cultural production as long as it stays in its place.

What must be rejected or expunged are, to repeat, the parts of oneself one finds intolerable (above all, violence and desire, the violence of desire, the desire for violence). The content of the stereotype, thus, is *per se* what threatens the self-image of the bigot and, more widely, what threatens the image that white culture makes of itself. So the stereotype can be utilized as an absolutely precise weapon against the dominant culture: what we've tried to make of you is precisely what compromises us most deeply. The oversexed and overdrugged black gangster is the perfect "shadow" self of white culture, its absolutely intolerable negative image. Thus the stereotype is invested with a preternatural power to threaten white culture and white personality; it can be used as a weapon.

An ascetic is constantly threatened with the re-eruption of his desires into his consciousness and the subsequent threat of their enactment in his life. That is why the logical conclusion of asceticism is suicide: Death expunges desire once for all. "The philosopher studies to die," says Socrates. White culture, understood as that which ejects its body—its violence, its sex, its addiction, the rhythm of its pulse—into the other, into the African-American, is continually threatened by the re-eruption of what has been ejected, which also constitutes its deepest desire. Rap peddles these desires to white culture as commodity, but that in itself constitutes an act of resistance; it is an artful destruction of white culture that is also the self-destruction of white culture.

We are now confronted with the other in ourselves; our children purchase it and desire it (that is, desire to desire), even as "concerned parents" such as Tipper Gore try to reinstitute the construction of ascetic culture and its slumming containments of the enjoyments of the body, cleaned up and made decent. We want to lose ourselves in desire; this loss is our death, but, more profoundly, the extrusion of the other is itself an act of suicide. What could the ejection of the body possibly signal except death, except the demented turning toward death of a body in pain? Thus, as I have said, white culture is a culture of death in a certain sense, though it views itself as a culture of immortality, of life purged of particularity, of life liberated from the material. Is it any wonder that this extrusion comes to be the site of desire, that in turning back toward life in its chaotic particularity we are pulled obsessively to what our construction of ourselves as already dead sought to shunt away? Thus the site of extrusion is the site of cathexis; it is where our desire is made and its objects determined; our desire to desire, to allow ourselves to desire, can only turn toward life by turning toward the other, and hence toward our own death as pure white selves. The historical irony is that the figure of the black, violent, thug threatens white people and white culture as the result of our own conceptual elaborations and the oppressions we have used them to impose. Our fear of the figure that Tupac Shakur explicitly invoked is the product in part of our shaping of that figure and applying it to people who look like Tupac. It is a position we manufactured, a composite of our ejections and oppressions, and it is beginning to speak in its own voice, and use the very power we have ascribed to it.

The amazingly shrill white response to rap is a desperate clinging to life lived in ascetic terms, but of course that desperate clinging is itself desire: desire turned against desire, the desire not to desire, and hence itself an inscription of suicide. That is why rap is invested with a preternatural power as art, as culture, as cultural critique, as the confirmation of stereotype. In it, we really do watch the threat of violence to ourselves as white people. But what we do not understand is that this violence is our own violence, returning to us from the ghetto into which we sought to confine it. Our lack of self-knowledge makes this threat incredibly intense, gives it the air of something surreal; in making ourselves what we are, we have made this violence, returned upon us, incomprehensible to ourselves. And since our self-construction is precisely a comprehension, we are threatened *at our core* by a violence we cannot understand or contain. It is for precisely that reason that rap is censored. Bizarrely, for example, MTV blanks out all guns from rap videos, and bleeps out words that refer to guns. But of course guns are ubiquitous on television in general; the policy applies *only* to black popular music. Violence and its signifiers are permissible in the "right" hands, and those hands belong to Sylvester Stallone, not to Doctor Dre.

Ice Cube's "What Can I Do?" turns the stereotype around on a dime. Let me say that there are snatches of this rap that are indistinct or which I do not understand. In fact, that is itself a feature of rap that gets used strategically; rap is designed to be partially incomprehensible to crackers like me. It makes me feel my exclusion, and hence intensifies my discomfort. Thus, it helps create an epistemic community among those who *do* understand it. It is a zone of concealment in which cultural reconstruction becomes possible. (We have seen the making of such zones since the slave narratives.) The song starts with a narrator out of PBS saying this:

In any country, prison is where society sends its failures. But in this country society itself is failing.

Cube then proceeds to describe, in the first person, the life of a drug dealer, which proceeds from wealth to prison to working at MacDonald's. The song concludes with the following:

> The white man's broke every law known to man to establish America. But he'll put you in the state penitentiary, he'll put you in the federal penitentiary, for breaking these same laws. Now we're gonna look and see if this motherfucker's guilty for the laws he'll put you in jail for. Drug using, drug selling, armed robbery, strong arm robbery, grand larceny, rape, racketeering, conspiracy to commit murder, extortion, aggravated assault, mayhem, sodomy of a black man, trespassing, embezzlement, perjury, kidnapping, smuggling, grand theft, brandishing a firearm, carrying a concealed weapon, breaking and entering, and pre-meditated, cold-blooded murder.
>
> Guilty on every charge.[19]

This amazing work is typical of the African-American tradition in many ways. First, it makes philosophy out of personal experience. Despite its realism, however, this can hardly be straight autobiography, since during the years in question, Cube wasn't doing time, but rather making great records. Second, in the tradition of Douglass, the charge is hypocrisy; the cure, truth.

The meaning runs deeper, however. First, the person whose story Cube tells in his own voice is a stereotype, though the picture may be precisely true of someone. The rich, black drug dealer with his bitches and mobile phone could be straight out of a police profile. In prison, he opts for body-building over books, a choice with economic consequences that raises the specter of a black man with sixteen-inch arms and an ax to grind. But the profound move is this: White folks have tried to eject their criminality into the "black underclass"; black disrespect for order is supposed to be mirrored by our effortless respect for it. Again, we are confronted with the content of whiteness, now rendered contingent. White self-constructions congratulate themselves on abiding by an order that white culture has *made*. Law, whether conceptual, scientific, or governmental, is at the center of our self-constructions; we are the people who order ourselves and one another, who comprehend and by comprehension command bodies. The making of that order, the one we follow and you proverbially break, has also been the history of oppression, of the breaking of bodies and the subjugation of peoples. But here Cube shows that this transcendental condition of white mythology is purely imaginary, is *merely* a mythology. The fact that we have imaginatively excluded criminality, transgression, from ourselves allows us (in a point that ought to be familiar by now) to ignore the most obvious facts about ourselves. It allows us, in fact, to practice criminality on a huge, generalized, worldwide scale while seeming to ourselves to be law-abiding citizens. As KRS-One puts in "Sound of Da Police," "Your laws are minimal / Cause you won't even think about looking at the real criminal." This is a particularly sharp formulation because it makes the matter turn on visibility. What we seek to make visible in black folks by an amazingly elaborate and publicly conducted process of enforcement is precisely what we seek to make invisible in ourselves; to see the real criminal, we'd have to look in the mirror. In fact, Cube's conviction of "the white man" is exactly right, because though relatively few of us are criminals as defined by the legal system, we all together constitute a criminal capable of robbing the world and practicing modes of exclusion that verge on annihilation.

Patricia Williams, in *The Alchemy of Race and Rights,* makes precisely the same point. Discussing a case she remembers from her youth, Williams writes,

> A black man working for some civil rights cause was killed by a white man for racially motivated reasons; the man was stabbed thirty-nine times, which prompted a radio commentator to observe that the point was not just murder but something beyond. I wondered what sort of thing would not die with the body but lived on in the mind of the murderer. Perhaps, as psychologists have argued, what the murderer was trying to kill was a part of his own mind's image, a part of himself and not the real other. After all, generally, statistically, and corporeally, blacks as a group are poor, powerless, and a minority. It is in the minds of whites that blacks become large, threatening, powerful, ubiquitous, and supernatural.[20]

Thus the violence that the white murderer does to the black victim is, imaginatively, the murderer's violence toward himself; the violence with which the black gangsta threatens white culture takes on a supernatural significance as a return of the excluded portions of white culture. Black bodies are not by *nature* supernaturally powerful or magical; we invest them with that potential to threaten us by using them in our semiotics of self-construction, and then hate and fear them in proportion to our constructions. Think for a moment about why black Tupac scared white people more than black Bob Marley. The racial constructions of American selfhood are not generalizable, and Jamaican culture and persons have not been the locus of white American ejection and oppression in the same way that American blacks have. We do not shiver with supernatural fear at Marley's assertions of black centrality and identity, or even at his descriptions of burning and looting.

A couple of pages later, Williams continues as follows with regard to Bernhard Goetz's shooting of four black teenagers in the New York subway:

> What struck me, further, was that the general white population seems, in the process of devaluing its image of black people, to have blinded itself to the horrors inflicted by white people. One of the clearest examples of this socialized blindness is the degree to which Goetz's victims were relentlessly bestialized by the public and by the media in New York: images of the urban jungle, with young black men filling the role of "wild animals," were favorite journalistic constructions; young white urban professionals were mythologized, usually wrapped in the linguistic apparel of lambs or sheep, as the tender, toothsome prey. . . . Locked into such a reification, the meaning of any act by the sheep against the wolves can never be seen as violent in its own right. . . . Thus, when prosecutor Gregory Waples cast Goetz as a "hunter" in his final summation, juror Michael Axelrod said that Waples "was insulting my intelligence. There was nothing to justify that sort of summation. Goetz wasn't a hunter." (*Race and Rights,* 74–75)

Thus the violence done by white people is rendered utterly invisible to white people; in the bizarre imaginary that dominated the Goetz trial, it was very hard to remember who did the shooting. When it was necessary to address the fact that Goetz did *shoot,* the attempt was made to cast him as the defender of the sheep. In contemporary American culture, violence by white people against black people is rendered invisible, while violence by black people against white people is conceived to be continual and ubiquitous. If white violence against blacks is so obvious that it must be noticed in some way, it is legitimized by the invocation of the specter of massive, threatening, chaotic black violence, a specter that arises from our ejections and is then naturalized by us, as if violence were an essential feature of blackness rather than a projection on our part and, relatedly, a result of our own violence. This erases not only the contemporary situation of massive dehumanization, exploitation, and cultural destruction, but also the history of appropriation and assault that marks white treatment of black bodies in America. Williams writes, "Whites must take into account how much this history has projected onto blacks all criminality and all of society's ills. It has become the means for keeping white criminality invisible" (*Race and Rights,* 61).

The moral talk of white America focuses on personal responsibility. Whenever the criminality of the "black underclass" is discussed in white America, there are two modes of explanation: first, absolving individual members of the underclass of responsibility because of their membership in that class; second, insisting on their personal responsibility, and perhaps blaming those who would absolve them for the very criminality in question. But in a case where the stereotype demands particularization and violence, the question of responsibility arises all too easily for the "black underclass." Both responses seem unable to conceptualize responsibility except by excusing or indicting the *black* person: whether there's responsibility or not, it seems, it's you that have it or lack it. In the case of white collective criminality, the discourse of responsibility has no place. This is a conceptual effort imaginatively to free the criminal exercise of power into a realm where it is nobody's doing at all. Thus our ethics has obvious applications to the excluded, but it breaks down completely when it comes to ourselves. An ethics of personal responsibility (typical of capitalism, for example), one might say, is designed to focus on certain sorts of criminal acts with vicious intensity, while it is completely incapable of detecting others, and those of the grandest scale. And the fact that "our" ethics detects "their" acts and leaves us blind to our own is hardly an odd coincidence.

To treat persons as irredeemably particular, passionate, violent, instinctive, is to make them over into persons who harbor within themselves the constant potential for criminality by the standards of the ethics of stereotype. Thus the black population of the United States is always a threat, a reservoir of transgression, a never-drained capacity for destruction. We practice exclusion while preaching inclusion, practice annihilation while preaching uplift. But we have a tremendous appetite for that which we have excluded or attempted to destroy. For one thing, what is excluded has the potential, as "What Can I Do?" demonstrates, to show us to ourselves. That is dangerous, but it can be desirable, especially once our self-image as reasonable white folks has begun to disintegrate. Thus we buy back the excluded zones of ourselves (our criminality, for instance) as commodity. This purchase is dangerous to white culture in certain ways, but the commodity is containable, saleable, ignoreable in time of crisis.

Nevertheless, it is the only possible way, in the current situation, that we could receive ourselves. When Khalid Mohammed, the former spokesman for Nation of Islam, speaks of the crimes of the white man, he can be dismissed as a demagogue, or simply fail to find an audience among whites. (Ice Cube, in fact, samples one of Khalid's speeches on *Lethal Injection*.) But rap, as I could pause to argue but won't, is art: art that is often of very high quality, art that immediately rivets the attention. (Hurston's aesthetics can teach us how and why it does this.) Rap transmutes violence into art, transmutes stereotype into art, transmutes degradation into art. This is in itself an amazing accomplishment, and typical of African-American culture, as we have seen in the discussion of Hurston. It also transmutes solutions to violence into art, the rejection of stereotypes into art, and uplift into art. (Latifah: "Who you callin a bitch?") Now perhaps Khalid is also an artist in his own way, but rap is an art of almost perfect accessibility; it sets its themes to beats and rivets you with them. In some ways, this insulates white folks from its message even as they listen; it's possible to dig the beats and ignore the words, or even enjoy the words and forget them when it becomes too dangerous to listen. But it leaves the words present in white consciousness as a sort of dystopian trace of the aesthetic experience, leaves the words of the excluded inhabiting the culture as a whole in virtue of market penetration, with explosive capacities.

Hear this by Sister Souljah, who enjoyed a briefly huge celebrity when she suggested (more or less facetiously, I imagine) that black people take a day off from killing each other and kill white folks instead. This became a campaign issue for Bill Clinton in the 1992 election. But on "360 Degrees of Power" she is up to something else:

> Being both feminine and strong represents no conflict.
> African women have always been powerful, decisive and strong.
> And, in a state of war, we must be even stronger!
> .   .   .   .
> Ancestors blessed me with the power of spirits.
> Dominate my thoughts, I'm not tryin'a hear it.
> I'm stronger than that, too bold deep and black.
> On a feminine curve with nerve.
> You thought I was a noun but no way I'm a verb
> An action word.
> A secret for centuries but now the cat's out the bag.
>
> Strong black woman you should be glad.
> You have 360 degrees of power girl, you bad!
> No adjective can describe my objective.
> Original cradle rocker, positive conquers negative.
> You started me braggin cause you played with my esteem.

Now you're mad cause I'm rising like steam.
Reduce me to a curve, a swivel, or a twist.
Cause my hips bring you pleasure and eternal bliss.
Don't mean to intimidate, relax while I insulate
Your children and your entire nation.
No buck whilin', no misbehaving.
Powerful but won't misuse it, take advantage or abuse it.
Keep in mind before you go, it's what you need if you're
gonna grow.[21]

This lyric turns stereotypes around with incredible power and precision. First of all, it glories in the "strong black woman" of popular belief, and it glories in womanhood in general in the image of the circle and the curve, both associated with femaleness (and particularly black femaleness). And the primary image is of fertility, of black women as a source out of which people and cultural transformation can arise ("I'm a verb, an action word": recall Hurston's aesthetics). There is art in the beat, and in the poetry. But there is, always present within that art, a fertility, a possibility for ramification into the culture as a whole. And Souljah does address the culture as a whole. On the same disk, she says, "We have the power to tell the truth, to say whatever is necessary, to do what needs to be done, whatever it is and no matter who it may hurt. Well if the truth hurts, you'll be in pain. And if the truth drives you crazy, then you'll die insane."

Ice T, star of disk, book, screen, and lecture circuit, has had particular success in transforming his life into art. (He says of the lecturing, "I'm going to Harvard or someplace to teach these people how to be real. Isn't that stupid?" Well, no. The people at Harvard *need* to be taught how to be real very badly.) Here is "Straight Up Nigga," which plumbs, like the Souljah rap, all of the themes I have been discussing.

Yo check this out. A lot of people be gettin mad cause I use the word nigger, know what I'm sayin? . . . They say I'm a black man. I tell them I'm a nigger; they don't understand that. I'm gonna say what I wanna say. I call myself what I want to call myself. Know what I'm sayin? They need to stay off my dick, you know? . . .

I'm a nigger, a stand-up nigger from a hard school.
Whatever you are I don't care; that's you, fool.
I'm loud and proud, well-endowed with a big beef.
Out on the corner I hang out like a horse thief.
So you can call me dumb or crazy,

Ignorant, inferior, stupid, or lazy,
Silly and foolish but I'm bad and I'm bigger.
But most of all I'm a straight-up nigger.

. . . .

America was stolen from the Indian, show and prove.
What was that? A straight up nigger move. . . .

. . . .

Those who hate me, I got something for ya.
I'm a nigger with cash, a nigger with a lawyer.
No watermelon, chitlin-eatin nigger down south,
But a nigger that'll slap the taste from your mouth.
A contemplatin, best-champagne drinkin,
Ten-inch-givin, extra large livin,
Mercedes Benz drivin, thrivin, survivin,
All the way live and kickin, high-fivin,
Strokin, rappin, happenin, deal doin,
Fly in from Cali to chill with the crewin,
Grindin, groovin, fly-girl grabbin,
Horny, gun-shootin, long-hair-havin
Nigger, straight up nigger.

. . . .

Now you keep me in a constant sweat.
But I'm a nigger that you'll never forget.
A black, bad, ironclad, always-mad
Fly nigger takin off from a helipad.
Rolex stylin, buck whilin', cash pilin,
Sportin chain links and medallions,
Intellectual, high-tech,
Cashin seven-figure checks and still breakin necks.
The ultimate male supreme, white woman's dream,
Big dick straight up nigger.[22]

As I have said, to seek to evade the stereotype may often be to intensify double-consciousness by producing a "white" surface. Ice T says, "If some square Tom politician is not a nigger, then I *am* a nigger, you understand? I am not what you want me to be" (*Ice Opinion*, 105). For this reason, the upwelling of black culture into the mass media and swirl of commodity exchange takes the form of a reinforcement of stereotype. In fact, and typically, though with particular gusto and sheer verbal agility, Ice T goes beyond confirming stereotypes to reveling in them and deploying them with perfect strategy.

This song intensifies the stereotype and makes it even more threatening than it is on its own. The black guy hanging on the corner like a horse thief, armed and every white woman's dream, is bad enough. But when that black guy has a lawyer and is cashing seven-figure checks—in short when he has the resources to burst out of the ghetto and into your face—*that's* a threat. This figure of the rapper as simultaneously hoodlum, poet, and successful entrepreneur is unprecedented in American history and is deeply subversive. This black man is, first, operating within white America's capitalist structures with complete success, in part by selling his product to white consumers. He's rich, and it's obvious that he's smart, and so forth. But he's also got ten inches for the bitches; he's also hooked into the gang structure in LA; he's also potentially violent. And it must be pointed out that he's supremely conscious of what he's doing: he's utterly at play in the racial signifier. He plays, but he's serious as well, and he knows exactly what he's doing as he lobs those words and images. Even as he insists that he can call himself whatever he wants, that he won't be named by white culture or even by black culture, he brings forward the history of the white man as nigger.

NOTES

INTRODUCTION

1. See, for example, Michael Eric Dyson, *Reflecting Black: African-American Cultural Criticism* (Minneapolis: University of Minnesota Press, 1993). As in several of his books, Dyson begins with an autobiographical excursus. In fact our stories, across the racial divide, run in an amazingly parallel course: we were born in the same year and raised in mostly black cities (Dyson grew up in Detroit); for both of us, the King assassination was a pivotal moment in the development of racial consciousness; we both spent some years in Tennessee and were both influenced by the work of Richard Rorty, who was my dissertation supervisor. There is a similar autobiographical excursus in the first chapter of Houston Baker's *Long Black Song: Essays in Black American Literature and Culture* (Charlottesville: University Press of Virginia, 1972). Patricia J. Williams consistently connects extremely sophisticated legal theory with intense personal description, as in *The Alchemy of Race and Rights* (Cambridge, Mass.: Harvard University Press, 1991) and *The Rooster's Egg* (Cambridge, Mass.: Harvard University Press, 1995).

2. Houston Baker, *Workings of the Spirit: The Poetics of Afro-American Women's Writing* (Chicago: University of Chicago Press, 1991), p. 48.

3. Hazel V. Carby, "The Multicultural Wars," in *Black Popular Culture*, a project by Michele Wallace, edited by Gina Dent (Seattle: Bay Press, 1992), p. 193.

4. A small sample of the field: David Roediger, *The Wages of Whiteness: Race and the Making of the American Working Class* (New York: Verso, 1991) and *Towards the Abolition of Whiteness* (New York: Verso, 1994); Michael Omi and Howard Winant, *Racial Formation in the United States* (New York: Routledge, 1994); John Garvey and Noel Ignatiev, eds., *Race Traitor* (New York: Routledge,

1996); Fred Pfeil, *White Guys* (New York: Verso, 1995); Ruth Frankenberg, *White Women, Race Matters: The Social Construction of Whiteness* (Minneapolis: University of Minnesota Press, 1993); William Upski Wimsatt, *Bomb the Suburbs* (Chicago: The Subway and Elevated Press Company, 1994); Theodore W. Allen, *The Invention of the White Race* (New York: Verso, 1994); Jane Lazarre, *Beyond the Whiteness of Whiteness: Memoir of a White Mother of Black Sons* (Durham, N.C.: Duke University Press, 1996).

5. This case is made beautifully by Brenda Dixon Gottschild in *Digging the Africanist Presence in American Performance* (Westport, Conn.: Greenwood Press, 1996).

6. Ralph Ellison, "Change the Joke and Slip the Yoke," reprinted in *The Norton Anthology of African-American Literature,* ed. Henry Louis Gates Jr. and Nellie McKay (New York: Norton, 1997), p. 1542.

7. This has been remarked by many black feminists, for example, Barbara Smith in "Notes for Yet Another Paper on Black Feminism, or Will the Real Enemy Please Stand Up," *Conditions,* 5, no. 3 (October 1978): 123–32. See also Elizabeth Spelman, *Inessential Woman* (Boston: Beacon, 1988).

8. This point is compellingly argued in many places, for example, by Gottschild in *Digging the Africanist Presence,* by Robert Farris Thompson in *Flash of the Spirit: African and Afro-American Art and Philosophy* (New York: Random House, 1983), and in Joseph E. Holloway, ed., *Africanisms in American Culture* (Bloomington: Indiana University Press, 1990).

ONE

1. Perhaps the definitive treatment of the genre is William L. Andrews's *To Tell a Free Story* (Urbana: University of Illinois Press, 1986). Andrews says that the slave narrative was dedicated "to the proof of two propositions: (1) that the slave was, as the inscription of a famous antislavery medallion put it, "a man and a brother" to whites, especially to the white reader of slave narratives; and (2) that the black narrator was, despite all prejudice and propaganda, a truth-teller, a reliable transcriber of the experience and character of black folk" (1).

2. South Carolina slaveowner Edward Thomas Heriot, for example, wrote, "I manage them as my children. . . . There is no class of people, as far as I have seen in this country, or Europe, of the same grade, where there is so much real happiness, where the wants of nature are so abundantly supplied, where the requirements of labor are as little, and where the guaranty against poverty and distress from all conditions of existence is so great" (quoted in Bruce Levine, *Half Slave and Half Free* [New York: Hill and Wang, 1992], p. 24).

3. A planter from Maryland wrote in 1837 that "the character of the Negro is much underrated. It is like the plastic clay, which may be moulded into agreeable or disagreeable figures, according to the skill of the moulder" (quoted in John W. Blassingame, *The Slave Community* [New York: Oxford University Press, 1979], p. 246).

4. The exemplary discussion of authorizing and authenticating procedures and of the use of supporting documents in slave narratives is by Robert Stepto in *From Behind the Veil: A Study of Afro-American Narrative* (Urbana: University of Illinois Press, 1979), chapter 1. I will limit myself to recounting two points made by

Stepto. First, documentation of the sort appended to Henry Bibb's *Narrative of the life of Henry Bibb, an American Slave* (see note 8 below) serves fundamentally to establish not only the writer's literacy and the truth of his story, but his very existence; second, the slave narrative rises to the level of true autobiography where the former slave is in control of his or her own story (as in Douglass's first narrative, according to Stepto).

5. William W. Brown, *From Fugitive Slave to Free Man: The Autobiographies of William Wells Brown,* ed. William L. Andrews (New York: Penguin, 1993 [1848]), p. 21. Subsequent quotations are cited parenthetically by page number in the text.

6. Joanne M. Braxton, *Black Women Writing Autobiography: A Tradition within a Tradition* (Philadelphia: Temple University Press, 1989), p. 16.

7. Frederick Douglass, *My Bondage and My Freedom,* in *Autobiographies* (New York: Library of America, 1994 [1855]), p. 367.

8. Henry Bibb, *Narrative of the Life of Henry Bibb, an American Slave.* reprinted in *Puttin' On Ole Massa,* ed. Gilbert Osofsky (New York: Harper and Row, 1969), p. 132. Subsequent quotations are cited parenthetically by page number in the text.

9. Malcolm X, *By Any Means Necessary* (New York: Pathfinder, 1992), p. 183.

10. Booker T. Washington, From an address delivered at Fisk University, 1895 (though these lines appear elsewhere in Washington's speeches and writings as well); printed in *Selected Speeches of Booker T. Washington* (New York: Doubleday, 1932), p. 37.

11. Booker T. Washington, *Up from Slavery,* reprinted in *Three Negro Classics* (New York: Avon, 1965), p. 37.

12. Sister Souljah, *No Disrespect* (New York, Random House, 1994), pp. 11–12.

13. Lunsford Lane, *Narrative of Lunsford Lane, Formerly of Raleigh N.C.* (1842), p. 31; reprinted in *Five Slave Narratives* (New York: Arno Press, 1968).

14. My discussion of surveillance and social construction, here and throughout, obviously owes much to Michel Foucault, *Discipline and Punish,* trans. Alan Sheridan (New York: Vintage, 1979).

15. Patricia J. Williams, *The Rooster's Egg: On the Persistence of Prejudice* (Cambridge, Mass.: Harvard University Press, 1995), pp. 232, 233.

16. James W. C. Pennington, *The Fugitive Blacksmith, or, Events in the Life of James W. C. Pennington,* pp. 6–7; reprinted in *Five Slave Narratives.* Subsequent quotations are cited parenthetically by page number in the text.

17. Henry Watson, *Narrative of Henry Watson, A Fugitive Slave* (Boston: Bela Marsh, 1848).

18. George Fitzhugh, *Cannibals All!* (Richmond: 1857), p. 200.

19. In 1857, the Reverend William G. Brownlow of Tennessee wrote, in a passage typical of many Southern religious justifications of slavery, that "the Scriptures look to the correction of servants, and really enjoin it, as they do in the case of children. We esteem it the duty of Christian masters to feed and clothe well, and in the case of disobedience to *whip well."* See *A Sermon on Slavery,* quoted in Blassingame, *The Slave Community,* p. 83.

20. This is also the fundamental approach of David Walker's famous *Appeal,*

as Houston Baker makes abundantly clear in *Long Black Song: Essays in Black American Literature and Culture* (Charlottesville: University Press of Virginia, 1972), pp. 58–79.

21. Douglass, *Autobiographies* (New York: Library of America, 1994 [1845]), pp. 97–98. Subsequent quotations are cited parenthetically by page number in the text.

22. Andrews, *To Tell a Free Story*, p. 103.

23. Quoted by Andrews in *To Tell a Free Story*, p. 139.

24. Linda Brent (Harriet Jacobs), *Incidents in the Life of a Slave Girl* (New York: Harcourt, Brace, Jovanovich, 1973 [1861]), p. x. Subsequent quotations are cited parenthetically by page number in the text.

25. Andrews, *To Tell a Free Story*, pp. 253–63.

26. *Narrative of Sojourner Truth* (Oxford: Oxford University Press, 1991 [1850]), pp. 29–30. Subsequent quotations are cited parenthetically by page number in the text.

27. Valerie Smith, *Self-Discovery and Authority in Afro-American Narrative* (Cambridge, Mass.: Harvard University Press, 1987), p. 29.

28. A very acute and very obtuse account of interracial erotics is given by Eldridge Cleaver in *Soul on Ice* (New York: McGraw-Hill, 1968). Cleaver investigates the isomorphism of racism and body/mind dualism, but his account is conspicuous for its sexism and extreme homophobia.

TWO

1. For rich documentation of this admittedly sweeping and simplified assertion, see Ivan Hannaford, *Race: The History of an Idea in the West* (Washington, D.C.: Woodrow Wilson Center Press, 1996), especially chapters 7 and 8. Hannaford discusses the origins of modern racial taxonomies in such figures as Linnaeus, Buffon, and Blumenbach, and its later "scientific" development in such figures as Cuvier, Retzius, and Humboldt. See also George Mosse, *Toward the Final Solution: A History of European Racism* (London: Dent, 1978).

2. W. E. B. Du Bois, *Dusk of Dawn: An Essay Toward an Autobiography of a Race Concept*, in *Writings* (New York: Library of America, 1986 [1940]), p. 654. Subsequent quotations from this volume are cited parenthetically by short title and page number in the text.

3. For an exemplary discussion of race as fiction and a reduction of race to ethnicity, see Naomi Zack, *Race and Mixed Race* (Philadelphia: Temple University Press, 1993).

4. Robert Stepto, *From Beyond the Veil* (Urbana: University of Illinois Press, 1979), p. 63.

5. W. E. B. Du Bois, *The Autobiography of W. E. B. Du Bois: A Soliloquy on Viewing My Life from the Last Decade of Its First Century* (New York: International Publishers, 1968), p. 125. Subsequent quotations are cited parenthetically by short title and page number in the text.

6. Du Bois quotes this from himself in *Dusk of Dawn*, p. 597.

7. W. E. B. Du Bois, *The Souls of Black Folk* (New York: Penguin, 1989 [1903]), p. 2. Subsequent quotations are cited parenthetically by short title and page number in the text.

8. W. E. B. Du Bois, "Starvation and Prejudice," *Crisis*, 2 (June 1911): 64;

quoted in David Levering Lewis, *W. E. B. Du Bois: Biography of a Race* (New York: Henry Holt, 1993), p. 434.

9. Lewis, *Du Bois*, p. 280.

10. James Baldwin, quoted in Henry Louis Gates, "The Welcome Table," in *Lure and Loathing*, ed. Gerald Early (New York: Penguin, 1993), p. 150. This book is an anthology of responses to the notion of double consciousness by African-American thinkers.

11. Martin Luther King Jr., "I Have a Dream," in *I Have a Dream: Writings and Speeches That Changed the World*, ed. James Melvin Washington (San Francisco: Harper, 1992), p. 104.

12. James Baldwin, "Stranger in the Village," in *Notes of a Native Son* (Boston: Beacon, 1983 [1955]), p. 167.

13. James Baldwin, *The Fire Next Time* (New York: Vintage, 1993 [1963]), pp. 5-6. Cited subsequently in the text.

THREE

1. That aspect of Du Bois's rhetoric—his celebration of "culture" in an Arnoldian sense—is discussed by Houston Baker in *Long Black Song*, chapter 6.

2. Malcolm X, as told to Alex Haley, *The Autobiography of Malcolm X* (New York: Ballantine, 1992 [1965]), pp. 64–65. Subsequent quotations are cited parenthetically by short title and page number in the text.

3. Kobena Mercer, "Black Hair/Style Politics," in *Welcome to the Jungle: New Positions in Black Cultural Studies* (New York: Routledge, 1994). Mercer emphasizes the *artistic* possibilities of hairstyles as a play on racial signifiers and provides a worthwhile counterpoint to Malcolm's rather simplistic take on the situation. See also Lisa Jones, *Bulletproof Diva: Tales of Race, Sex, and Hair* (New York: Anchor, 1994).

4. Richard Wright, *Black Boy*, in *Later Works* (New York: Library of America, 1991), pp. 253–54. Subsequent quotations are cited parenthetically by short title and page number in the text.

5. See Molefi Kete Asante's "Racism, Consciousness, and Afrocentricity," in *Lure and Loathing: Twenty Black Intellectuals Address W. E. B. Du Bois's Dilemma of the Double Consciousness of African Americans*, ed. Gerald Early (New York, Penguin, 1994), pp. 127–43.

6. Shirley Taylor Haizlip, *The Sweeter the Juice* (New York: Simon and Schuster, 1994), p. 14. Subsequent quotations are cited parenthetically by page number in the text.

7. Patricia J. Williams, *The Alchemy of Race and Rights: Diary of a Law Professor* (Cambridge, Mass.: Harvard University Press, 1991), p. 236.

8. James Weldon Johnson, *The Autobiography of an Ex-Colored Man*, reprinted in its entirety in *The Norton Anthology of African-American Literature*, ed. Henry Louis Gates Jr. and Nellie Y. McKay (New York: Norton, 1997), pp. 777–861.

9. Malcolm X, *By Any Means Necessary* (New York: Pathfinder, 1992), p. 181. Subsequent quotations are cited parenthetically by short title and page number in the text.

10. Malcolm X, *The Last Speeches* (New York: Pathfinder, 1992), pp. 152–53.

11. Indeed, Cornel West has argued that that is also what black folks admired

most about Malcolm. "His early rhetoric was simply prescient: too honest, too candid, precisely the things black folk often felt but never said publicly due to fear of white retaliation, even in the early sixties. . . . Malcolm X did not hesitate to tell black and white America "like it is," even if it resulted in little political and practical payoff." (I would dispute that last claim, by the way.) See Cornel West, "The Paradox of the African American Rebellion," in *Keeping Faith: Philosophy and Race in America* (New York: Routledge, 1993), p. 281. Michael Eric Dyson also celebrates Malcolm as a truth-teller in *Making Malcolm: The Myth and Meaning of Malcolm X* (New York: Oxford University Press, 1995).

12. Hortense Spillers, "Mama's Baby, Papa's Maybe: An American Grammar Book," reprinted in *Within the Circle: An Anthology of African-American Literary Criticism from the Harlem Renaissance to the Present,* ed. Angelyn Mitchell (Durham: Duke University Press, 1994) p. 457.

13. Evelyn Rosser, "Chocolate Tears and Dreams," in *Life Notes: Personal Writings By Contemporary Black Women,* ed. Patricia Bell-Scott (New York: Norton, 1994), pp. 44–45.

14. Maya Angelou, *I Know Why the Caged Bird Sings* (New York: Bantam, 1993 [1970]), p. 2. Subsequent quotations are cited parenthetically by page number in the text.

15. Richard Wright, *Native Son,* in *Early Writings* (New York: Library of America, 1991) p. 535. Subsequent quotations are cited parenthetically by page number in the text.

16. See Malcolm X, "The Founding Rally of the OAAU," in *By Any Means Necessary,* pp. 33–67.

17. For excellent and contrasting discussions of Descartes in relation to oppression, see Naomi Zack, *Bachelors of Science* (Philadelphia: Temple University Press, 1996), and Susan Bordo, *The Flight to Objectivity: Essays on Cartesianism and Culture* (Albany: State University of New York Press, 1987).

FOUR

1. For a trenchant critique of reversed racial essentialism, one that is also thoughtful about the origins and goals of that essentialism, see Michael Eric Dyson, *Reflecting Black: African-American Cultural Criticism* (Minneapolis: University of Minnesota Press, 1993): "The quest for racial unity has largely represented the desperate effort to replace a cultural uprooting that should never have occurred with a racial unanimity that actually never existed" (xv).

2. Here are some examples of feminist treatments of *Their Eyes Were Watching God:* Nellie McCay, "'Crayon Enlargements of Life': Zora Neale Hurston's *Their Eyes Were Watching God* as Autobiography," in *New Essays on Their Eyes Were Watching God,* ed. Michael Awkward (Cambridge: Cambridge University Press, 1990), and Elizabeth Meese, "Orality and Textuality in *Their Eyes Were Watching God,*" in *Modern Critical Interpretations: Their Eyes Were Watching God,* ed. Harold Bloom (New York: Chelsea House, 1987).

3. Zora Neale Hurston, *Their Eyes Were Watching God* (New York: Harper-Perennial, 1990 [1937]), p. 23. Subsequent quotations are cited parenthetically by short title and page number in the text.

4. Zora Neale Hurston, *Dust Tracks on a Road* (New York: HarperPerennial, 1991 [1942]), p. 202.

5. Zora Neale Hurston, *Mules and Men,* (New York: HarperPerennial, 1990 [1935]), p. 120.

6. Zora Neale Hurston, *Tell My Horse* (New York: HarperPerennial, 1990 [1938]), p. 54.

7. Mary Helen Washington, for example, writes that "significantly, even in this seemingly idyllic treatment of erotic love, female sexuality is always associated with violence. . . . Janie is beaten by her glorious lover, Tea Cake, so that he can prove his superiority to other men." See "'The Darkened Eye Restored': Notes Toward a Literary History of Black Women," reprinted in *Within the Circle: An Anthology of African-American Literary Criticism from the Harlem Renaissance to the Present,* ed. Angelyn Mitchell (Durham: Duke University Press, 1994), p. 448.

8. Zora Neale Hurston, *Jonah's Gourd Vine* (New York: HarperPerennial, 1990 [1934]), p. 9.

9. Deborah G. Plant, *Every Tub Must Sit on Its Own Bottom* (Urbana: University of Illinois Press, 1995), chapter 1.

10. See Ruth Frankenberg, *White Women, Race Matters: The Social Construction of Whiteness* (Minneapolis: University of Minnesota Press, 1993), especially chapter 3.

11. Robert Hemenway, *Zora Neale Hurston: A Literary Biography* (Urbana: University of Illinois Press, 1977), p. 260.

12. McCay, "'Crayon Enlargements of Life,'" p. 54.

13. Henry Louis Gates Jr., "Zora Neale Hurston and the Speakerly Text," reprinted in *Zora Neale Hurston: Critical Perspectives Past and Present,* ed. Gates and K. A. Appiah (New York: Amistad, 1993), p. 158.

14. Zora Neale Hurston, "Characteristics of Negro Expression," reprinted in *The Sanctified Church: The Folklore Writings of Zora Neale Hurston* (Berkeley: Turtle Island, 1981), p. 49. Subsequent quotations are cited parenthetically by short title and page number in the text.

15. Richard Wright, review in *New Masses,* October 5, 1937. Reprinted in *Zora Neale Hurston: Critical Perspectives Past and Present,* ed. Henry Louis Gates Jr. and K. A. Appiah (New York: Amistad, 1993), pp. 16–17.

16. This problematicity was driven home for me when I read Hazel Carby's essay "The Politics of Fiction, Anthropology, and the Folk: Zora Neale Hurston," in *New Essays on Their Eyes Were Watching God.* Carby writes that "Hurston could not entirely escape the intellectual practice that she so despised, a practice that reinterpreted and redefined a folk consciousness in its own elitist terms. Hurston may not have dressed the spirituals in tuxedos, but her attitude toward folk culture was not unmediated; she did have a construct that enabled her particular representation of a black rural consciousness" (76). She goes on to say that Hurston's construction was a response to the urbanization and northern movement of African-Americans, and that she created a "representation of 'Negroness' as an unchanging, essential entity, an essence so distilled that it is an aesthetic position of blackness" (77). My answer to that, as will be clear, is "yes and no." My view is that she deployed such an "essence" strategically, and could not have been more explicit in her final rejection of it as an adequate account of her own or anyone else's identity. Nevertheless, Carby's criticism is also trenchant even on that level, and focuses suspicion exactly on white appropriations (such as mine) of

Hurston's aesthetics. Ann duCille discusses what she calls "Hurstonism" in *The Coupling Convention: Sex, Text, and Tradition in Black Women's Fiction* (New York: Oxford University Press, 1993) as the construction of an "authentic" blackness by critics such as Baker, and mounts a compelling critique of that sort of essentialism, especially as it gets used to dismiss figures such as Jessie Fauset as "inauthentic."

17. Langston Hughes, *The Big Sea* (New York: Hill and Wang, 1963), p. 239. Subsequent quotations are cited parenthetically by short title and page number in the text.

18. Amiri Baraka, "The Myth of a 'Negro Literature,'" reprinted in Mitchell, ed., *Within the Circle*, p. 167.

19. Maya Angelou, foreword to *Dust Tracks on a Road*, pp. x, xi–xii.

20. Alice Walker, from the ravishing and shattering essay "In Search of Our Mothers' Gardens," widely reprinted; see Mitchell, ed., *Within the Circle*, p. 404.

21. Zora Neale Hurston, "How It Feels to Be Colored Me." The essay has been collected in *Folklore, Memoirs, and Other Writings* (New York: Library of America, 1995); this quotation appears on p. 827.

22. Zora Neale Hurston, *Moses, Man of the Mountain* (New York: Harper-Perennial, 1991 [1939]), p. 282.

FIVE

1. For a treatment of the various direct and indirect connections of rap to Malcolm X, see Michael Eric Dyson, *Making Malcolm: The Myth and Meaning of Malcolm X* (New York: Oxford University Press, 1995), chapter 3.

2. Michele Wallace, "Afterword: 'Why Are There No Great Black Artists?': The Problem of Visuality in African-American Culture," in *Black Popular Culture*, a project by Michele Wallace, edited by Gina Dent (Seattle: Bay Press, 1992), p. 345.

3. Houston Baker, *Black Studies, Rap, and the Academy* (Chicago: University of Chicago Press, 1993), p. 89. This book is, for my money, the best, and it is certainly the most readable, "academic" discussion of rap. Subsequent quotations are cited parenthetically by short title and page number in the text.

4. MC Lyte, "Act Like You Know," on *Act Like You Know* (Atlantic Records, D110737, 1991).

5. Ice T, as told to Heidi Siegmund, *The Ice Opinion: Who Gives a Fuck?* (New York: St. Martin's, 1994), p. 94. Subsequent quotations are cited parenthetically by short title and page number in the text.

6. Guru, from the introduction to *Jazzmatazz*, vol. 1 (Chrysalis Records, D125063, 1993).

7. Public Enemy, "Burn, Hollywood, Burn," on *Fear of a Black Planet* (Def Jam Recordings, AAD 45413, 1990).

8. Langston Hughes, quoted in Maya Angelou's foreword to Zora Neale Hurston's *Dust Tracks on a Road*, pp. vii–viii.

9. Kool Moe Dee, "Funke Wisdom," on *Funke Funke Wisdom* (Jive Records, 1388-2-5, 1991).

10. Snoop Doggy Dogg, "Murder Was the Case," on *Doggystyle* (Death Row Records, 792279-2, 1993).

11. Scarface, "I Seen a Man Die," on *The Diary* (Rap-a-Lot Records/Noo Tribe Records, 8 39946 25, 1994).

12. Mercer, *Welcome to the Jungle*, p. 109.

13. Andrews, *To Tell a Free Story*, p. 9.

14. Fesu, "Fallin' Off Da Deep End," on *War with No Mercy* (Nuff Nuff/Continuum Records, COND 1940 4, 1994).

15. Sister Souljah, *No Disrespect* (New York: Random House, 1994), p. 350.

16. Sherley Anne Williams, "Two Words on Music: Black Community," in Dent, ed., *Black Popular Culture*, pp. 167–68.

17. Claude Brown, *Manchild in the Promised Land* (New York: Macmillan, 1965), p. 109.

18. Henry Louis Gates Jr., *Colored People* (New York: Knopf, 1994), pp. xiii–xiv.

19. Ice Cube, "What Can I Do?" on *Lethal Injection* (Priority Records, P2 53876, 1993).

20. Williams, *The Alchemy of Race and Rights*, p. 72. Subsequent quotations are cited parenthetically by short title and page number in the text.

21. Sister Souljah, "360 Degrees of Power," on *360 Degrees of Power* (Epic Records, EK 48713, 1992).

22. Ice T, "Straight Up Nigga," on *O. G. Original Gangster* (Sire/Warner Bros., 9 26492-2, 1991).

INDEX

aesthetics, 85, 102, 159
  Hurston's, 128–31, 143–48, 153,
    164, 193, 194
  rap and, 165, 167, 193, 194
affirmative action, 12, 14
Afrocentrism, 117, 121, 122, 164,
  173
Allen, Theodore W., 9n
Allen, Woody, 184
Andrews, William, 21n. 1, 22n. 5,
  38, 44, 176
Angelou, Maya, 111–12, 131, 137,
  153
anthropology, 55–56
Appiah, K. A., 143n. 13, 149n. 15
Arrested Development (rap group),
  161
art, 73, 76–77, 85
  Hurston and, 125–26, 129–32,
    138, 143–48
  rap and, 165–66, 167, 193
Asante, Molefi Kete, 93
authorship, racial content of, 6,
  22–26, 33, 41, 64–67, 150

autobiography
  Hurston and, 153
  power of, 39–40
  stereotype and, 33, 104
  theory and, 5–8
Awkward, Michael, 124n. 2

Baker, Houston, 6, 7, 37n, 88n, 161,
  163, 171, 182
Baldwin, James, 9, 10, 80–84,
  130–31
Baraka, Amiri, 151–52, 181
Beastie Boys (rap group), 170–71
Bell-Scott, Patricia, 111n. 13
Benedict, Ruth, 153
Bibb, Henry, 22, 26, 34–35, 44, 150
Big Daddy Kane (rapper), 168
Biggie Smalls (rapper), 13, 161, 163,
  174, 176
Blassingame, John W., 21n. 3, 36n
Bloom, Harold, 124n. 2
blues, 122, 146, 151, 169, 170
Boas, Franz, 153
Boone, Pat, 130, 167